Sex, Love,
and
Dharma

Sex, Love, and Dharma

ANCIENT WISDOM
FOR MODERN RELATIONSHIPS

SIMON CHOKOISKY

Destiny Books
Rochester, Vermont • Toronto, Canada

Destiny Books
One Park Street
Rochester, Vermont 05767
www.DestinyBooks.com

Text stock is SFI certified

Destiny Books is a division of Inner Traditions International

Note to the reader: *This book is intended as an informational guide. The remedies, approaches, and techniques described herein are meant to supplement, and not to be a substitute for, professional medical care or treatment. They should not be used to treat a serious ailment without prior consultation with a qualified health care professional.*

Library of Congress Cataloging-in-Publication Data
Chokoisky, Simon.
  Sex, love, and dharma : ancient wisdom for modern relationships / Simon Chokoisky.
       pages cm
  Includes index.
   ISBN 978-1-62055-287-2 (paperback) — ISBN 978-1-62055-288-9 (e-book)
  1. Self-actualization (Psychology) 2. Love—Religious aspects—Hinduism. 3. Interpersonal relations—Religious aspects--Hinduism. 4. Dharma. I. Title.
  BF637.S4C4986 2015
  294.5'441—dc23
                                                                           2015007210

Printed and bound in the United States by Lake Book Manufacturing, Inc. The text stock is SFI certified. The Sustainable Forestry Initiative® program promotes sustainable forest management.

10 9 8 7 6 5 4 3 2 1

Text design and layout by Virginia Scott Bowman
This book was typeset in Garamond Premier Pro and Gill Sans with Parma Petit, Gill Sans, and Agenda used as display typefaces

To send correspondence to the author of this book, mail a first-class letter to the author c/o Inner Traditions • Bear & Company, One Park Street, Rochester, VT 05767, and we will forward the communication, or contact the author directly at **www.spirittype.com** or **siddhadeva@yahoo.com.**

Contents

Discovering Your Dharma

A long time ago, the visionaries of the Indian subcontinent, called *rishis*, or seers, discovered three basic truths about human life. First, all beings want to be happy. How we define happiness differs among individuals and cultures, but this one truth remains constant. Second, they found that for long-term happiness, it is better to live with rather than against nature. Dr. Robert Svoboda quotes his mentor, the Aghori Vimalananda: "Learn to live with nature or nature will come live with you."[1] This means that, while jumping off a cliff may feel exhilarating in the short term, the breeze lifting your hair as you slice through the air, nature inevitably catches up to you. Short-term pleasure is easy; keeping it up is not. Activities that give us pleasure do not necessarily lead to happiness—and those that promote happiness are not always pleasurable! If you want to fly while keeping your organs intact, it is best to study gravity and the laws of aerodynamics first, and apply them judiciously in your attempts at flight.

The rishis of ancient India did just that (though not necessarily in the realm of aerodynamics), and passed down their secrets to us via oral tradition. They called the laws of nature, as well as the practice of following them, dharma. This is the third insight: dharma is one, but it is useful to see it through the lens of five important subcategories.

TABLE I.1. THE FIVE SUBCATEGORIES OF DHARMA

LEVEL OF DHARMA	ASSOCIATED SCIENCE	AREA AFFECTED
Physcial	Ayurveda	From the skin in: how to care for and relate to your **body**
Environment	Vastu shastra	From the skin out: how to care for and relate to your **physical environment**
Social	Dharma types	Nonphysical environment: how to care for and relate to your **society**
Spiritual	Yoga	Ethics and morals, nonphysical, local environment: how to care for and relate to your **spiritual self**
Cosmic	Vedic astrology— jyotisha	Outer space, from the skin of the planet out: how to understand your karma and relate to the **planets, stars, and cosmos**

Table I.1. illustrates the five levels of dharma, or natural law, and the disciplines that help us live accordingly. Note that the dharma types, being in the middle, straddle the others, and are implicated in living a dharmic life on every level. They are also particularly useful because they are not hard to learn. While mastering ayurveda or Vedic astrology can take a lifetime (or more!), getting a handle on the dharma type is far less demanding. The purpose of this book is to introduce you to all of these traditions for optimal understanding of how to make the most of your role in the universe.

THE FIVE LEVELS OF DHARMA

The first level—the level of self—is dedicated to everything that is you, from the skin in. It is the realm of ayurveda, which teaches us how to understand diet and lifestyle in order to experience lasting fulfillment from the physical body. Good relationships are possible when you're sick, but they are much easier when both partners are healthy and vibrant. Accordingly, chapters 4 and 6 of this book are dedicated to addressing this vital aspect of relationship health—health itself.

The second level of dharma deals with how you relate to your physical environment, everything from your skin to the skin of the planet, the atmosphere. This entails learning how to turn our houses into homes—comfortable living environments that support our physical, emotional, and spiritual well-being, as well as that of the planet. This is explored in chapter 5.

Next is the level of social fulfillment. This is where the dharma type is particularly useful. You are born with special gifts, and your dharma type will help you find and express them. How to do this using the BE FIT program is detailed in chapter 3.

The fourth level of dharma is devoted to ethics and morals and how you relate to your spiritual self. Techniques for how to incorporate spiritual practices from tantra and yoga are detailed in chapter 10 for this purpose.

Finally, the fifth level relates to everything outside our earthly environment. Broadly speaking, it is the realm of the cosmos and how we relate to the macrocosm. Our ancient ancestors believed in the maxim "as above, so below"—that the position of planets and stars in the heavens have a lot to say about the nature of our karmas, past, present, and future. Jyotisha, Vedic astrology, helps us make sense of those karmas by unraveling the map of our lives displayed in the heavens, including how to time anything for optimal success. This is covered in chapter 11.

The remaining chapters explore how these levels of dharma intertwine in our daily lives.

The word *karma* is often associated with reincarnation, but you don't have to believe in reincarnation to realize that you are affected by the past. A look at your genetic heritage over many generations is a look back at the karma (actions and their consequences) of your ancestors and how that is playing out today. From alcoholism and diabetes to behavioral and spiritual attitudes, we are influenced by the past while possessing the free will to act on it and create our future. In this way, karma is both fate and free will, separated by time.

Karma is both fate and free will, separated by time.

The free will of today creates our experience of tomorrow. Indulge in ice cream and candy often enough and you suffer the effects of this sugar abuse in the form of diabetes and poor health. Likewise, if you have inherited patterns of self-neglect from your predecessors, you can do something about it starting today to create a balanced life for yourself tomorrow. Just how to do that is the realm of dharma, and in this book we will look at how to follow the natural laws of your being in every sphere, from the physical to the spiritual, and learn how, by doing our dharma, we mitigate undesirable karma.

**Doing your dharma erases your karma—
or at least mitigates its effects.**

PART ONE

Dharma

✦

*Creating a Framework
for Success in Life and Love*

1

Inside Us All

The Origins of Dharma

Have you ever wished human beings came with an instruction manual? Have you wondered why most material things in life come with directions, like your car or your toaster, but how to have a happy marriage and how to determine your purpose are usually left for us to figure out for ourselves? From caring for our bodies to raising our kids, life's essential lessons are not taught in school; instead, we have to pick them up from family, mentors, or personal experience, especially in the West. In the ancient East, specifically the Vedic culture of India, questions like "Who am I?," "Where do I come from?," and "What am I here to do?" were considered more crucial than multiplication tables, and were addressed early on.

The rishis of ancient India, who tried to answer these questions, used keen insight as well as trial and error to understand the basic nature of every human being, what they called dharma. In Sanskrit, *dharma* means "purpose," the natural law of your being. By living in accordance with your dharma, you maximize positive experiences and minimize negative outcomes in your life. The dharma types are an instruction manual for how to live a fulfilled life, the details of which are discussed in my previous book *The Five Dharma Types*.

In this book, I will show you how to hack into and start using your dharma software from day one in love, work, knowledge, and beyond. In brief, the dharma types are:

Warrior—whose purpose is to fight for a just cause, solve problems, lead, and to protect that which cannot protect itself

Educator—whose purpose is to enlighten others, bringing good counsel to the world

Merchant—whose purpose is to unite people and things in a way that fosters enjoyment and prosperity, the happiness brokers of the dharma type family

Laborer—whose purpose is to love, serve, support, and build communities, without whom society as we know it cannot exist

Outsider—whose purpose is to seek out freedom, new experiences, and a unique expression that reforms and refreshes the world

These are the five archetypes, and they have more to say about living your best life than simply what your profession should be or what your personality is like. There is a specific diet, lifestyle, exercise regimen, favored entertainment, and even sexual expression for every dharma type. Finding yours will help you flow with nature in a way that makes life and your relationships more fulfilling. Why is this? Because dharma means living with nature rather than fighting against it.

> "In order that people may be happy in their work, these three things are needed: they must be fit for it; they must not do too much of it; and they must have a sense of success in it."
> JOHN RUSKIN

THE ORIGINS OF DHARMA

The word *dharma* comes from the Sanskrit root *dhr,* which means "to sustain." This is the same root from which we get the English words *firm, farm,* and *throne,* and is related to *truth, tree,* and *betroth*—all things that indicate permanence and sustenance. That which sustains our bodies, minds, emotions, and the universe itself is dharma. Long ago, before the carbon-neutral movement, recycling, and "being green" were in fashion, our ancestors talked about real sustainability; that is, living in accord with our nature. That's why reducing our carbon footprint is less important than minimizing our karmic footprint, which is done by walking in dharma.

> **More important than reducing our carbon footprint is minimizing our karmic footprint, which is done by walking in dharma.**

Have you ever told a lie? Think about how much effort it took to keep it up over time. You had to build a backstory and constantly cover up to make it plausible. It takes effort to sustain *adharma,* dharma's opposite. It is wasteful and pollutes not only the external environment but your inner self as well. There is a fractious energy around you when you go against dharma, and others feel it at a subtle level, even if they can't express what they're feeling. This can create a snowball effect that eventually leads to calamity. Little things add up to big problems when you go against the grain of your nature. Rejecting your purpose or doing another's dharma not only harms you, but others as well, which creates karma. Undesirable karma, in turn, generates *duhkha,* or suffering. These three concepts—karma, dharma, and duhka—are jewels in the crown of Vedic philosophy, and the most valuable of these is dharma. Walking in dharma reduces your karmic footprint, minimizes duhkha, and increases *sukha,* joy and happiness.

Ultimately it is easiest to just tell the truth, even if hurts in the short term. There is nothing to hide and no energy wasted in being true to yourself. It is only uncomfortable when you don't have the tools to express your nature. The first step in learning exactly how to reclaim your dharma and make it work for you is finding your dharma type.

Let's begin! Take the following self tests to figure out your dharma type.

DISCOVER YOUR DHARMA TYPE!

So let us now discover your dharma type. In Self Test 1 choose the answers that describe you best; you can choose up to four for each multiple choice question if you are unable to decide. Next, read the paragraphs in Self Test 2 and choose two that describe you *best*. Not all of their qualities have to fit, though they should at least elicit a gut reaction of "yeah, that's me"—even if you don't necessarily like them! There are two paragraphs for each type. If it is difficult to decide, you may pick as many paragraphs as you like and narrow the results later. Check the answer key at the bottom of each test to tally your choices. The two that receive the most tallies likely indicate your dharma type and the Life Cycle you are in.*

It is useful to have friends or relatives help us with the tests and descriptions. Often we see ourselves differently from how the rest of the world perceives us. We may also be in a cycle that makes it difficult to access our essential dharma type. Life cycles can tint our basic expression like different colored lenses—some enhance our

---

*Another way to find your dharma type is to consult your Vedic life map. This requires an accurate birth time and place, though it is often possible to use general information such as "around 10 a.m." This technique not only zeroes in on dharma type, which remains the same, but also on the sequence of life cycles (different periods experienced as we travel through life and assume different roles and karmas). Dharma type practitioners can be found at www.spirittype.com.

light while others sometimes diffuse it—so take your whole life into consideration when reading the following descriptions, and have a friend or relative help you in the process. Looking at yourself from childhood to now will provide a complete portrait that should help determine your type.

◈ SELF TEST I

Circle the answers that best apply to you. You may choose more than one answer for each question if applicable. Try to think of qualities that are permanent in you, how you have always been, rather than how you are at times or during recent changes in your life. Tally them up at the end to determine your dharma type.

1. **Circle the word that means the most to you or describes you best.**
   a. Freedom
   b. Loyalty
   c. Wisdom
   d. Honor
   e. Prosperity

2. **Circle the phrase that means the most to you or describes you best.**
   a. Independence and Bliss
   b. Love and Devotion
   c. Worldliness and Knowledge
   d. Discipline and Perfection
   e. Entertainment and Fun

3. **Circle the phrase that means the most to you or describes you best.**
   a. I love being alone. Sometimes I hate people, sometimes I like them, but they usually don't understand me.
   b. I don't mind being alone as long as I have something constructive and productive to do.

c. I love being alone. I like people but I need time to spend by myself for quiet contemplation and rejuvenation.

d. I don't mind being alone, as long as I have a goal to accomplish.

e. I hate being alone. I prefer the company of people, even if I don't know them.

4. **Circle the phrase that means the most to you or describes you best.**

a. I like strange, dark, or wild and remote places no one has ever thought of or been to.

b. I like the plains and wide expanses of earth. I like living close to the ground, on ground floors rather than in high-rise apartments.

c. I like high and remote places. I like upper floors, high-rise buildings, and living above others looking down.

d. I like challenging places, places that are high, but not so high as to be remote. I like fortified and strong places.

e. From the Beverly Hills to gently rolling slopes, I like places where the action is, places that are easy to get to, but also exclusive. I like living in the middle ground, not too high, not too low, where there is activity and access to the world.

5. **Circle the sentence that describes you best.**

a. I am the rebel or black sheep of my family. As a parent, I give freedom to my kids and let them individualize themselves from others.

b. I am deeply bonded with my family. As a parent, I nurture my kids by making sure they are well fed, healthy, and content.

c. I tend to teach my family and urge them to improve themselves. As a parent I make certain my kids learn how to think for themselves, get a good education, and understand the world.

d. I am the strong one in my family. As a parent I lead by example and earn my kids' respect with discipline and order.

e. I actively support my family with shelter and resources. As a parent I provide for my kids and make sure they understand the value of money, self-effort, and making your way in the world.

6. In religion I *most* value the following:

   a.   Going my own way.

   b.   Faith and devotion.

   c.   Study and scripture.

   d.   Penance and discipline.

   e.   Rituals and observances.

7. In marriage I *most* value the following:

   a.   An unconventional spouse, one who understands my particular quirks and desires.

   b.   A dutiful spouse who is loyal and provides for me: a woman who cooks and cleans/a man who brings home the bacon.

   c.   A sensitive, intelligent spouse.

   d.   A challenging spouse with whom I can do activities.

   e.   A beautiful spouse.

8. I mainly watch TV for:

   a.   Horror, alternative political and spiritual viewpoints, science fiction (like the sci-fi, FX, indie, and alternative channels).

   b.   Family, drama, history, and community programs (like soap operas, reality TV, daytime shows, cartoons, entertainment gossip, and reruns).

   c.   Educational, thought-provoking, human-interest stories and entertainment (like National Geographic, PBS, Syfy, and documentary channels).

   d.   Sports, action, news, and politics; adventure stories and entertainment (ESPN, CNN, etc.).

   e.   Fun programs, drama, music, comedy, game shows, financial and motivational stories and entertainment (like HBO, the Comedy Channel, and Spike).

9. **Under stress I tend to:**
   a.   Bend the rules or lie to get my way; feel invisible and self-deprecate.
   b.   Become lazy, close down in my own space, and worry a lot.
   c.   Be scatterbrained, feckless, and wishy-washy.
   d.   Become anger prone, inattentive, and reckless.
   e.   Be moody, depressed, loud, and restless.

10. **At my best I am:**
   a.   A revolutionary, an inventor, a genius.
   b.   A devoted friend, a hard worker, a caregiver.
   c.   A counselor, a teacher, a diplomat.
   d.   A leader, a hero, a risk taker.
   e.   An optimist, a self-starter, a promoter, an adventurer.

Answer Key for Self Test I

Tally your answers now. The most selected letter likely reflects your dharma type. For confirmation you should now move on to Self Test II.

   A. Outsider
   B. Laborer
   C. Educator
   D. Warrior
   E. Merchant

 **SELF TEST II**

Select *two* paragraphs that describe you best. Then refer to the answer key on page 18 to determine your type.

1. Sometimes I think no one really understands me, and no one ever will. I love freedom and need to feel independent and free most of all. Although I can fit into many crowds, I never really feel a part of any of them. I wear many hats but none of them defines me. People may see me as secretive or mysterious, but I am just the way I am—different. By fate or choice I am attracted to foreign lands, cultures, religions, and values and have embraced some of these. I have talents and abilities that are not always recognized, and it can be hard to make a living if I do not compromise with my society. My ambitions are somewhat unique, and I have a quirky way of seeing the world. Sometimes I feel lost and don't know what my true purpose is, but when I look at others I am reminded of what it is not: I can't conform to somebody else's lifestyle just for the sake of security, even though I may not have found my own.

2. I have often dreamt of owning my own business and being financially independent. From an early age I have felt a need to provide and be provided for. I have a strong sense of the value of money and I don't mind working long hours to generate security for myself and my family. I don't pay much attention to my body, unless it is part of my business or I have the leisure time. I like giving and the feeling that it creates, but in this competitive world it is most important to secure my own and my family's needs first. I have a good practical sense and know how to take care of mundane obligations. I believe that anyone can make it in today's society if they're willing to apply themselves. I am motivated and self-driven and can't understand idealistic or so-called spiritual people who deny the importance of financial security.

3. I like to protect those who cannot protect themselves. I believe in standing up for a good cause whether it is social, environmental, ecological, etc. Money is less important to me than securing justice in the world. I have strong convictions and character, and people often look to me for leadership. I have an inner strength that drives me to achieve. I can usually outperform others by sheer force of will. I have an eye for deception and can tell when someone is lying. I admire wisdom and like to associate with smart and educated people, though I may not have the time or opportunity to cultivate these qualities in myself. I can be highly disciplined and therefore acquire skills quickly. At my best I am courageous, noble, and self-sacrificing, but I can also be distracted, anger prone, and judgmental.

4. I love the camaraderie of working with others to construct something useful. I am handy, skilled, practical, and not averse to work. I am devoted to friends and family, and though not an intellectual I have a good sense about things, though I can't always explain it in words. My needs and tastes are simple, and it doesn't take a lot to make me happy: good food, good company, and a solid roof over my head are the essentials in life. I like being of service and feeling needed. Being useful to someone is more important than how much money I make, though I don't like to be cheated. I believe in hard work and don't understand lazy people. I can be superstitious and have deep-seated beliefs about things that often stem from my childhood and cannot be easily rationalized.

5. I prefer intellectual work to physical labor. I can be idealistic and focus on concepts and philosophies rather than living in the real world. I become disheartened by the ugliness and injustice of life and often lack energy to change it. I have always been smarter and more perceptive than most of my peers, though not inherently practical. I like to counsel others, though I don't always practice what I preach. I have a knack for encouraging and finding the best in people, and as a

result people come to me for advice. I don't have a killer instinct and that's a disadvantage if I try to compete in physical or other cutthroat professions. I like to live in a peaceful environment, rather than the hustle and bustle of the busy world. I often know what needs to be done but don't necessarily have the energy or skills to do it. It is often easier for me to tell others what to do rather than to do it myself.

6. I set strong standards for myself and expect to live up to them. I love competition, debate, and testing my limits. I even compete with myself when others are not around. I have a huge heart, and my generosity sometimes gets me in trouble. I like to lay down the law in my family and with others. From early on I was blessed with physical and mental strength, though I often abuse these by pushing too much—I play hard and party hard. I like to care for those who cannot fend for themselves: the innocent, the elderly, and the underprivileged.

7. I hate constrictive social, religious, and moral institutions, and I feel it is my right to speak and act out against them. I also feel justified in flouting an unjust law and not conforming to artificial regulations. I am physically, emotionally, and/or spiritually different from others, and because of this I find it hard to fit in. I can see through people's bullshit, and that makes me want to run away from society. Sometimes I resent normal people who were born with opportunities that I don't have. I would rather overthrow the status quo to allow fresh growth than try to patch things up piece by piece. I respect an authority that allows me to be who I am and understands the gifts I have to offer.

8. I am a devoted, loyal, patriotic person and have a deep connection to the things that are dearest to me: my family, friends, God, and country. I believe it is important to abide by the codes and principles of my country, church, and society. I love to build community. I guess you could say I'm sentimental about the things I value. A dutiful worker, I believe in getting a job done right and am faithful to my word. I am also very good at what I do and specialize in well-developed skills. I secretly

admire widely read and cultured people and wish I were a bit more like them, but I just don't have the time to waste on that and prefer to be better at what I do than to know a lot of trivia. I have to touch, see, hear, or feel something; otherwise it is not real for me.

9. I love attention and being the life of the party. I am quick and clever and find it easy to get along with others. I can be very likable, though I don't necessarily like other people and am more attached to the few people I can really trust—myself and my family. I am naturally glib and gregarious, and people tend to believe what I say. I have good taste and appreciation for the finer things in life, things that have beauty and value. However, I sometimes feel an emptiness that I have to fill with outside things, though it is never really filled until I give or do something for others. Sometimes I feel that I am not worth anything, and that if people really knew me they wouldn't like me. Because of this I respect those who have raised and supported me, and I work hard to pay back their love in return. I am also very emotional and can go to extremes of depression and elation. This volatility may cost me in relationships and in my health, and I sometimes like to numb it with drugs, sex, and entertainment. I enjoy all sorts of fun, from performing for people and being the center of attention to watching others do the same.

10. I consider myself a rather cultured, mild-mannered person. I don't tolerate vulgarity or crass behavior. I have special food preferences and daily regimes that require me to be alone for parts of the day so I can tend to my rather delicate constitution. I tend to be solitary in my personal habits and prefer losing myself in a book more than engaging in the hustle and bustle of the world. I like the realm of ideas and concepts, though I am rarely able to embody them in the real world. I don't have abundant physical energy, though I enjoy sports, games, and being in Nature for their recreational and inspirational value.

Answer Key for Self Test II

1 and 7: Outsider

2 and 9: Merchant

3 and 6: Warrior

4 and 8: Laborer

5 and 10: Educator

2

The Roles We Play

General Principles of Dharma

"I just don't know what to do. I'm stuck and overwhelmed, and I feel like such a failure. I mean, the best part of my day is probably walking the dog."

This is my Vedic life-mapping client, let's call her Jane, a few minutes into our dharma session. Complaints like this are increasingly common, and Jane is one of a new set of well-intentioned but confused purpose seekers.

"Does your dog think you're a failure?" I ask.

"Well, no, I guess not," she chuckles. "I probably take care of him better than I take care of myself."

"I wish you could see yourself through his eyes, because you're definitely doing something right with him. And if we called your son, your boss, or your friends and asked, 'Do you think Jane is a failure?,' wouldn't they say you're at least doing okay in their eyes, if not better?"

Instead of categorically pronouncing ourselves failures, it helps to isolate what we're not happy with, and also to focus on things that are working.

"Well, yeah . . . but I still feel like something's missing."

"What if life were a stage and you were a character, with a

specific script to follow, marks to hit, and so on. Would it be easier to know your purpose and feel fulfilled?"

"Yeah, sure. It would be nice to have a set of instructions."

Most of our obligations in life are simply roles we play. We are *master* to our pets, *spouse* or *main squeeze* to our significant other, *parent* to our kids, *child* to our parents, *employee* to our boss, and *pain in the neck* to our employees. These are roles pretty much every human being has had to play from prehistoric times to the present day. In traditional cultures, happiness came from fulfilling your obligations to family and society.

Not satisfied that these roles are enough, in the modern West we have put a twist on this arrangement and begun to glorify the individual, seeking our happiness from our personality and not our role. We say, "I matter," instead of "my role matters," in part because the roles we choose are not enough to fulfill us. But the truth is that even when we exalt the individual, exclaiming, for example, "You're great!," we're still only saying, "You're great . . . at something," like making money or cooking. When I worked in sales, I noticed that when numbers were high everybody was my friend, but when sales dipped I began getting the suspicious "What's wrong with that guy?" look. This is nothing but your role affecting how people see you.

Our roles are important, but so are we. Part of the reason we have rejected them and set up selfhood as our primary source of happiness is because we have lost connection to the roles that really matter. Somehow *friend*, *hockey fan*, and even *parent* are not enough anymore. That is because dharma is missing from our life. Dharma is purpose, the blueprint that not only outlines how to play our daily roles, but also points the way to personal happiness. That sense of a life well lived comes in part from doing our job as a mom or a friend, but also from having fulfilled our purpose on this planet. Everybody is born with a purpose, a destiny. It just takes skill to find it.

✦✦✦

A Sanskrit aphorism states, "There is no sound that is not a mantra, no plant that is not medicine; no person who does not have a use, but people skilled at finding these things are themselves hard to find." The Vedic culture believed that nothing in nature is useless, that everything has a purpose. Accordingly, they arranged the sounds of the alphabet to create the perfect vibrational language, Sanskrit. They found the medicinal value of every vegetable, animal, and mineral substance in their environment and organized it under ayurveda, the study of life. They distilled the five essences of individual purpose, called the dharma types, and passed this wisdom down to us via oral tradition.

To understand yourself is to understand your dharma type. Knowing your weaknesses is knowing the weaknesses of your type. Your faults and strengths are written in you just like characters in a play, and in the play of life you are free to improvise and create, but the basic script you work with has been already penned by creation itself. The canvas of your life is sketched; it is up to you to fill in the lines.

> To understand yourself is to understand your dharma type.
> Knowing your weaknesses is knowing the weaknesses
> of your type. The canvas of your life is sketched;
> it is up to you to fill in the lines.

When Michelangelo painted the Sistine Chapel he took great care to craft the sketches of the figures, but sometimes left his assistants to fill in the paint. The sketch was everything; such is the importance of a blueprint. Similarly, your dharma type is your basic blueprint, and in this book we will learn how to use it to color in and fulfill all your heart's desires.

Jane is intrigued, but her face is twisted in a puzzled look. She asks, "Okay, if there are seven billion people on the planet and five dharma types, how does that make me unique?"

I reply, "Can you think for a moment what life would be like if you didn't know your gender?"

For most people this is a nonquestion, a theoretical exercise, but think about how confusing life would be if you didn't know whether you were a man or a woman. These two simple categories—male and female—affect us almost every waking moment. Everything from the clothes we wear to the way we walk and talk, even our names are determined by sex.

I tell her that the answer is simple: like knowing your gender, understanding your dharma can turn the guesswork of day-to-day choices into easy and intelligent decisions. Even more important, it can help you find your purpose. Like a compass, your dharma type always points in the right direction; you simply have to learn how to use it. And though it is not as visible as gender, I believe, as did the ancient seers who discovered these archetypes, that your dharma type is fixed in you—just as sexual preference, eye color, and other traits are.

For example, your archetype can help you navigate relationships and harness the laws of attraction. Knowing who you are will help you find the right mate and protect you from those who are not right for you. Knowing who you are is sexy and promotes deep attraction. When you commit to walking in dharma, both men and women become drawn to you because people are attracted to those who live their purpose. Doing your dharma influences people and benefits the environment in ways you can't imagine. That's why the message of our Vedic elders is simple: play your role to the best of your ability and leave the results to the universe. As an example, Jane, who is an Educator, has a charm that comes from wisdom and gentleness. When Educators try to take on the party heartiness of the Merchant type, they lose their natural grace and fall flat.

Knowing who you are will help you find the right mate and protect you from those who are not right for you. Knowing who you are is sexy, whether you're a man or a woman, and promotes deep attraction.

We all play multiple roles every day—father, boss, employee, sports fan, and so on. But these roles are limited and cannot fulfill us completely. These roles are also automatic. When you drive, do you ever think about your duty as a licensed chauffeur—a law-abiding member of the driving class—a role that comes with many privileges and not a few perils? Do you consciously consider your responsibility not to run over people, not to damage property, and to stay in your lane and obey traffic signals? You don't, but this is your obligation as a driver, and the world expects nothing less from you, and nothing more. Do you ever come home and say, "Man, I did a terrible job driving today. I could have been home a minute and a half earlier if I hadn't switched lanes behind that dump truck!" Even if you do have this kind of internal dialogue, how much of your time is spent being depressed about it? Probably not much, because unless you drive for a living (in which case this becomes your profession), your commute doesn't rank high up on your list of priorities. Treat your dharma this way: become consciously competent yet unattached to its fruits. This is the first step to freedom.

KARYAM

The Sanskrit word *karyam* is generally translated as "work." The word actually means "that which has to be done." Typically you don't think of feeding a baby or changing a spare tire as work—these things just "need to be done" for life to flow smoothly. In much the same way, your dharma is karyam, what has to be done for you to have health, wealth, and spiritual success.

By taking the personal element out of it—the *I need to do, I need to be*—we eliminate the tension these statements engender. It is not you but your dharma that matters. Your personal feelings aside, the car doesn't care who changes its tire. The kids don't care who feeds them, as long as they are fed. In that moment, it is not you, but your role as a mechanic or a parent that matters most, and your feelings toward the karyam, the work, are less important. Your body doesn't care how you feel about giving it proper maintenance, as long as you do it. In the end you'll be happy you did.

Whether you know it or not, the role you are given to play largely determines your experience and expectations. Every role is set up by the scriptwriter: the secret is that you are also the coauthor of your destiny. The difference between feeling successful or feeling like a failure is not how well you play your roles, but how you view them.

"What if I told you that, as an Educator, your duty is to bring wisdom and understanding to people?"

"I can relate to that," Jane replies. "I've always loved teaching and learning new things. But my husband is a businessman, and sometimes it's hard because he's always thinking about the bottom line. I'm different—that's not a priority for me—and it causes problems between us."

"Merchant types have to make money because they use this to make life better for others. Is your husband involved in any charitable activity?"

"No, except for the Little League he coaches on weekends. He does spoil the kids, though, taking them on trips, buying them meals, and treating them to a good time. And that's the thing—he thinks my doing yoga and meditation is a waste of energy and money, whereas he's either working or gone on the weekends."

I explain to Jane that Merchants and Educators speak different languages, and that to understand each other you have to understand what makes each other tick. Merchants are ruled by the Water element. Water is emotion and, like the tides, Merchants can be changeable or even volatile. Water also rules taste, and Merchants have a zest for life, a zeal that can make them temperamental or tempestuous. Finally, Water is value—homes on the beach are always more expensive than those inland. The world's greatest civilizations prospered from the rivers they were founded upon: the Nile, the Indus, the Tigris and Euphrates. Water is money, an essential blessing to Merchant types because it allows them to fulfill their spiritual dharma, which is giving back.

"For your husband, the greatest spiritual practice is charity—to give what he has in abundance to others. If he's working hard and giving back, he doesn't need to meditate or do yoga, which is why he probably can't understand why you need to."

"But as an Educator that's sort of my thing. I love to read five books at a time, and he can't understand why I spend so much money on two-hundred-hour yoga certifications if I'm not doing anything with them, like making a living!"

For optimal compatibility, two people have to understand their dharma types and what drives their purpose in the world. They have to communicate this to the other and find a way to compromise that's satisfying to both of them.

"What if you tried to make some money from what you know, by seeing clients here and there or teaching classes, to show him that this stuff is marketable? On the other hand, he should accept that ideas are more important to you than material possessions, that they amount to wealth in themselves, whether marketed or not. Show him you understand what he values, and support him in being even more charitable."

THE MODERN CAVEWOMAN

The second part of Jane's concern is that she's run-down and doesn't even know it. While carrying out her roles as mother, spouse, and all-around good girl, she has neglected her own physical needs.

"Jane, what does it mean to be successful and fulfilled, in your mind?" I ask.

She cocks her head and her eyes move up and out, searching her mind.

"I guess I just want to feel happy, like I've done my job in the world, like I've been a good wife and mother, connected myself to something greater than my own life, something higher in the universe."

It's an answer I hear from many women. Unfortunately, many of them also overextend themselves, trying to be all things to all people without devoting enough time to their own needs. Wanting to be happy but not acting like it produces frustrating results.

"Are you easily startled, say, by loud noises?"

"Yeah, I guess. My husband says I'm jumpy," Jane replies.

Being on edge is a sign that your body is in stress survival mode.

"You know, dharma works in two ways—outward and inward," I tell her. "You have a dharma to fulfill in the world, but also a duty to your own body and mind."

A wise man said that "behavior is everything," meaning that when our actions are inconsistent with our thoughts and desires, problems arise. We want happiness, but we do not act as if we do.

"When you spend your last bit of free time answering emails so people don't feel hurt, or attending to the needs of others without making time for yourself, you create an imbalance, a 'disturbance in the Force,' in *Star Wars* terms."

She laughs, getting the analogy and, more important, its reality in her life.

"Women are raised to believe that if they work hard enough taking care of others—their parents, kids, spouses, coworkers, neighbors—they will magically find fulfillment. If you only soldier on, ignoring your needs and the rhythms of nature, you can make it and achieve the American dream. You have to look no further than how we view the menstrual cycle—as a nuisance, an unwelcome visitor. Women are taught to ignore this call from nature to relax and reset, and push through it instead. After all, there are deadlines to meet.

"Being busy is not a virtue," I tell her. "You want to give it all—to your family, to your job, to your country—but you also have a duty to yourself, and abandoning that is like leaving someone stranded on the side of the road. Ignoring the dharma of your body and your mind is like abandoning your dharma type."

In modern parlance, forsaking your biological needs for replenishment and rest translates into increased stress. When you overextend yourself your body enters survival mode; you begin to run on the stress hormones cortisol and norepinephrine. Over time, running on stress shuts down reproductive function and digestion. Then symptoms like menstrual pain, low hormone levels, fatigue, and fuzzy thinking set in. When digestion is impaired, a whole host of problems crop up. And that's just the beginning.

"With your body in constant survival mode, which it enters when you do not devote time to replenishing it, functions like fat burning and rejuvenation, which are less crucial to survival, are shut off, since fat is a slow-burning fuel that does not work as well as sugar for emergencies. As a result, your body demands more sugar and, long story short, before you know it, you've put on fifteen pounds.

"The infomercial people with the really ripped abs are telling you that you need to work out harder. So you do, creating more stress in the process, which increases cortisol levels and exacerbates the vicious cycle. Despite training harder, your weight remains the same. Instead of speeding up, you need to cool down."

Rather than training harder we need to train smarter, and in the following chapters I will show you self-care tools that will help you burn fat the right way, by turning your attention to the dharma of the body. In a revealing TED talk every woman (and man!) should see, Dr. Libby Weaver examines the implications of being a modern "juggling woman" while living with cavewoman biochemistry.* She notes that despite doing two hours of cardio a day, she couldn't burn fat. But once she took up t'ai chi, the weight melted off. Why? When you are stressed your body holds onto fat for protection. When you learn to relax, it too relaxes and lets go of its security blanket. Taking a deep breath and getting out of stress mode will make you healthier and more attractive and improve your relationships.

For both men and women, stress hormones are great at getting us out of immediate danger but they are lousy to live with. Stress is the opposite of attraction. Learning to deal with it and create attraction in our relationships is one of the purposes of this book.

STOUTENING AND LIGHTENING

The classic texts of ayurveda tell us that when body and mind are stressed or emaciated, *brimhana,* or anabolic food and therapy, should be used. When a person is suffering from obesity or stagnation, *langhana,* or catabolic food and therapies, are called for. Anabolic foods include milk, meat, sugar, butter, ghee, and oily foods. Perhaps part of the reason modern Western culture, from Europe to the Americas, indulges in these foods is because our lifestyles have become so stressful and emaciating that we feel a natural need to counterbalance them with heavy foods and sed-

---

*This talk is "The Pace of Modern Life versus Our Cavewoman Biochemistry: Dr Libby Weaver at TED." It can be found at www.youtube.com/watch?v=tJ0SME6Z9rw.

entary habits. Bacon for breakfast, chicken for lunch, and beef for dinner is a common American meal plan (sometimes called the standard American diet, or SAD). This was unheard of among our ancestors. Back then, butchering an animal was reserved for special occasions, and even the hardiest meat eaters did not partake of meat at every meal.

Modern Merchant society has instilled the credo of busyness into our culture to such a degree that even the things that are supposed to ease our efforts and relax us, like cell phones and TV, actually take up more time and attention than they free up. Watching TV after a hard day's work deadens the mind and body, but it is not relaxing or nourishing to either. Cell phones and computers are supposed to free us but end up tying most people down, tethering them by the thread of instant communication and information. Going into zombie mode in front of the TV and eating heavy, salty, and sweet food on the go are not good long-term strategies for breaking the cycle of stress. The lifestyle suggestions in this book will naturally put you in a fat-burning, calm, and steady state.

"So the dharma type can show me what to do for health too?" she asks.

"Your dharma type has some things to say about diet and lifestyle. For example, you're an Educator and your digestion is finicky. You should always devote at least an hour to your lunch or dinner, eating in a relaxed, stress-free environment. Whatever your schedule, block out this hour every day for yourself, and honor it. Take time to lie on your left side to let your food digest. And replace one hour of TV every night with a warm bath. That's it. Do those two things and you'll see a big difference."

**You are only as old as your digestive system:
keep it healthy and it will keep you young.**

Diet books are always on the best-seller list because no one diet works for everyone, yet every book resonates with someone. But it's not just about the food you eat; it's about what your body can do with it. If you eat on the go all the time, no diet will work for you. If you don't allow your digestive tract to rest from time to time, by fasting intermittently and allowing time between meals, your health and immunity will suffer. You are only as old as your digestive system: keep it healthy and it will keep you young.

THE FOUR SUPPORTS

In Hindu society, when people talk of dharma they usually refer to two things: *varna* and *ashrama*—your dharma type and the season of life. The life seasons are broad, helpful ways to know what's expected of you personally and socially, based on your age.

The four seasons of life—Spring (Laborer), Summer (Warrior/Merchant), Autumn (Educator), and Winter (Outsider)—are bolstered by the supports we need during those stages: parents, spouse, children, and the Divine, respectively (see table 2.1).* In the first, the springtime of our lives (roughly from birth to age twenty-two), we rely on our parents to raise, shelter, feed, and otherwise nourish us while we are learning to stand on our own. Through our childhood and teenage years, it is the job of parents, grandparents, aunts, uncles, and the extended family to look out for our safety and teach us how to nurture ourselves physically, emotionally, and intellectually so we grow into mature men and women. This includes lessons in sexual maturity that are quite different for men and women, as discussed in part 2.

---

*For more on the four seasons of life see my book *The Five Dharma Types*.

TABLE 2.1. FOUR SEASONS OF LIFE
AND THE DHARMA TYPES

DHARMA TYPE	SEASON	AGE SEASON ENDS
Laborer	Spring	22–25
Warrior/Merchant	Summer	44–50
Educator	Autumn	66–75
Outsider	Winter	Death

During the summer season (ages twenty-two to forty-four), we lean on our spouses to help us become whole. This is when we join together to produce something more than we can ever be ourselves. Statistics routinely show that married couples are healthier, make more money, and have higher status (that is, occupy higher social rankings) than unmarried people. Statistics also astonishingly favor marrying in the Summer over the Spring season. That is because couples who marry before age twenty-five have an over 60 percent divorce rate!* This may be partly because the requisite training young men and women need has not been completed. In chapter 8 we discuss the need for male and female education and initiation. When young people marry too early, the Spring support (parents and elders) is yanked away too soon and the Summer support is not yet strong enough to sustain the relationship. Unless you have very strong extended families, as is the case in Indian and other traditional societies, couples breaking away from the nest too soon to

---

*Sixty percent of marriages for couples between the ages of twenty and twenty-five end in divorce. "Those who marry under the age of 20 have the highest rate of divorce. These couples are nearly 1.5 times as likely to get divorced as those who get married between the ages of 20 to 24 years old. Those who marry after the age of 25 are even less likely to get divorced." ("Marriage and Divorce Statistics," National Center for Health Statistics [April 12, 2010], www.avvo.com/legal-guides/ugc/marriage-divorce-statistics.)

get married risk severely high odds of divorce. In more traditional settings, married couples tend to live in the same house or at least very near the family home. If you do not have such a setup, consider waiting until at least age twenty-five before getting married.

Because the desire to share your life as a couple is strongest during the Summer season, loneliness and depression are not uncommon in singles who fail to find a partner during this time. This loneliness will only increase in the Autumn season, when leaves start falling from the trees and our attachments to the world slowly grow weaker. The needs for partnership should be fulfilled in the Summer; it is too late to look for partnership in the Fall, for nature has other plans for us at that time.

Thus, it is important to know where we are in life and what our expected supports are. Love (and marriage) is a Summer game, one that continues to support us well into the Fall season of our lives. But in the Fall, as Winter approaches, we must recuse ourselves from the crutches of Summer and become more and more independent. What is life but an ongoing search for independence? In Spring, our parents and elders teach us who we are and how to behave as well-raised individuals. In Summer, our spouses help us become the best we can be—to be more than the sum of our parts. An old adage holds that "If it weren't for women, men would still live in caves." That desire for improvement, for material comfort and success, for civilization itself is a result of the male/female bond and the Summer season of life.

In the Fall we gain even greater independence. We are relieved of the fever of struggle for success and released from the responsibilities of changing diapers, going to work, and holding down the fort of the family unit. We are free to travel (Air element), to study, and to refine our individuality. This is often when we begin to take courses for general self-improvement, in line with the Educator nature of the season.

During Autumn, we turn to intangible supports: to wisdom, dharma, and Spirit. We become teachers, and our children and students become secondary supports. That is, we learn from teaching and passing down our wisdom. Without the crutch of young people, wide-eyed and open-eared, we cannot complete the Fall stage of our lives. They help us consolidate our knowledge and experience. This is why initiation rituals are so important, both for elders and for adolescents. These rituals help us understand our roles during every stage of life. The questions and issues raised by students and children help us rethink our positions and assumptions so that we distill what we've learned into wisdom.

Finally, our greatest independence comes when, releasing everything, we embrace the Winter season and its Space element. This is the stage of wisdom, when our limited, localized personalities begin to identify with something greater than themselves. Like Space, consciousness is everywhere; in the stream, in the field, in our next-door neighbor. Real compassion comes when you see yourself in another—when another's suffering and wisdom become yours.

In the Winter, all our physical props fall away: our parents are dead, our spouses have given their contributions to us and have moved on to taking care of their own Fall and Winter responsibilities. Our kids have now moved on to the Summer of their own lives and are busy with spouses, children, and careers of their own. In the Winter our material supports fall away to make room for the Spirit. God, Love, Creation—whatever you want to call the substratum of your existence—this is the top level of the dharma pyramid, and the pillar of the fourth stage of life. From our midsixties onward—the appropriately named (and timed) retirement years—our support is the invisible hand, not of the market but perhaps of the darkness, as the Spirit is utterly invisible to our five senses. Or, perhaps more optimistically, we might consider this the invisible hand of the Light.

Don't worry if you don't understand these concepts just yet. We will come back to them later and show you just how and why they can help you build not only successful relationships, but a successful life.

The title of this book is *Sex, Love, and Dharma,* but really *dharma* should be first. Without making dharma primary, we are like a blind person in a dark room looking for something that isn't there, to paraphrase a famous quote. Without dharma, sex cannot fulfill us over the long term, and love is elusive. By putting the truth of who we are first, and following that, we find not only love, but also prosperity and success.

3

BE FIT

Your Dharma Type as a Guide for Life

In this chapter we will look at how to master your dharma type and use it to reach your potential in every area of your life. Even if you are completely new to these archetypes, the BE FIT five-step plan will take you from zero to hero in no time.

> **"Speak truth and do your dharma."**
> TAITTIRIYA UPANISHAD

"B"—BE YOURSELF

The first step is to get to know your dharma type. Once you've taken the test and narrowed it down to one or two types, read the summaries below and take them out for a spin. Get an idea of the strengths and weaknesses associated with each type.*

Educators
Strongly idealistic, but not necessarily practical
Noted for intelligence and grasp of abstruse concepts

---

*For more detailed information on each dharma type, refer to my book *The Five Dharma Types*. Or you might consult with a dharma type practitioner to help you understand your type, the life cycles, and the specific challenges at any given time.

Generally not forceful, physically less resilient than other types

Good counselors, but unable to follow their own counsel

Motivated by truth rather than money, but prone to indiscretions like anger, lust, or greed due to a lack of control over their senses

Sanskrit terms: jnana, dayaa, kshanti: wisdom, compassion, forbearance

Outsiders

Culture, beliefs, race, physicality, and other traits make them different from their immediate environment

Travels to or lives in foreign lands and different or unusual places

Absorbs and adopts foreign ideologies and concepts

Incredibly adaptive, able to blend in and wear many hats

Resents establishment and the "normal" life of others

Keenly aware of injustices in society, be they economic, educational, or political

Values personal freedom over other things

Sanskrit terms: ananda, kaivalya, svatantriya: bliss, isolation/independence, freedom

Warriors

Motivated by challenge to improve self and others

Interested in protecting those who cannot protect themselves

Responds to defiance and competition

Values knowledge, wisdom, and innocence in others

Sanskrit terms: yukti, virya, viveka: skill, strength, judgment

Merchants

Strongly motivated to secure personal and family interests

Needs to be around others, feels lonely or empty without company

A smooth talker: likeable, glib, socially active, and highly entertaining

Feels best when giving, at first to family, then to community, and eventually the world

Understands how the Merchant society functions and is good at taking advantage of it

Sanskrit terms: shakti, rasa, danam: energy, juiciness, charity

Laborers

Strong likes and dislikes

Deep sense of community and belonging

Emotional ties and loyalty to their own things: family, country, job, home team

Good physical strength and endurance, and a powerful work ethic

Capable of great service and self-sacrifice

Strong intuition and specific intelligence, but not well rounded

Sanskrit terms: bhakti, seva, dhriti: devotion/love, service, solidity/endurance

Once you are sure of your type, memorize the key emotions associated with it from table 3.1 on page 38. Remember that you cannot act outside of your dharma and be happy over the long term. You cannot pretend to be someone else and find lasting success, because that is a crime against wisdom. The root of all dis-ease is crimes against wisdom, which pull you away from your core purpose.

TABLE 3.1. COMMON EMOTIONS
FOR EACH DHARMA TYPE

DHARMA TYPE	NEGATIVE EMOTION	POSITIVE EMOTION
Outsider	Deception, anxiety	Empathy, wonder
Educator	Lust	Compassion
Laborer	Sloth, jealousy	Love, loyalty
Warrior	Anger, pride	Generosity
Merchant	Greed	Conviviality, enthusiasm

> You cannot act outside of your dharma and be happy over the long term. You cannot pretend to be someone else and find lasting success, because that is a crime against wisdom. The root of all dis-ease is crimes against wisdom, which pull you away from your core purpose.

"I want someone to love me for me. I don't want to try to be someone else." Clients who are single often say this to me, bemoaning the fact that it is so hard to express their true selves *and* find someone who loves them for themselves. My follow-up question is this: "Okay, do you want someone to love you for the ice-cream-eating, haven't-showered-in-two-days, couch-potato version of you, or the socially engaged and dynamic part of you?

"Wouldn't you agree that the dynamic you *is* trying to be someone else—someone different from the couch-potato you? In reality, both of these are in us. Which one we express determines how the world sees us. So which part of you do you want your potential mate to meet first?"

The answer is obvious, but many of us have forgotten how to be ourselves. The best way to do this is to know your role in any interaction, and your dharma type is the compass that will help you find it. Let it show you your role and lead you to your true self. In any interaction, each dharma type has a purpose.

Dharma Type Roles

Educators

An Educator should give people more wisdom and guidance than they had before. No matter what the situation, your role as an Educator is to create understanding. People open up to Educators, often without knowing why, because there is a harmlessness about you, a "safe space" you create that allows others to tell you anything. Be that compassionate, nonjudgmental, peacemaking Educator and see what happens the next time you talk to the guy at the bus stop or the lady across the counter. Even if you are secretly judgmental, that's okay; suspend acting on that inclination for a moment. Educators are deeply passionate, but emotionalism should not rule your interactions. Think of Gandhi or your favorite teacher or priest: Educators are exemplars of truth, purity, and wisdom, and always leave you knowing more than before you met them. That's your role, dear Educator, in everything you do. Kick the tires, take it for a spin, and see what happens.

Warriors

Warriors are born to protect that which cannot protect itself. They are made to lead, and qualified to do so because they also know how to follow orders. As a Warrior, your role in any interaction is to offer solutions to problems and take control, if necessary, to get the job done. This should not be in an aggressive or boisterous way, because aggression is a sign of weakness. The best Warrior gets things done quietly, efficiently, with the fewest casualties and the most benefit for all involved. From protecting health by combating disease or teaching yoga to fighting for human rights, the smartest Warriors choose their battles. Don't go chasing windmills just because you can. Pick the smart fight and finish one job before starting the next.

Merchants

The Merchant's job is to make people happy, using humor, food, entertainment, or anything that lifts the spirit and brings joy to the heart. Whether you give a compliment, a gift, or a free backrub is entirely up to you, but in your next interaction, see how you can bring *shakti*, positive energy, to others. You are the happiness broker to the world, dear Merchant, and there is no job as delightful and easy as yours, so get to it! You will find that your own happiness is linked to how much you give to others. This is the ironclad law of cause and effect that every evolved Merchant learns: you have to give to get.

> **Merchants' happiness is linked to how much they give to others. This is the ironclad law of cause and effect that every evolved Merchant learns: you have to give to get.**

Laborers

The Laborer's questions are "How can I help?" and "How can I be of service?" When you approach any interaction with this feeling in your heart, you cannot *help* but be useful, for Laborers are the most handy and useful of all the dharma types. As a Laborer you love to care for and nurture friends and family, and when you approach everyone as potential family you will grow your circle wider than ever. Think of Mother Teresa and Oprah Winfrey: the power that you have to build family and community reaches beyond borders and bloodlines. And when you have your family around you, you get the security and sense of belonging you need.

Outsiders

The Outsider's dharma is to refresh the world by conveying a unique perspective. Outsiders are often anxious about sharing new or unusual information for fear of how they'll be viewed. Don't worry about that: in any interaction, ask what you can do to give people options they never considered before or bring a sense of awe and mystery to their lives. Outsiders combine different elements to forge innovative solutions to long-standing problems. Dear Outsider, discover and share your unique expression; you will benefit others and yourself.

"E"—EVOLVE

The key to attracting your ideal mate lies in having a larger vision for your life. It doesn't matter where you may be now. It doesn't matter that you haven't attained the prosperity, health, or professional success that you want. What matters is that you are engaged in pursuing your dharma. Once you understand the core tenets of your dharma type, you can maximize your potential and minimize your weak points by evolving.

To do this, find which type you tend to evolve into (see table 3.2). Each of us has a complementary archetype that represents the qualities we need to incorporate to become the best we can be.

TABLE 3.2. EVOLUTION AND DEVOLUTION OF THE DHARMA TYPES*

MUTUAL DEVOLUTION	MUTUAL EVOLUTION
Warrior–Merchant	Warrior–Educator
Laborer–Educator	Merchant–Laborer
Outsider–All	Outsider–All

*Though certain dharma types evolve into each other, they never *become* another type. Instead, by taking on qualities of their complementary type, they become the best they can be.

The Dance of Evolution and Devolution

Educators evolve when they take on qualities of the Warrior, like discipline and the ability to stick to a goal. Educators fail to "walk the walk" when they devolve by adopting the traits of the Laborer; they need the Warrior's oomph to keep them honest. Warriors, on the other hand, benefit from the Educator's patience and ability to see both sides of a story before making decisions.

Merchants evolve into Laborers and vice versa, because each one has what the other needs. Laborers are sometimes too closed off from the world and need the fun and variety of the Merchant type to bring them out of their shells. Merchants, for their part, learn stability from the Laborer.

When types devolve their worst qualities emerge and their talents are prevented from coming to the fore. This doesn't mean that Educators cannot work in service professions or that Laborers shouldn't teach. However, all factors being equal, these types are not as well-suited for these jobs. By taking someone's place in the workforce when it goes contrary to your dharma type, you not only curb your own self-expression, you deprive others of the opportunity to do that job.

When Educators devolve into Laborers, they become stuck in a mode of thinking or attached to their knowledge in an egotistical way. When Laborers take on Educator values, they lose their own inherent strength and intuition. Educators think with their heads, Laborers with their guts. Switching these around creates confusion and leads you away from your dharma.

When Warriors devolve into the Merchant type, their strength turns to bravado, and instead of championing a noble cause they glorify themselves, fighting for the highest bidder. They become mercenaries to money, which often favors the strong, going against their dharma to protect the just and the defenseless. Merchants devolving into Warriors paint a similar picture of unnecessary force in the name of currency, not courage.

Warriors: To the Highest Bidder

Medicine is by and large a Warrior profession; it takes Warrior doctors to fight on behalf of patients against a common enemy—disease. In a Merchant society, however, doctors find it difficult to practice medicine the way they would like to. America is a Merchant nation, and it has a poor record of dealing with its Warriors—both those on the battlefield as well as those working in the trenches of its health care system. In contemporary America, hospitals have become more like sales centers for the corporations that own them than centers of healing. This is evidenced by the practices they follow: imposing patient quotas, including requiring doctors to see a certain number of patients per hour or per day; procedure quotas, meaning pushing doctors to order a certain number of tests and surgeries every day; and pharmaceutical quotas. Such practices may work for car dealerships but not for healing institutions, which is why the results have been catastrophic: medical mistakes in hospitals are the third leading cause of death in America, behind heart disease and cancer.*

*For more on this subject, see *Unaccountable* by Marty Mackary and *When Doctors Don't Listen* by Leana Wen and Joshua Kosowsky.

Evolution occurs more readily when you interact with the dharma type you're evolving into. If you're a Warrior, you should keep company with an Educator and vice versa, because by being around these types some of their qualities rub off on you. Merchants need to work with Laborers to incorporate some of the Laborer's energy into their own. You can never become another dharma type, but you learn much by absorbing the energy of the dharma type that promotes your evolution. This does not mean that you should avoid dharma types that encourage your devolution. However, being around them is less conducive to your personal growth because devolution pairs speak very different languages.

Take special care to communicate exactly what you mean around types you devolve into because the potential for misunderstanding in these situations is high. Imagine that they are from another city, country, or even another planet, because, for some intents and purposes, they are! Slow, careful communication will ensure that your intentions are understood and will head off potential problems before they arise.

Examples of How Each Dharma Type Can Devolve and Evolve

Educators

Educators may read fitness articles but never actually do the work, claiming their job or family limits their time. This is devolution. Instead, snap up some of the Warrior's gusto and get your butt to the gym to put all that knowledge into practice. For Educators to evolve they must take on Warrior traits. You need to move, walk, ride, and tone your body so your mind will be firm. Express your passion through movement and creativity; your work life and your love life will flow more smoothly.

Merchants

A Merchant might look at the corporate ladder and try stepping on everyone to reach the top. This is devolution into the Warrior. Fighting is not the way to happiness for Merchants; building relationships is. Building friendships and cultivating people who owe you favors is a much smoother way to the top than making enemies. Just as with cause and effect, you gotta give to get. So get going giving!

Educators: Living Your Purpose

"Simon, how did you learn all this stuff? Do you actually follow any of it?" asks Jane.

As an Educator, I know firsthand that one of the hardest things for my type is walking the walk, following through on the precepts we counsel others to embrace. But for Educators to grow into their dharma, they must actually live what they preach. Dr. Martin Luther King Jr. said, "It is possible to affirm the existence of God with your lips and deny his existence with your life." This is true of many people today. A look at examples like Dr. King and Gandhi—the latter an Educator, the former an Outsider playing an Educator—reveals the power Educators harness when they live their purpose instead of just talking about it.

"To tell you the truth, for a long time it was just theory, and nothing happened in my life," I reply to Jane. "That's why it took so long for me to write my first book. When I started practicing every principle I counseled others to follow, my life opened up. That's why I'm convinced it will work for you."

For Merchants to evolve, they need to make something real in order to appreciate its value. The price of a house or a stock depends on the market. What was worth $100,000 yesterday may fetch only $50,000 today and its value may go even lower tomorrow in a market economy. Value is an idea, one often linked to emotion. But a brick is a brick, a turnip is a turnip. Once Merchants connect to the process of building a house or preparing a home-cooked meal, they begin to appreciate the value of shelter and good diet. Then it becomes harder to eat nothing but junk food (which Merchants like) or to simply dismiss someone's foreclosure, because health and shelter are no longer abstract concepts; they are concrete realities.

Merchants do well to get in touch with the Earth element, and taking a cooking class, volunteering at a homeless shelter, or learning a trade are great ways for them to ground themselves in their Laborer point of evolution.

Laborers

A Laborer trying to outsmart her date with tricks and trivia is going to crash and burn. Instead, try invoking your date's senses through touch, taste, smell, and sight. This could mean anything from horseback riding (touch) to having wholesome, down-home food (smell and taste). Use these to get to know your date and, more important, to show him you are "real" and down-to-earth, for this creates genuine chemistry. Cooking, dancing, or even gardening together is a better way to communicate with your partner than trying to figure out what he's thinking. Communication via body language is much stronger than communication through words. Which do you want to use to say what you really want?

For Laborers, lightening up and enjoying themselves is a first step to evolution. Taking a salsa class, traveling, singing, and playing, especially in a communal spirit, uplifts the Laborer type. By evolving into Merchants, Laborers also find their own true worth. When you do not value yourself others won't either, and that's why Laborers often work at jobs with little recognition or compensation. By evolving into the Merchant, you learn to stand up for your skills and get your due in society. Other Merchant values involve learning the money game and how economics works, from compound interest to real estate. Taking a financial literacy class, for example, is a great way to get a grasp on money matters and manage your finances.

Warriors

In today's Merchant society money is power, and Warriors are drawn to it as a source of strength and security. But when Warriors cultivate money and power for self-serving reasons or at the cost of their higher purpose, their spirit wilts. Such Warriors die early of heart attacks or fall into vices like gambling or drinking. Being successful is fine, as long as you also fight malaria in Africa or devote time to eradicating illiteracy in the inner city. Whatever your cause, Warrior, if you want to feel truly alive, find your passion and put your considerable skills behind it! Learning anything boosts your edge. You probably did not like school when you were young; there was much more interesting stuff going on outside the classroom. But later in life Warriors begin to appreciate knowledge, as maturity brings the insight that knowledge is power. Read a book; get tutoring or counseling. Go to an astrologer or palmist or try psychotherapy. Any kind of one-on-one mentorship is supremely useful for Warrior types. Constantly improve yourself, and remember that knowledge whets the sword of good judgment.

Outsiders

You may have noticed that so far we have not discussed the Outsider's points of evolution and devolution. That is because Outsiders take on traits of other types, along with their evolution and devolution points. For example, an Outsider playing a Merchant evolves into the Laborer and devolves into the Warrior type. An Outsider playing a Warrior becomes the best Warrior they can be by learning the Warrior's dharma and evolving qualities from the Educator.

In addition, all Outsiders need to learn meditation or prayer to discover their unique worldview and calm their anxious minds. Outsiders run on residual anxiety and do well to find mystical ways to deal with material problems. Also, since deception comes easily to you as an Outsider, you have to hold yourself accountable. Have people call you on it when you're exaggerating or outright lying and find ways to practice taking responsibility for your actions. Taking responsibility for everything in your life is the best practice for an Outsider. Be accountable for the good and the bad, even the things you have no control over, like how you were raised and the traumas of your early childhood. This is the real sense of "turning the other cheek"—recognizing and taking responsibility for your karma—a core teaching of Christianity, though one not popularly practiced even by Christians. Taking responsibility for your karma makes you powerful and *able to respond*. Running away from karma results in powerlessness, and only delays your evolution. In the words of Jesus, who was himself an Outsider and knew this well, "Truly I tell you, you will not get out until you have paid the last penny" (Matthew 5:26).*

 ### DEVOLUTION EXERCISE FOR ALL TYPES

Think about the areas in your life where you have devolved in the past. Have you encountered problems with money? relationships? exercise? food?

Write down several examples in as much detail as you can.

Now consider how you can shift from devolution to evolution in those areas. Read about and promote your best traits!

Understand Your Weaknesses

Educators are lusty and can become trapped by their desires. They have to remember to be pillars of truth and wisdom for others and not succumb to second-class behavior.

Merchants are insecure and feel empty. Their antidote is giving energy, resources, or comfort to others.

Warriors don't know enough and make bad decisions. They need to educate themselves through schooling or, better yet, through one-on-one mentorship, to equip themselves to be the best Warriors possible. Otherwise they slip into cynicism and anger at the world and themselves.

---

*For more of Jesus's specific teachings for Outsiders, see *The Five Dharma Types.*

TABLE 3.3. ATTRIBUTES OF EACH DHARMA TYPE

DHARMA TYPE	SKILLS	STRENGTHS	WEAKNESSES
Warriors	Both gross and fine motor skills; usually a combination of the two that allows for the achievement of a goal (i.e., a soccer player).	Generous and self-sacrificing. Can achieve anything in the name of a good cause.	Pessimistic, cynical, materialistic. Do not believe in saving grace, and become prone to a dog-eat-dog mentality.
Merchants	Fine motor skills. Less goal-oriented, more focused on refinement (i.e., a violinist).	Inspirational and charitable. Entertaining and funny. Can motivate people.	Insecurity. Need constant validation from others to believe in her or his own worthiness.
Educators	Mental skills. Possess less motor skills than other types; often clumsy or uncoordinated.	High minded, pure, and noble. Sources of wisdom and purpose to others.	Wishy-washy, feckless, no backbone. Schism between ideals and reality, especially as pertains to base emotions like lust.
Laborers	Gross motor skills, usually applied for self-sustenance, as in a trade or hobby.	Loyal and devoted. Hardworking and unaffected. The backbone of functional society.	Intense jealousy. Attachment to people, things, or ideas to the point of irrationality.
Outsiders	Can mimic any of the types. Usually have affinity with Laborer types.	Born to free other beings. Instigate revolution, progress, and positive change.	Blame, self-deceit. Refuse to accept responsibility for their own actions; blame the world for their problems. Cannot see their own faults and shortcomings.

Laborers get stuck in their ways. They may also feel overwhelmed or inferior in situations that call for them to interact with too many people. Their antidote is to cultivate an attitude of service and love. This burns through any possible obstacle they may face in life.

Outsiders are anxious and self-deceptive. They lie to themselves and others. They need to take responsibility for everything in their lives, even if it wasn't "their fault."

See table 3.3 on page 49 for more attributes of each dharma type.

"F"—FIND YOUR WORD, FIND YOUR NAME

The "F" part of the BE FIT acronym stands for "Find your word and find your name." What kind of Educator are you? A counselor? Preacher? Scientist? Are you a Merchant who is a mover or are you sexy, hilarious, or charitable? What about you, Outsider? Solitary? Mysterious? Deep? You can use adjectives like this, or you can use nouns, verbs, and even prepositions like "in"—as in "I am always 'in' with fashion or 'in the know.'" Or you can think of a nickname that describes you. In the distant past, last names were given according to profession, like Smith, Fletcher, Tanner, Baker, and Farmer for people who worked with metal, arrows, leather, bread, or the land, respectively. Names were also given based on where you lived—Underhill, Rivers, Brooke, Woods, Ford, Bridges—or who your father was: Richardson or Davidson. Some were nicknames that stuck, like Smart, Young, Strong, Black, or White. Other cultures made descriptive names like this into an art form. *Umiko* in Japanese means "plum blossom child."[1]

How to Find Your Name or Word
Here are three different ways to discover your Name or Word:

Find Your Name

In a group, challenge friends and family to give each other accurate "names"—a noun, verb, adjective, or nickname that feels right. Take turns coming up with descriptive names from any language or tradition to spur your imagination. Who knows? Some of them might stick for life! It helps to see yourself through the lens of your good friends. Oftentimes they have insights into your character that you never considered.

Find Your Word

If you don't like names, consider finding your personal word. This is a secret mantra that resonates with you on a deep level. It can be a foreign or English word that reminds you of who you are and who you want to become. *Value* is a word one Merchant uses to remind herself to always give more than she gets. *Endeavor* is a Warrior's secret word that describes his personality, to always strive to be better. *Carney* is an Outsider's word, and he lives up to it. Always outside the system, he lives on a communal farm and travels, entertaining others.

Find Your Sacred Sound

Your sacred, or primordial, sound is another way to find a name or word that resonates with you. One person's sound, *peh* (pronounced "pay"), immediately made him think of Petros, the Greek name for Peter. Petros (and Petra) mean "rock," and in the Bible, Jesus said, "I shall build my church on this rock," referring to Peter as his apostle.* He got shivers down his neck because he had always seen himself in Peter's role in the Gospels.

Your sacred sound is based on your Vedic horoscope and the

---

*This, like countless other biblical statements, is open to interpretation, but such polemics are beyond the scope of our discussion here.

time and date you were born. You can find it by consulting a dharma type practitioner.*

To use these words, consider combining them with your dharma type. What kind of Educator/Warrior/Laborer/Merchant/Outsider are you? Narrow it down. Are you a *compassionate* Educator, a *wise* Educator, an *investigative* Educator, or a *poet, dreamer,* or *seeker*? Use your special word to refine your role and your dharma. Keep it secret. Let it be the filter through which you give energy to the world.

Discover Your Spirit Animal

Another way to refine your special name is to find your spirit or totem animal. Native American traditions are storied for their use of power animals as guides.

> In most cultures through the ages, animals have been—and still are—regarded as messengers of spirit, ambassadors of wisdom, and guides to other states of consciousness. As vehicles of connection to the sacred, animals . . . help us open to the deeper mysteries of life.[2]

This description, from Dawn Baumann Brunke's book *Animal Voices, Animal Guides,* is followed by a definition of *totem animal*:

> The origin of the word *totem* is linked to the idea of family or tribe. . . . Many Native American clans identify with totem animals—Bear, Eagle, Wolf. There are national totems (the

---

*For a dharma consultation or to find your sacred sound, visit www.spirittype.com. For more information on Primordial Sound Meditation, which uses this sound as part of a special meditative practice, visit www.chopra.com/our-services/meditation/primordial-sound-meditation.

American bald eagle), state totems (in Alaska, the ptarmigan), and group totems—the Elks, the Loyal Order of the Moose, the Lions Club. Even sports teams have totems—the Miami Dolphins, the Seattle Seahawks. If you start looking you will see animal totems used everywhere: in television and film (the NBC peacock, the MGM lion), as car names (Jaguar, Mustang, Beetle), on sports equipment (Arctic Cat, Puma).[3]

Your totem animal can guide you to the diet, lifestyle, and spiritual path appropriate for you. Trying to be a vegetarian while living with wolf energy may be a futile exercise; or being a meat eater with a deer totem may seem cruel to your body and mind. Bird totems mirror a high-flying consciousness, one always ready for travel or longing for distant vistas. An ant totem represents hard work and a communal spirit, while the solitary bear may reflect a curious, omnivorous, even lazy nature. Your totem animal matches you not only spiritually but also in its thoughts, instincts, and behavior. How much sleep you need, how fast you walk, and the aforementioned dietary habits are just one link that can help you find balance in your life. Whether you actually "look" like a wolf or not, having wolf energy makes you resonate with that animal's basic essence.

This resonance also extends to compatibility between partners. A wolf and a deer totem type may find they have a lot to work out before moving in together. So would cat and dog or rat and cat spirit animals. It would be wise to consider your partner's totem before making any major decisions together.

Finding your spirit animal can happen quickly or take some time. Just as you did when finding a name above, consider asking friends and family to help you. Some people have definite similarities to their totem animals, like webbed feet or even vestigial gills. But others may need to meditate or pray, asking for a dream or a vision to give them a clue. Keep your eyes open and look for signs from nature.

Putting It All Together

Once you understand your spirit animal, consider adding your special word or name to it. What kind of owl/snake/crow/dog are you? Are you a Trusty Owl, a Wisdom Owl, a Chatty Owl, a Fierce Owl, or a Mystic Owl? Then add your dharma type to complete the description. Are you a Happy Owl Educator, a Strange Owl Outsider, or a Mother Owl Laborer? This combination of animal spirit with keyword and dharma type gives you a personal mantra to use whenever you need to find your center. Some people use it as a spiritual name that remains with them for life. Or the name may change based on your life experience, growing and shifting to reflect the life cycles you are in. Your dharma type and spirit animal almost never change, but the names and words that guide their expression do. Use them to home in on your purpose and help you find your destiny.

By knowing who you are, you attract the right mate. In part 2 we will discuss how physical chemistry affects who we attract. But the deepest long-term compatibility happens at the spiritual level, and if you do not know who you are at your core, you will never invite deep love into your life. How can we expect others to love and understand us if we don't understand ourselves?

> The deepest long-term compatibility happens at a spiritual level, and if you do not know who you are at your core, you will never invite deep love into your life.

"I"—IMAGINE WELL, INTEND WELL

Now that you've learned who you are and how to evolve into your best self, it is time to harness your dharma type's element as a vehicle for your intention and imagination. This is a tool for helping you shape and co-create your future. If you fail to plan, then you plan to fail; using your element will help you grow into the life you want to live. There are five elements and they each correspond to a dharma type (see figure 3.1).

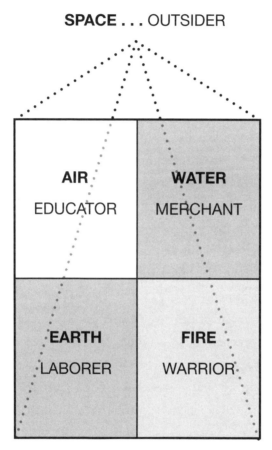

Figure 3.1. The five elements and their corresponding dharma types

Fire—Warriors

Fire, the Warrior's element, relates to sight and vision. If you're a Warrior type, write out your goals, put them on the fridge or on a whiteboard in your room, and look at them with intent for five minutes every day. A valuable trick some Warriors use is to spread posters of what they're working on all over the walls of their house. From police detectives looking for suspects to lawyers structuring an argument, giving visual flow to a project is highly inspiring for Warrior types.

Another useful tool to kindle inspiration is lighting candles. Try this when you eat, or to make an ordinary evening special. If you or your partner are Warriors, you will respond to the Fire element in your surroundings with rekindled passion and hunger. Honor this need for light in your life any way you see fit, using salt lamps, chandeliers, even torches. These work especially well in the southeast corner of your property, house, or room. In chapter 5 we will look at the ancient art of vastu and how to use it to create passion, love, and health by honoring the southeast corner (which represents the Fire element) and placing hot things there, like stoves, lamps, and technology devices such as your computer or stereo system. Having a night-light or a salt lamp constantly turned on in the southeast corner of your house is a nice way to pay homage to the Fire element in you and your home.

By this logic, the southeast is also a good place for a fire ceremony or a barbecue. Warriors love being outside because the sun is their primordial source of light and life. Earlier we touched on the tendency among Warriors to ditch the classroom in favor of the outdoors. This is why: the sun is your friend. Use the sun's energy to fill up and give you more of your own. From getting a tan to installing solar energy panels, connecting with the cosmic source of fire will help you heal your body and mind.

Reciting the Gayatri mantra is a great way to greet the sun every morning. In the Vedic tradition, Gayatri is the most important mantra and all Brahmins are initiated into its use at an early age.*

---

*For a recitation of the Gayatri mantra and a special way to combine it with yogic breathing, visit www.spirittype.com.

Other spiritual practices include *dharana,* gazing at a candle flame with unbroken attention for five to fifteen minutes a day. This is excellent for improving eyesight and creating focus in your life.

Also consider using technology—computers, cars, tools—to help you achieve your goals. Look at what you want with single-minded attention and envision yourself possessing it already. If you do this often enough, with intensity, nothing can stand in your way, Warrior!

Air—Educators

For Educators to connect to their inspiration, they need to harness the Air element. Go to a mountain peak and feel the breeze on your face. Ride a horse, motorcycle, sailboat, or bicycle, or simply run. T'ai chi and *pranayama* (extension of the breath) are excellent practices to cultivate your breath and create inner peace and inspiration. Walk every day, first thing in the morning, if possible. The transition between your bedroom and the outdoors can wake you up filled with inspiration and set the tone for the rest of your day.

While you are out, do not walk aimlessly; learn to make the most of your time in nature. There are two ways to walk: with focus or with feeling. When you are focused on a problem, the movement of breath and body can help stir up new solutions. A brisk walk while concentrating on a particularly thorny issue can help fresh ideas you never considered before rise to the surface of your consciousness. The other way to walk is with sensation. Feel the muscles in your body working or focus on your breathing. The phantom breath is phenomenal for producing a deep meditative state while walking. It is a variation on alternate-nostril breathing (see page 108) that doesn't require the use of your hands. You can do it anywhere, even walking to work, without anyone knowing what you're up to. Alternatively, you can focus your attention outside the body, meditating on the exceptional beauty of your surroundings.

 THE PHANTOM BREATH

As you inhale, visualize air coming in only through your left nostril.

As you exhale, feel it leaving through the right.

It doesn't matter where the air is actually moving, what matters is your attention, because where your mind goes, your prana—life force—follows.

Now, on your next inhale, breathe in through your right nostril, hold your breath for a split second, and exhale out your left nostril, all without using your hands to close or open your nostrils. This is one round.

Keep breathing this way for five to fifteen minutes, or for a set number of rounds. You'll find it's difficult to keep track, as a profoundly calm and trancelike state is usually induced by the phantom breath.

For a more powerful experience, try to visualize your life breath (called prana or chi) about twelve inches outside your nostrils. Picture it as tiny light particles glistening in the air, like effervescent molecules dancing in a ray of light. As you breathe in, see them line up and ascend into your left nostril, making a loop at your third eye and exiting out your right nostril. Repeat, beginning with the right nostril.

Prana is intelligent and it follows your intention. If you simply (and humbly) ask it to move for you, it will, and its benefits, such as improved health, focus, and inspiration, will astound you!

MEDITATING ON YOUR SURROUNDINGS

Notice the feel of the sun and the breeze, the sounds and smells of the trees and grass.

If your eyes are open, let them soften and take in your surroundings.

If you are inside, you can still practice noticing your surroundings. Take in the feeling of the air, the sounds and smells around you—all the little things you might not normally notice.

Commit to settling into this awareness for a set amount of time, maybe even just five minutes.

Becoming aware of the world around you can move you to tears if you let it. There is no emotion without motion, and the Air element governs the movement of thought, sensation, and feeling. The skin and the nervous system are responsible for giving us messages about our environment, and Educators should keep these nourished with oil massage and good nutrition. Educators are essentially communicators—to keep your lines of communication flowing, make sure your Air element can also flow freely. That means keeping windows cracked open to allow for energy to circulate, as well as paying special attention to the northwest direction in your home, which is governed by the Air element. Setting up your office in this area and doing yoga and exercise or simply reading there can stir up new inspiration.

Air is also words. Use them as tools—affirmations, mantras, and prayers can produce good results for you, dear Educator. Offer up your life breath as a prayer and surrender it without attachment to the results. When you hold on to Air, it cannot do its job. Words are your tools, so say them out loud, sing—in the shower or in your pillow if you need to. Write your prayers, thoughts, emotions, and intentions in a journal, a blog, an article, or a book. What begins as a blog may become a blockbuster, so speak your truth and speak it often to anybody who cares to listen (even if that is only your cat!).

Water—Merchants

Merchants need to be around water. Even if you live in the desert, Merchant, having a fountain in the northeast corner of your home is a way to invite water and the abundance it represents into your life. Have fun, surf, bathe, swim, and drink lots of water. Merchants should never be dehydrated. Water is linked to enjoyment and taste. If your tongue is dry, even the finest morsel tastes like cardboard. Therefore, drink lots of water and, for Merchants, alcohol is also okay, especially with good company.

What's the Big Deal about Oil?

Ancient wisdom and modern science attest to these benefits of oil:

- Oil is lipophilic, meaning that it attracts other oils and fat-soluble toxins to itself. Whether taken internally or applied to the skin, this chelating effect means that when the oil is removed from the body, the toxins it attracted are also removed. That is why internal and external oleation is the mainstay of detoxification therapy in ayurveda. It literally pulls heavy metals and environmental toxins from your body.
- Oil nourishes the tissues, feeding and moisturizing whatever it is applied to and helping to fill and lubricate the spaces of the body.
- Oil calms the nervous system. As most nerve endings live on the skin, it is a primary defense against stress and nervous exhaustion.
- Oil boosts immunity. By feeding the healthy microbes on our inner and outer skin (the intestines, colon, and nasal passages included), oil ensures optimal immune function. Dry skin is weak and subject to disease. Oil-nourished skin has a layer of protection against possible invaders.
- Oil has a saponifying effect. Combined with water, oil creates bacteria-fighting suds that can clean the body without using harsh soaps and chemicals.
- Oil, especially ghee (clarified butter), is rejuvenating, promoting strength, vitality, and virility.

Use water as a spiritual medium: pray near a waterfall, do *abhiseka* (anointing), or offer milk and water to your favorite deity. Water and fire sanctify any spiritual ritual, be it Christian, Hindu, or even Zen Buddhist. Water symbolizes desire, purity, wealth, and nourishment. Use it to make yourself pure and to make deals with God: "Lord, help me do X and I will do Y." Making deals or "bribing" celestial powers with gifts, vows, and good intentions is allowed for Merchant and Laborer types, provided you follow through on your end of the bargain! In India it is customary to offer a glass of milk and cookies to Ganesha, the remover of obstacles, before engaging in any new endeavor. Just like Santa Claus, he knows if you've been naughty or nice, but even if you've been naughty, he is the easiest of the gods to please.

Water also represents money, emotion, and sex. Make love by the ocean (or in the shower). Use money to make money. If you're overweight, fast or drink only hot water on Mondays, Thursdays, or Fridays (days of the week associated with water, surplus, and luxury, respectively) to balance your excesses. Water is the vehicle of emotion, so move it. If Air rules the movement of impulses in the nervous system, Water is our neurochemistry, our emotion molecules carried by the Air element. To produce them in adequate quantities, our bodies must be hydrated with water and its energetic equivalents—love and zest for life. Love is like hydrogen, you need it in two parts; relish is the oxygen in one part. Together they make H_2O. To create this zest for living you must move your emotion, or it will stagnate. Cry to God if you want, but use emotion to soar to high inspiration and focus your intention.

Earth—Laborers

Earth represents food and the sense of smell. Laborers can use farming or gardening to spur their imaginations. Let the earth host and foster your intention. The Buddha put his pinky (earth finger) to the ground to witness his enlightenment. Bring your bed down and sleep close to the earth, or simply lie down under a tree, look up at the sky, and imagine.

The Earth element also represents working with material reality.

Build something useful, whether it be a house or an ant farm; the measure of a Laborer's accomplishments is what she's left behind and how well she has nurtured and sustained her family and society. Offer food to your family, your neighbors, and your deity. A great guru once said, "Feeding people is the best spiritual practice." By nourishing and cooking for others you create community. To a Laborer type, there's nothing as inspiring as belonging and being part of a family. Use your devotion to serve the Divine as you serve your neighbors.

Fasting is also useful for Laborers. Fast once a week on the day of your planetary period. You can find this in your Vedic horoscope or through a dharma type reading. If you don't know it, fast on the day of your birth. If you were born on a Friday, fast on Fridays. Alternately, fasting on Saturdays is generally well accepted for everyone. This is a way to pay homage to Saturn, who also rules the earth and material reality.

Space—Outsiders

Outsiders require space to be who they are. Space and time are one, and the remedy for today's time-pressed, stressed-out lifestyle is to give ourselves space and time. It's okay to leave that email unanswered. It's okay not to please everyone or not to be all things to all people. Sacrificing your health and sanity because of stress and time pressure attacks your inner space. Learn to create boundaries that nurture you.

Outsiders instinctively search for freedom from restrictions and limitation. This may take the form of anything from driving too fast to violating sexual taboos. However, the lesson of space is not to break external laws but to transcend the barriers of your consciousness. This is the Asian way of inner freedom. As Pandit Rajmani Tigunait says, "Westerners live freely and think in structured ways, while Easterners think freely and live in structured ways."[4]

Learn to structure yourself externally, Outsider, while freeing yourself within. This is the path to self-mastery. Using sex, meditation, sensory deprivation, even consciousness-raising substances is par for the course for Outsiders, though many get trapped in the drug experience, which itself becomes a subtle prison. Release your attachments to external crutches and explore the Space element in your consciousness, using the self to know the self.

In practical terms, this means taking care of the spaces of your body and home by keeping them clean and uncluttered. Outsiders love cleanses and detox programs because of this instinctual pull to feel pure. But a lifestyle regimen that does this for you without the need for harsh purgation is the way to long-term mastery of your physical inner space. The same applies to your external living space. When they're unbalanced, Outsiders clutter their home with junk and their bodies with toxins. To find balance, take on the monumental task of clearing your inner and outer spaces by creating a clutter-free environment in your home, and a pure body by following the regimens in the chapters that follow. This frees you to imagine your life any way you want, without the limiting structures of a toxic body and a dirty, cluttered home.

Key Values for Intention

Finally, you can use key values of your dharma type to help you focus your intention and imagination. For example, Educators need to surrender, and live and let be. Native American smoke ceremonies teach this ethic well. Taking smoke or air into your lungs and holding it there, speak your intention with your heart. Then release the air or smoke and let go of your intention with it. Surrender it to nature and the Air element outside of you. Give your intention to the universe and do not interfere with its realization. Do your dharma and leave the results to the cosmos. This is a practical lesson for the Educator type.

Similarly, Warriors can use focus and control to attain what they want, while Merchants can create, contribute, clothe the needy, and be charitable. Laborers can serve, devote, and build, while Outsiders may reform and innovate. Use the values of your dharma type to imagine just how you can share your gifts with the world. Not only will this make you more powerful, but it will make you attractive to anyone with whom you interact.

"T"—TIME YOUR MOVEMENTS

The final step in the BE FIT program is to time your movements. Now that you understand how to be your most authentic self, you must learn the season you are in and exactly what it is good for. The top two results from your dharma self tests typically show your dharma type and life cycle. That is, if you scored 8 Educator and 6 Warrior, one of these types is likely your dharma type, the other the life cycle you are in.

Knowing your life cycle can help you focus your intentions to get the most from even the toughest periods of your life. Will you be in school for the next two years? Surrender to that reality while carefully planning for the future. Are you in a job, relationship, or location that obliges you to be in one place for a certain time? Be there while actively creating your future. Respect your life cycle, and work to generate more choice so you can accommodate future cycles. To see how each cycle affects your dharma type, refer to my book *The Five Dharma Types*.

FIND WHAT BEFITS YOU AND BE FIT

Aristotle said that every great work of art displays the same quality— unity. All of its features work together to express its purpose. The same can be said of an enlightened person; every element in your life must align to express your destiny. In Sanskrit, this concept of unity is called yoga.

Become a yogi, a complete person. Yogis are not just people who can turn themselves into pretzels, but people who are whole, healthy, unified with their purpose. Everything they do reflects their dharma type, and from the grandest stage to their innermost moments, every step and every breath pulses with the essence of their dharma. The greatest yogis sometimes can't even touch their toes, but they can reach the dizzying depths and indelible heights of awareness!

Let us review what makes each dharma type tick:

> **For Laborers** to work and serve, they must love unconditionally, without jealousy, pride, possession, lust, anger, or need. Treat others like your son or daughter, sister or brother, father or mother. Just love. No presumptions. No conditions.
>
> **For Warriors** to protect what cannot protect itself and offer radical solutions to problems, they must acquire knowledge through mentorship and wield wisdom like a weapon.
>
> **For Educators** to teach and learn, they must embody the truth they propound—walk the walk, live the lesson, and practice what they preach.
>
> **For Merchants** to enjoy and grow their prosperity, they must engage in charitable enterprises, or give to live. Sharing is caring, and giving is better than receiving.
>
> **For Outsiders** to refresh and reinvent themselves, they must find their unique purpose, even if it goes against what the world believes, or even what they themselves believe, even if it's not convenient.

4

From Ama to Agni

Lessons from Ayurveda and
Your Dharma Type to Create Full-Body Health

Now that you understand your dharma type, it is time to get a handle on your health by learning the dharma of the body: what makes it tick and what obstacles prevent you from living a long, fruitful life. What practices lead to happiness and which lead to pain and suffering, what promotes longevity and how you measure these things—these are the purview of the ancient art of ayurveda. Ayurveda is the oldest healing system in the world, having been tested and proved for some five thousand years. It is popular today because of celebrity authors like Dr. Deepak Chopra, Dr. Andrew Weil, Dr. Mehmet Oz, and perhaps most vitally, Dr. Vasant Lad, who is largely responsible for translating ayurveda's vast wealth of wisdom for the West.*

In this chapter I have distilled the ayurvedic action steps you need to take right now to reclaim your health and vitality, and, by doing so,

---

*Even modern allopathy recognizes ayurveda's contributions to surgery, internal medicine, and pharmacology. Sushruta, a famous ayurvedic surgeon, is recognized as the father of plastic surgery. His famous text the *Sushruta Samhita* details over three hundred surgical instruments and thousands of substances, mixtures, and medicines for ailments as varied as colic to cancer.

your sexiness. These action steps apply equally to all dharma types.

It's hard to be sexy when you're sick. Though our noses are not nearly as sensitive as those of many animals, humans are still wired to sniff out when people are not well, and to avoid them. But the reverse is also true: radiant health is very attractive to both men and women, and it makes sense to cultivate it if, for nothing else, to attract a quality partner. A well-known aphorism says, "The root of dharma, prosperity, enjoyment, and freedom is good health. Diseases take this away, as well as goodness and life itself."

This reminder of how important health is, not only to love and romance but in practically every area of life, comes from the ayurvedic author Charaka. Health stands as an asset and disease is a liability when it comes to achieving our goals, which is why, even in a book on sex, love, and dharma, we must consider health one of the greatest aphrodisiacs. Lucky for you, the most important step to achieving it is summed up in just two words: *eliminate ama.*

If humans are wired to find health attractive, then *ama* is the destroyer of attraction. There is no equivalent for this Sanskrit term in English, but it amounts to "toxic sludge" or "morbid mucoid plaque." Ama can be gross, like the whitish mucus you see if you stick out your tongue in the morning, or it can be subtle, circulating systemically, causing inflammation, cell toxicity, and congestion. You can bet that if you have it on your tongue it's also in your body, making all kinds of mischief. According to ayurveda, ama is the root cause of all disease. Modern research is catching up to ayurveda's wisdom in recognizing the deadly effects of ama, though it is still a long way from knowing what to do about it.

Ama creates tolerable problems like bad breath and flatulence, as well as serious issues, like heart disease, autoimmune disorders, Alzheimer's disease, and even cancer. Needless to say, romance is dampened when your body is full of sludge, and delectable lovemaking becomes impossible. So how do you know if you have it?

THE BREATH, POOP, AND WEIGHT TESTS

If you wake up in the morning with foul-smelling breath it is a sign of putrefaction, which means you have ama in your system. More than likely, you will also have a whitish coating on part or all of your tongue, which you should scrape off immediately using a tongue scraper. Ama on the tongue means there is ama in the body. But if you wake up with fresh-smelling breath and no ama on your tongue, then you are *nirama*—without excessive toxic sludge—and your body is better prepared to respond to stress. Ama is the reason some people get sick when they're exposed to stress or a cold virus while others do not. Ama is inflammatory, compromising your immunity and the body's ability to resist external and internal threats. And, as we shall learn later, it is a key factor in aging.

If you can burp and taste last night's dinner when you wake up, your digestion is sluggish, and ama is probably present. If this is the case, skip breakfast and allow the body to finish digesting your last meal before giving it a new challenge. Here's a simple way to know if you are ready to eat any time: if you can still taste and burp your last meal, then wait a little while, or try some of the herbal remedies outlined below.

The poop test is simple: if your bowel movement floats, it is a sign that you are relatively ama free and getting enough fiber. Because ama is sticky, cold, and heavy, it makes fecal matter sink (and stink!). On the other hand, healthy digestion will promote the float. Other signs of low ama include almost no smell to the feces; fecal matter comes out easily, shaped like bananas; and very little toilet paper is needed afterward. All these signs indicate good flora in the gut and adequate fiber intake. Research now tells us that our prehistoric ancestors ate up to one hundred grams of fiber a day. We are lucky to get twenty grams in our standard American diet, so be sure to get substantial fiber in your diet.

Dr. Lad is fond of saying that the greatest happiness is waking up to the call of number two. If you easily go every morning without the need for coffee, food, or laxatives, it generally means your GI tract is functioning well. If you're not quite ready for a movement first thing in the morning, make it a point to drink a tall glass of room-temperature water (sixteen ounces) after scraping your tongue. This practice works well for everyone. Drinking a glass of room-temperature water first thing in the morning serves two functions. First, it hydrates your body, since you've been waterless for at least the past eight hours. Second, it encourages peristalsis and the flushing of any remaining toxins from your system. This first glass of water in the morning is the most important drink of the day. Even if you forget to drink the rest of the time, at least you've started well by hydrating your body and brain to function optimally at work, at school, or at play.

The next test is the most interesting. To do it, weigh yourself before eating, then thirty to sixty minutes after eating weigh yourself again. You will need a precise scale for this. If your weight goes up after consuming food, your body is not making the most of its nutrition. If your weight stays the same, you are metabolizing your meals properly. If your weight goes down, that might be a sign of hyperthyroidism or an overactive metabolism.

STEPS TO AN AMA-FREE BODY

Eliminating ama is essentially synonymous with kindling the digestive fire, called *agni* in Sanskrit.* Agni is one of those good four-letter words you want to remember, because it stands for all the enzymatic and metabolic processes in the body, including the transformation of food into consciousness. Agni is the opposite

---

*Though technically kindling agni and removing ama are two distinct processes, doing one typically leads to the other.

of ama, and when one is high, the other is low. Impaired agni is a factor behind many modern addictions—tobacco, coffee, alcohol, even sex. When our metabolic fire becomes sluggish, our bodies turn to substances or activities to stimulate them. A shot of whiskey temporarily burns ama and we feel good. That cigarette after a meal kindles agni and helps us digest our food. Good agni even digests our mental and emotional experiences, which is why emotionally impaired people are more likely to turn to hard drugs to cope with mental ama—unprocessed thoughts and emotions that literally clog our brain chemistry and make us feel crappy. But habitual crutches like this are simply substitutes for our own inner pharmacy.

According to ayurveda, burning ama—toxic sludge—and building strong agni do away with the need for drugs and alcohol to prop up our bodies and minds. Then we are able to digest both our physical and our emotional experiences, and depression and sickness fade like shadows before a flame. Part of the enduring popularity of juicing and certain restrictive diets like the lemonade cleanse lies in their ability to burn ama and kindle agni, at least temporarily. Below we will look at proven techniques for how to do this permanently as part of your daily lifestyle.

DAILY SELF-CARE TO PROMOTE AGNI

Have you noticed how often soap opera and silver-screen lovers wake up in the morning and start making out? They must have very little ama and perfect agni to pull that off! Giving that first morning smooch with sweet-smelling breath is a sign of great health, and something we can work up to.

But bad breath is not only lousy for lovers; it's a sign of putrefaction in the body. Common sense dictates that you cannot be romantic if you suffer from halitosis, poor digestion, or gas. Blotchy skin, rotten teeth, and arthritic joints are not exactly sexy. Therefore, ayurveda recommends a daily self-care routine designed to make you healthier and more attractive and energetic, whether you have a partner or are single and looking to attract one.

Start with one or two of these recommendations and add in more every week until this routine becomes a lifestyle. Each of these sections—Bedroom, Bathroom, and Kitchen—have steps that can be done in order or moved around to fit your needs.

Bedroom

Wake up. Your daily routine starts in the bedroom. It begins by waking up early enough to take advantage of the spiritual qualities of the dawn. Ayurveda says that our bodies are a microcosm of the universe. The galaxies of neurons within mirror the galaxies of stars without. Dr. Claudia Welch, in her book *Balance Your Hormones, Balance Your Life*, extends this thinking to our lifetimes, equating one day with the span of our lives. Thus, if sunrise equals birth and sunset is death, we live our lives during the day while night represents our time between worlds, the afterlife. You can take control of your healing by doing practices at the times that correspond to life traumas:

Twilight—In Utero
Sunrise—Birth
Midday—Midlife
Sunset—Death

Waking up a little before dawn is tantamount to reliving our time in utero, just before birth. This allows us to heal traumas that occurred in the womb, traumas that neither we nor our parents may be aware of. Pranayama is one way to help reset your emotional and hormonal systems. When performed just before dawn, healing practices have the potential to create wholeness and reprogram our lives. Let your body's microcosm match nature's macrocosm by rising with or just before the sun.

> "A regulated daily routine puts us in harmony with nature's rhythms. It establishes balance in our constitution and helps to regularize our biological clock. It indirectly aids in digestion, absorption, and assimilation of food and generates self-esteem, discipline, peace, happiness, and long life."
>
> DR. VASANT LAD, *THE COMPLETE BOOK OF AYURVEDIC HOME REMEDIES*

Look at and rub your hands. Take a moment to look at your hands while saying a prayer or remembering what is good in your life. Give thanks for the opportunity to express your dharma. Now rub your hands together and move them over your face, neck, shoulders, and down to the rest of your body. This cleans your aura and helps wake you up.

Bathroom

Scrape your tongue. Tongue scrapers are inexpensive and worth their weight in gold. In fact, a silver or gold tongue scraper makes for an unconventional and romantic gift. It is "bathroom bling" that holds its value and shows your lover how much you care about her health. Gold and silver have healing properties, and ayurveda makes clever and varied use of these precious metals (which we will explore more later).

Otherwise, a copper or regular metal tongue scraper works just fine for this purpose. First thing in the morning, head to the bathroom and gently scrape your tongue downward (no more than fourteen times; don't overdo it!). You will see the toxic mucoid plaque that has built up overnight come right off. A coated, sticky tongue in the morning means there is ama in the GI tract: in the colon if it is only on the back of the tongue, in the small intestine if it is in the middle, or in the stomach if it is toward the front of the tongue. If the entire tongue is coated, then ama is present throughout the digestive system. This is something that brushing your teeth or gargling typically does not remove. Scraping your tongue gently also massages the organs represented there. Like the feet, your tongue has reflexology centers and scraping in the morning wakes them up. Doing this with a copper or gold tongue scraper adds antimicrobial benefits, as copper has been shown in studies to be harmful to the bad bacteria in the mouth and beneficial to the good, health-promoting bacteria.* This in turn leads to reduced cavities and better oral hygiene.† Even hospitals are now using copper fixtures to help stop the spread of disease.‡

Remember that ama is the toxic ground of disease and breeds harmful bacteria and toxins that clog the entire body. Cholesterol in the arteries is a form of ama in the circulatory system that leads to heart attacks. Plaques in the brain are forms of ama that engender Alzheimer's Disease. Getting rid of ama is one of the main jobs of a good ayurvedic self-care routine.

Evacuate your bladder and bowels. Emptying the bladder and regularly moving the bowels creates "good space," which is the literal meaning of the Sanskrit word *sukha*. Sukha is commonly translated as "happiness," and in ayurveda it is created through regular and

---

*For more on this see Santo, et al., "Bacterial Killing by Dry Metallic Copper Surfaces," *Applied and Environmental Microbiology* 77, no. 3 (February 2011): 794–802.
†For more on this see Almas, Al-Sanawi, and Al-Shahrani, "The Effect of Tongue Scraper on Mutans Streptococci and Lactobacilli in Patients with Caries and Periodontal Disease," *Odontostomatol Trop Journal* 28, no. 109 (March 2005): 5–10.
‡For more on this see Karpanen, et. al., "The Antimicrobial Efficacy of Copper Alloy Furnishing in the Clinical Environment: A Crossover Study," *Infection Control and Hospital Epidemiology Journal* 33, no. 1 (January 2012): 3–9. For a complete list of studies associated with the above, see Dr. John Douillard's online article "The Science of Tongue Scraping with Copper" at www.lifespa.com.

unsuppressed movement of urine and feces out of the body. Suppresing these urges can be extremely stressful to the body and mind, leading to a backed-up digestive system. If you are constipated or have scanty or irregular stools, consider supplementing with *triphala* (see pages 83–84) and putting more fiber and good bacteria in your diet.

After evacuation, wash the anal orifice in a bidet or in the shower, then wash your hands with soap. If you have hemorrhoids or anal sensitivity, try spraying rose water on some toilet paper and applying it every day.

Brush your teeth with a nonfluoride toothpaste. Fluoride for most adults is not only harmful, but has little use after tooth enamel has finished building. Fluoride has been linked to cancer and calcification of the pineal gland, and should be avoided, according to modern ayurvedic practice. Instead, use a neem toothpaste, and add a little baking soda if you have bleeding or receding gums, inflammation, and systemic acidity. Using baking soda with neem toothpaste will help to whiten teeth and alkalize your mouth.

Do oil pulling, or kavala. *Kavala* is an ayurvedic practice that has received widespread attention on the Internet in the past few years. In English it is called oil pulling, swishing oil in your mouth for up to twenty minutes in the morning or evening. According to ayurveda, oil pulling improves gum health; alleviates nasal dryness, TMJ (temporomandibular joint disorder), and neck pain; strengthens teeth; bolsters liver and spleen function, breast health, thyroid function, and appetite; and even eliminates wrinkles! Oil pulling also improves the voice and stimulates secretion of hydrochloric acid (HCl) in the stomach.

These may sound like outsized claims, but evidence is mounting that this five-thousand-year-old practice has merit and should be included in your daily routine. It does take some dedication to see full results, so stick with it and in two to three months you may post one of those YouTube testimonials!

Oil has a chelating effect, meaning that it pulls toxins out of any surface it's applied to (that's partly why it's called oil pulling). Swishing oil also cleans your teeth and removes plaque just as effectively as mouthwash, with all the added benefits of chelation. It also fills the spaces between your teeth and nourishes your gums.*

A healthy mouth also promotes a healthy heart. Studies have shown that gum disease and cavities increase the risk of heart disease and a plethora of other problems, as morbid bacteria in the mouth can easily circulate to other areas in the body. Keep your mouth clean and nourished by incorporating oil pulling into your daily routine.

✦ OIL PULLING—KAVALA

In the morning after brushing your teeth, take two tablespoonfuls of sesame oil in your mouth and swish it around. You can easily do this while you shower or shave.

Do not overfill your mouth because, within a few minutes, the saliva will begin to flow and increase the volume.

Do this for fifteen to twenty minutes. If it's difficult to hold for that long, work up to it. You may have to get used to the feeling of oil in your mouth. After ten minutes or so it will begin to feel like water, as saliva mixes with the oil. This is what you want. This oil is helping to pull toxins out of your system.

When you're done, spit it out. *Do not swallow the oil!*

Massage your gums with your finger and rub a dab of oil on the outside of your cheeks. Use a tongue scraper to scrape off excess oil from your tongue and voila! You're done.

This regimen, along with the benefits enumerated above, is also great for singers and public speakers, as it supports the voice and throat.

---

*For more on this go to www.lifespa.com/oil-pulling.

THREE SQUARE MEALS:
THE "EAT AS MUCH AS YOU WANT" DIET

It has become common in body building and fitness circles for people to eat five to six small meals daily in the belief that this keeps their metabolism high by forcing the body to digest all day long. While this may yield good results in the short term by prompting people to reduce their portion sizes, constantly pouring food into the body doesn't allow any rest for your system. As a result, ama builds up. People don't notice ama in the early stages because exercise often accompanies such meal plans, and exercise burns ama. But just like your dishwasher, you should allow your body's digestive cycle to finish before putting anything new into it. When you allow four to six hours to elapse between meals, your body has time to complete digesting and then focus its energies on other matters, like cleaning house, rejuvenating, and balancing your hormones. Bogging down your body with food promotes aging: fasting at least four hours between meals counters aging. Modern longevity research supports this, together with the health benefits of infrequent eating.

By grazing all day like livestock, we have less time to focus on other things in our lives, and our bodies don't have the full resources to devote to things like rejuvenation and burning ama. In the words of fitness guru Pavel Tsatsouline: "I don't have time to graze." Eating three solid meals a day may seem difficult at first and old fashioned, but with a little practice it becomes second nature. And feeling good when your body is not bogged down by dirty dishes all day long will make you a believer. Here's how it's done:

1. Start your morning examining your breath, tongue, or poop to determine if you have ama. If you do and you're still burping up last night's meal, then you may skip breakfast altogether and just have a tall glass of lukewarm water. But if you won't make it to

lunch without snacking, have a light breakfast. Fruits with a scraping quality, like grapefruit or apples, are great because they stimulate peristalsis while banishing your hunger. If you eat fruit, eat it alone, and be sure to avoid consuming fruit and dairy together. If ama is not present or if you're really feeling hungry after your morning routine and water, then have a hearty breakfast that will take you through to lunch.

2. At lunch, eat as much as you want! Make lunch the largest meal of the day. Ayurveda says that digestion is at its peak at midday (it peaks again around midnight), so having your biggest meal between 11 a.m. and 2 p.m. ensures that your body can handle all the extra nutrients. Allow yourself at least an hour for lunch, and sit and enjoy your meal. Believe it or not, relishing your food in a relaxed fashion not only helps you digest and absorb it better, it creates a sense of fullness and satisfaction that resonates throughout your day. Just as good sex leaves you with a smile all day long, enjoying a sumptuous meal at lunchtime with few restrictions on how much to eat can have the same effect.

3. Don't snack. The first few days it may be difficult to break this habit, as it takes forty-eight to seventy-two hours for our bodies to adjust to this style of eating. But don't give up. By the third day you will get used to waiting for the evening meal with relish. Or you may not even be hungry for dinner. Your body will make the proper adjustments and you will feel light and energetic all day long without needing to reach for a snack at all.

4. Have a light supper. Dinner should not be the biggest meal of the day, but it should be enough to get you to breakfast without late-night-snack cravings.

5. Go to bed early, before 10 p.m. if possible. Between 10 p.m. and 2 a.m. our body's agni wakes up again, so to avoid those late-night-snack cravings, just go to bed and allow your metabolic cycle to burn ama instead. You will wake up with a cleaner tongue and

more energy in the morning. If you do burn the midnight oil, no need to beat yourself up: you will get hungry. (Try drinking some warm milk or juice in that case.)

6. Finally, take time to cook at least two to three times a week. As we'll see in part 2, connecting to the sensuality of eating by preparing and cooking food makes you a better lover. To be sensual means to be connected to your senses, and working with the scents, tastes, sights, textures, and even sounds of your food will make you more sensitive in every area of your life. You may even find that you eat less when you prepare your food. When all your senses have been stimulated by the process of cooking, your taste buds won't need to make up for any lack in the other four senses. Your palate will require only what it needs and no more.

> When all your senses have been stimulated by the process of cooking, your taste buds won't need to make up for any lack in the other four senses. Your palate will require only what it needs and no more.

One of the reasons we overeat is that our senses are not adequately stimulated, and we feed our need for pleasant sights, sounds, smells, and other sensations by consuming food. Haven't you noticed that when you're engrossed in a book or listening to really good music the time just flies by and you don't notice any hunger? That is because your other senses are being sumptuously gratified to the extent that they satisfy even your sense of taste. Take some time to increase your sensitivity by exposing yourself to beauty, whether by going to a rock concert or hiking the Rocky Mountains. Taking in a symphony, if you truly enjoy it, will actually help you eat less and lose weight.

Boredom is one of the main reasons for overeating. The other is stress. When you make time to stimulate your senses and divert your mind away from stress and boredom, you will need less food to combat these symptoms. Food is medicine, and we often use it to fill us up when other areas of our life feel empty. Practicing your dharma and good self care will remove the need to self-medicate with food and help you to become the best you can be.

One final note on the Three Square Meals plan is that you can use it with almost any diet. There are many good books on healthy eating. Whether you follow the *Eat Right for Your Type* blood-type plan or Michael Pollan's healthy food guidelines, or a mix of two or three eating strategies, it doesn't matter: you can use them all in the context of Three Square Meals. From Paleo to the Zone to healthy vegetarian cuisine, ayurveda as the mother of all medicine embraces individual preferences rather than homogenizing them. It recognizes our unique cultural tastes and allows us to adopt a cus-tomized dietary and supplement program for our mind/body and dharma type.

Food Compatibility

Even though you can eat as much as you want on the Three Square Meals plan, there are certain food combinations you should avoid, such as yogurt and bananas, or fish and milk (see table 4.1, page 80). Mixing bananas with milk or other dairy products disturbs the intestinal flora and can lead to sinus congestion, allergies, hives, and rash. Consuming dairy and fruit together is a general no-no because this combination creates a big ama factory in your belly. Fruits and dairy are digested at different speeds and, when consumed together, will cause fermentation in your gut. The same goes for dairy and meat as well. This is a case of mixing proteins, which also builds ama. If you're going to have fruit, eat it as a stand-alone meal (for breakfast, for example) or at least forty-five minutes before your main meal. This would still count as your one meal and not a snack. You can make a smoothie in the morning with fruit, green drink powder, and water or apple juice, but never mix fruit and dairy, even in a shake. That means all those fruity yogurts, banana splits, and fruit-and-milk shakes are out if you want to destroy ama and become a healthy, sexy lover!

TABLE 4.1. FOOD COMBINATIONS TO AVOID

FOOD	WHAT IT'S INCOMPATIBLE WITH
Milk	Fruits (except dates) and bananas especially; plus fish, meat, yogurt, beans and other legumes, yeast bread
Yogurt	Fruits, especially citrus fruit, melon, and bananas; plus milk, fish, cheese, eggs, meat, starches, hot drinks
Melons	Always eat melons alone; they are incompatible with other foods, especially grains, cheese, and fried foods
Nightshade vegetables (like potatoes, tomatoes, and eggplant)	Nightshades should not be eaten with yogurt, milk, cucumbers, or melons
Starches (like potatoes, bread, and rice)	Fruits in general, especially bananas and dates; plus eggs and milk
Lemons	Yogurt, milk, cucumber, and tomatoes
Fruit in general	Fruit, especially melon, should be eaten alone; cooked-fruit combinations are okay, as is mixing dates and milk

Adapted from information from the Ayurvedic Institute (www.ayurveda.com)

The second big no-no is heated honey. Never bake or cook with honey. Not only are honey's good qualities spoiled, it turns into ama when heated. Raw honey is nectar; cooked honey is poison. If you want to use it to sweeten hot drinks, you can add honey after they have steeped for a while and are ready to drink. It will still mix quite easily without turning into toxic sludge. Heated honey is not only toxic to humans but to bees themselves, as noted "Barefoot Beekeeper" Phil Chandler attests.*

Raw honey is nectar; cooked honey is poison.

Eating Based on Your Dharma Type

While the Three Square Meals plan tells you when to eat, it doesn't tell you what to eat. Here are some suggestions, based on your dharma type:

Educators

Cultivating ahimsa (nonviolence) and the welfare of humanity as their prime aim, Educators typically require diets with less meat and more fruits, nuts, and dairy. Educators, who have delicate constitutions and need easy-to-digest foods, often find it best to supplement with herbs and vitamins to feel balanced. They may have what appear to others as finicky tastes, require the most attention to their diets, and have the greatest dietary limitations.

Warriors

Warriors require more protein and fewer carbohydrates to feel their best. In medieval times in Europe, venison (meat) was typically reserved for the ruling class and their armies, with peasants kept on a high-carbohydrate, low-protein diet (the Robin Hood story has its basis in this prohibition on hunting). They are ideal candidates for Paleo-style diets, though they can do just as well as vegetarians, as long as they keep their proteins and vegetables high and sugars and grains relatively low.

*Visit Phil Chandler's website, www.biobees.com, for more information. Or see https://groups.yahoo.com/neo/groups/TopHive/conversations/messages/1014.

Laborers

Laborers typically do well on higher-carbohydrate (grain) and medium- to low-protein diets. They can subsist just fine on vegetarian cuisine: rice, corn, beans, wheat, quinoa, lentils, and vegetables. A little meat can be a treat for a nonvegetarian Laborer, and in ancient times meat was consumed sparingly. The modern overabundance of flesh foods has blighted our health because most dharma types—except perhaps the Warrior—cannot handle meat for breakfast, lunch, and dinner. This is one of the reasons for the epidemic of obesity and heart disease in the Western world.

Merchants

Merchants appreciate luxury. Sumptuous chocolate, rich foods (including lots of ghee), and even fine wine are okay for easygoing Merchant types. Since their dharma is to bring laughter and joy to the world, they are allowed to enjoy their delicacies, with one catch: they must do it in moderation. Moderation, however, can be tricky for the fun-loving and sometimes moody Merchant type.

Outsiders

Outsiders like to go outside the box in search of new and cool trends. From Mongolian barbecue to strict vegan fare, from Spam to seitan, they sample everything and usually settle on their own unique blend of foods. When imbalanced, however, they are most likely to turn to "dead" and packaged foods, such as frozen dinners, canned food, chips, hot dogs, and the like. Because Outsiders deal in extremes, they straddle both sides of the spectrum, from the purest to the most putrid. Like the Buddha, their path is to strike a balance that reflects their eclectic nature.

THE BENEFITS OF TRIPHALA

Triphala (three fruits) powder is fitness for your belly. Triphala is an herbal compound that cleanses, tones, and rejuvenates any tissue it touches, an ayurvedic panacea that has received attention from Western science and herbalism alike. One of its ingredients (*emblica officianalis,* or *amalaki* in Sanskrit) has one of the highest concentrations of bioavailable vitamin C of any food on the planet (twenty times greater than an orange!). In addition, it is heat stable, so its effects aren't lost when it's dried or made into a tea. Amalaki is anti-inflammatory, antacid, and antipyretic, while also being rejuvenating for the body.

The next ingredient is *haritaki,* which is often depicted in the hands of the Medicine Buddha. Haritaki (*terminalia chebula*) breaks up hard fecal matter and promotes peristalsis; its astringency also tones the GI tract and helps with hemorrhoids and even leaky gut syndrome.

Finally, *bibhitaki* (*terminalia belerica*), whose name means "fearless of all disease," is triphala's third ingredient. It is an expectorant, bronchodilator, and laxative. It is especially good at clearing phlegm and congestion from the body. Together these three herbs work synergistically to create an effect greater than the sum of their parts. Triphala's components have anticancer, antioxidant, and rejuvenative properties that go far beyond helping you go to the bathroom (which it does). It can also be used as an eyewash. Triphala is a must-have staple in any home, especially since it is also ridiculously inexpensive.*

 THREE WAYS TO TAKE TRIPHALA

1. The easiest way is to simply put half a teaspoon of the powder in your mouth and chase it with water. Take a half teaspoon at night before bed or

---

*Do *not* take triphala if you are pregnant, menstruating, or suffer from chronic diarrhea or loose stools. For more information about this powder, refer to Sebastian Pole's definitive book *Ayurvedic Medicine.*

in the morning to scrape away ama. If you drink milk before bed for better sleep, then take triphala in the morning, or an hour or two before bedtime, because it is incompatible with dairy.

2. Stir a whole teaspoon of triphala in a glass of water in the morning. By nighttime the heavy residue will have settled and only light brown water will remain. At bedtime, without stirring it, drink the water and leave the residue on the bottom. Then add more water and stir. Leave this overnight and drink it in the morning the same way. Discard the remaining residue and repeat this process.

3. Add half a teaspoon of triphala to a cup of hot water. Let it steep for ten minutes, strain, and drink. You can add honey to it for taste.

An additional "benefit" of triphala is its horrible taste. Most people with ama find triphala disgusting and resort to taking it in tablet form. But you should avoid this because one of triphala's magic properties is telling you which flavors you need in your diet! If triphala tastes bitter when you take it, then you need to eat more bitter greens or supplement with herbs like milk thistle, dandelion, or the ayurvedic herb *kutki*. If taking triphala makes your mouth pucker, you need to consume more beans, raw vegetables, pomegranate, and turmeric, as these provide the astringent taste. Sour taste can be supplemented by citrus, yogurt, and fermented foods. You will rarely taste sweet, but when you do, that is a sign that ama is disappearing from your system. Because of its high vitamin C content and three astringent herbs, there will always be some sour and astringent taste to triphala, but a person whose GI tract is clean will find the sweet taste equally predominant.

KILL SUGAR

For some people, this will be the single most important step to burning ama, kindling agni, and restoring health. Recent studies published in the *Journal of the American Medical Association International* show that sugar kills, especially the added sugars found in soda, ketchup, juice, cakes, breads, and other comfort foods. People who got 20 percent of their calories from sugar had an almost 40 percent increased risk of death from cardiovascular disease, compared to those who got less than 10 percent of their calories from added sugars.[1]

In addition, sugar feeds the bad bacteria and yeasts in the gut that promote ama. More ama, in turn, creates a breeding ground for these rascals, and a vicious cycle is created whereby we feel worse and worse while craving more and more sugar, the very thing that makes us feel that way. That is because gut bacteria know how to make us crave the foods that feed them.

Ayurveda says that people with healthy agni are attracted to food that is good for their system. People with low agni and high ama, however, crave the opposite—food and drink that feed bad bacteria and make them feel worse. Modern science agrees.

> "Microbes have the capacity to manipulate behavior and mood through altering the neural signals in the vagus nerve, changing taste receptors, producing toxins to make us feel bad, and releasing chemical rewards to make us feel good."
> ATHENA AKTIPIS, PH.D., DIRECTOR OF HUMAN AND SOCIAL EVOLUTION, UNIVERSITY OF CALIFORNIA AT SAN FRANCISCO

Some of the most exciting medical research today focuses on the microbiome* and how these microorganisms affect our moods, immunity, and general health. Since the gut is connected to the nervous, immune, and endocrine systems, these little guys pack a huge punch when it comes to dictating whether we feel vibrant and alive or sluggish, sick, and depressed.

---

*The term *microbiome* refers to the totality of microorganisms and their collective genetic material present in or on the human body.

A therapist once told me, "Simon, sugar equals pain." Inflammation and, for women, painful periods result when we cannot process all the sugar we ingest. Chronic inflammation breaks down our tissues and creates multiple factors that bring on disease. The suffix *-itis* means "inflammation." Think about how many painful medical conditions carry this suffix—cystitis, appendicitis, arthritis—and all of these are exacerbated by excess sugar intake. Consider that sugar also robs your skin of elastin and collagen, accelerating aging and wrinkles. Combine this with cognitive decline and you have a serious case for doing something to curb this sweet killer.

The best way to kill sugar is to fast from it for five days. You can ease into this by gradually reducing your intake of soda, doughnuts, cereals, and other sugary foods or you can go cold turkey and stop consuming all elective sugars at once. The term *elective sugars* means foods that have processed sugar added to make them taste good, rather than, say, vegetables or grains, which have small amounts of sugar naturally present.

Start by eliminating soda, candy, and all elective sugars these first few days. See how you feel. Fasting is a natural part of life, and doing it intelligently will help you heal your body. You can still enjoy green apples, carrots, and the sugar naturally present in many vegetables, but avoid sweet fruits. Though natural, they slow down the removal of ama. You can have grains, but avoid sugary cereals. Read the labels on everything you buy, and try to ingest less than twenty grams of elective sugar a day. This will bring you down to "Paleo" levels—the amount of sugar eaten by our cave-dwelling ancestors.

After the first few days, you may like the feeling of a sugar-free body so much that you want to keep going. That's fine; continue until you feel the need to reintroduce sugar back into your diet. Then return to your normal diet slowly, adding limited amounts of sugar back into your life and enjoying every little bit of it. Be like the Swiss, who savor their delectable chocolates as bite-size pieces, as opposed to consuming the massive blocks of dark brown ama that we ingest in America.

The Five-Two Sugar Fast

You can also try the five-two regimen: fasting from sugar for five days and allowing yourself to have it for two. The five-two regimen has worked for body builders and fitness enthusiasts who want rapid fat loss. Eating this way is said to improve performance both in the gym and the bedroom by boosting testosterone and putting the body in a fat-burning mode. In addition, it allows you to be social and splurge on weekends or at parties without compromising your fitness plans. Do what your body and mind allow you and never force yourself. Harsh starvation diets end up sabotaging your efforts in the long run. This is not a diet, but a tool for reducing ama and inflammation. Using this in the context of the Three Square Meals plan is a great way to burn ama and boost metabolism.

When you feel that your digestion is back on track and have determined your ama is under control, you can return to eating more sugar with awareness. Pay attention to the signs of ama and, when you need to, be ready to take up your sword and kill the many-headed sugar hydra again. Some people will love the feeling of a sugar-free body so much that this becomes their lifestyle. Whatever option you choose, consider going on a sugar fast at least four times a year. Your mind and body will thank you for it!

Note: Diabetics and people prone to hypoglycemia should not do this sugar fast without consulting their doctor. Please consult your health care professional before making any dietary changes or starting an exercise program.

EXERCISE

Exercise improves sex and health by burning ama and kindling agni. When your muscles "feel the burn" they are also melting ama, squeezing out toxins, and galvanizing your metabolism to get rid of waste. Regular exercise is better than once-in-a-while workouts because it trains your metabolism to be an ama-burning machine. If you don't have time or a gym membership, there are a few exercises that you can easily do at home.* The two best movements for men include push-ups and kettlebell swings. For women, full-body squats, plank pose, and bridge pose are excellent. Below are brief descriptions of three of these movements as well as a useful breath practice.

ROCK-HARD PUSH-UPS

Everyone knows how to do a push-up . . . or they think they do. Here are some tips that will transform this exercise from good to great:

First, when performing a push-up it is important to "grab the ground" with your hands and try to *pull* yourself down, instead of falling into the movement. Pulling yourself engages the latissimus muscles of your back and creates stability.

Second, with your body aligned in one straight line from heels to head, squeeze your glutes and hold.

Then tense up every muscle in your body, from your toes to your quadriceps, abdominals, trapezius, and latissimus muscles, as well as your hands. You can even tighten the muscles in your face, but don't clench your teeth.

With this tight-as-a-bowstring configuration, pull yourself down and begin your push-ups.

When you're finished, relax your body completely and move around or

---

*To see these exercises performed online along with a complete workout plan, please refer to www.spirittype.com/exercise.

stretch. Tensing and relaxing this way is great for flushing your lymph system, releasing stress, and creating deep relaxation.

✦ *LION'S BREATH*

During any intense exercise, expecially these rock-hard push-ups, you can incorporate the Lion's Breath for maximum results.

Stick your tongue out, lift your eyebrows, roll your eyes up, and exhale to a low hiss as you push up. This is great for releasing pent-up anger, frustration, or unexpressed emotions.

Doing Lion's Breath during the contraction portion of an exercise will help you squeeze out extra reps while squeezing your muscles to the max!

Tensing your muscles this way is like wringing out a wet dishcloth: it squeezes toxins out of your system and teaches your body strength. Strength is a skill; weight lifters practice these tension-and-release exercises to build up their tendons, ligaments, and muscles.

✦ *PLANK POSE*

While on your elbows, follow the same directions as for the rock-hard push-ups and simply hold. Squeezing every muscle in your body teaches you self-control and body awareness. Start with ten seconds of this rock-hard plank and work up to twenty seconds at a time. Do at least three sets.

✦ *FULL-BODY SQUAT*

Squatting is the most natural of human movements, and is instrumental to proper bowel movement and health. By sitting in chairs for most of the day many of us have lost the ability to squat properly. But chairs can also help to retrain us to do this movement correctly.

Standing in front of a chair, slowly reach your butt back and down as if trying to sit. You can extend your arms forward for balance.

As your butt touches the seat, reverse direction and come up to standing position.

At the top, squeeze your glutes and quadriceps tightly for a second or two. Repeat.

As you get better, you can use chairs that are lower to the ground, thereby increasing your range of motion.

When I teach clients this movement I emphasize that the most important muscle in the squat is the abdomen. They don't believe me at first, until they try the movement. If you don't have a tight abdomen while squatting, your core becomes compromised and you can't lift the weight, risking injury and losing strength. As you reach the bottom of the squat, squeeze your abs super tight and let them push you up. It sounds counterintuitive, but in practice you will see that the abdominals are key to proper squats, and, if done right, they get a great workout too!

Time to Hit the Pot—the Neti Pot

If you wake up with nasal crust or have difficulty breathing or blocked sinuses, consider the yogic practice of *neti,* or nasal irrigation. In addition to exercise, nasal irrigation with half to one teaspoon of xylitol mixed with salt (a sixty-forty ratio) dissolved in twelve to sixteen ounces of water can clear out stuffiness and congestion and relieve allergy symptoms as well. If you suffer from any of these, doing neti will be a revelation. You can also add a tiny pinch of baking soda to this xylitol-saline solution for an extra cleansing touch.

According to ayurveda, ear wax, nasal crust, and smegma are waste products of the muscular system. If you find these accumulating in your body, it's time to fire up your muscles and exercise. Working out also helps to flush out mental ama and is one of the best ways to refresh the mind, especially for Educator types who are not always fond of exercise. Along with pranayama, movement is the best medicine for fighting depression, loneliness, and hormonal imbalances.

The right amount of exercise depends on your body type but, as a general rule, when you generate a light sweat in your armpits, at your temples, and on the nape of your neck, you have reached your limit. For some of us this is barely a warm-up, but ayurveda says that harsh exercise is not good for long-term health. Recent studies seem to confirm this, with results suggesting that more frequent but less intense training is better than long bouts of exercise done once or twice a week.* Remember, we are treating exercise as medicine and as a tool for detoxification and rejuvenation. When done right, along with the other recommendations in this chapter, it will prolong your life, not shorten it. For athletes and others for whom exercise is recreation or a profession, higher intensities are normal. But note that higher-intensity exercise taxes the body instead of nourishing it, and there is a price to pay for working out this way. As long as you're willing to pay this price and feel that your sport gives back something in return for the toll it takes on your body, then you should be okay with the consequences.

The key to proper exercise performance is your breath. Shallow, upper-chest breathing activates our stress response, just as being startled makes the body think to fight or flee. On the other hand, deep, lower-lobe breathing that expands the rib cage and activates our parasympathetic nervous system creates a calm, stress-free, and

---

*Kenneth Cooper, M.D., who did the original research still posted on most health club walls, initially said that you must exercise at between 60 percent and 80 percent of your maximum heart rate to achieve any cardiovascular benefits. Recently he said that, according to new research, "If you want *health* and *longevity* benefits from exercise you should exercise at a heart rate below 60 percent of your maximum heart rate" (emphasis mine) (www.lifespa.com/enjoy-exercise-every-time/). For more on this refer to Dr. John Douillard's book *Body, Mind, and Sport.*

anabolic environment. In his book *Body, Mind, and Sport*, Dr. John Douillard explains the studies behind this and how to consistently achieve the "runner's high" using your breath as a guide. He advocates what he calls Darth Vader Breath, or *ujjayi pranayama,* which you can learn on your own or by consulting a yoga professional.

Ujjayi entails breathing in and out through your nose, but during the inhale and especially during the exhale constricting your epiglottis slightly to create a hissing sound in the back of your throat. This type of breathing ensures that you are oxygenating the lower lobes of your lungs and encouraging your body to burn fat as a fuel. It is also a guideline for exercise. When you have to open your mouth to breathe, you are pushing too hard. Reduce your exercise intensity and work up to being able to breathe through your nose using Darth Vader Breath, even while running or working out at full capacity. This will be a revelation for your body and mind. You should perform ujjayi during all the exercises outlined in this section.

This kind of breathing also activates your abdominals, which are critical to proper exercise performance. If you've ever heard the *tsss* sound boxers or martial artists make when punching, or the *kiaiii* yell of a karate master breaking bricks, you've seen abdominal breathing at work. That is because the abdomen has to be pressurized to make these forceful sounds. A pressurized abdomen functions as your own safety belt.

SLEEP

Sleep deprivation produces mental ama—toxic sludge in the brain. This is nothing new to medical researchers, who have long recognized the destructive effects of sleep loss on cognitive function, or to military leaders who use it as a form of torture. During sleep our bodies process the stress, emotions, and experiences of the day and safely release their toxic by-products. When the body is not allowed enough time for this, ama builds up. We already know that amyloid plaque, a form of ama in the brain, is a factor in Alzheimer's disease and mental decline. But sleep loss also leads to systemic ama that clogs the arteries and brings on heart disease. Research shows that adequate sleep and an early bedtime (before 10 p.m.) reduce calcification of the blood vessels and vulnerability to cardiovascular issues.[2] This mirrors ayurvedic recommendations for sleep.

> **"Every important mistake I've made in my life,**
> **I've made because I was too tired."**
> **BILL CLINTON**

Many people resort to drugs to help them calm down, but diazepam and other tranquilizers prevent the neurons from discharging and rejuvenating our brains, thereby reducing much of the benefit of sleep and rest. Take time to meditate, relax, and get enough sleep in order for your brain to process the day's emotions and discharge accumulated toxins. Emotions are stored in our neurochemistry, and when our brain's chemicals get overwhelmed, they create both short- and long-term problems. Sleep. Meditate. Rest. Repeat.

Help for Sleep

Insomnia is an uncommonly common disorder
in the modern world.

DR. VASANT LAD, *THE COMPLETE BOOK*
OF AYURVEDIC HOME REMEDIES

- Breathing for life (beginning on page 106) is key to relaxing your mind and easing stress, which will give you a good night's sleep.
- Putting oil on the soles of your feet at bedtime and regular oil massage also work well to help you sleep.
- Try warm milk at bedtime with a pinch of nutmeg. Also, garlic

milk works well: Gently bring to a boil a cup of milk and one clove of chopped garlic. Let cool and drink before bedtime.

For additional tips and home remedies, refer to Dr. Vasant Lad's *Complete Book of Ayurvedic Home Remedies.*

TIPS FOR KINDLING AGNI THROUGH FOOD AND DRINK

To get a jump start on your digestion, you can arm your body to wipe out ama with the following herbs, recipes, and hydration tips. Try them and you'll turn the tide in the war against sludge!

Here are a few basics to get you started:

+ Before each meal, add a few drops of lime juice and a pinch of salt to a small slice of fresh ginger. Chew and eat. This will promote digestion.

+ Take the herb trikatu, an ayurvedic combination of ginger, long-pepper, and black pepper before meals. Trikatu also addresses lung congestion, asthma, and heaviness in the body. For chronic indigestion, combine one part trikatu with one part kutki and two parts chitrak—other digestive herbs that will help clear your liver and stoke your agni. If you follow the Three Square Meals diet, along with the other recommendations above, your digestion should normalize quickly. If you are still having digestive issues, it may be time to see an ayurvedic doctor.

+ Sip hot water every fifteen minutes throughout the day. This simple practice will clear out stagnated lymph and liquefy your ama, allowing it to be excreted more easily through urine, feces, and sweat. You can add lemon to it for an extra digestive kick. You will be amazed at how hydrated and clear you feel after just a few days. *Note: This regimen is best practiced during winter and spring, and may be too heating for some people in the summer.*

+ Instead of dessert, try takram—a delicious, nutritious after-meal drink that will help you digest and assimilate your food. Takram is the preferred after-meal drink in ayurveda because it is slightly astringent and, according to ayurveda, you should end meals with astringency rather than sweetness.

HOW TO MAKE TAKRAM

Add together a cup of buttermilk (use yogurt if you can't find buttermilk) and a cup of water, along with half a teaspoon of roasted cumin powder and black salt to taste.*

Stir well or mix in a blender.

Drink following a meal.

Takram is an exceptional digestive aid that will help you feel light and strong all day.

Those are some "do's" for kindling digestion; now here's a "don't": do not drink ice water, especially before, during, or after meals. Some fitness experts recommend drinking cold water because it forces the body to warm it up, thereby burning a few extra calories. The bad news is that cold water also dampens digestion, creating lymph stagnation and toxic sludge, which is a whole lot worse for you and your fitness goals. The only time ayurveda advises consuming cool drinks is in the summer, when the body easily overheats.

Water and Digestion

Drinking water does more than replace sweat and fluids; it is also vital for boosting our metabolism and energy levels. But most of us do not know how to use it to optimize nutrient assimilation and instead suffer from fatigue, bloating, and other symptoms of

---

*Black salt is a healthy delicacy available in Indian and Asian markets. It is a type of rock salt that helps liquefy ama and kindle agni. Because of its high trace mineral content, it smells like sulfur and tastes like something out of this world: once you try it, you'll never go back to eating regular salt!

improper digestion. The best way to drink water is to have eight to sixteen ounces first thing in the morning after brushing your tongue, and the same quantity fifteen to thirty minutes before every meal. This ensures that your stomach's bicarbonate layer (called *kledaka kapha* in ayurveda) is fully buffered, which then signals your body to produce more hydrochloric acid (HCl); this acid in the stomach breaks down food and kills bacteria. The more acid, the better your body can handle heavy foods like dairy, eggs, and gluten. A dry or dehydrated stomach does not produce optimal amounts of HCl, and this can lead to indigestion and other problems as the undigested food moves down the GI tract. Your stomach doesn't have teeth; it has hydrochloric acid to digest what you give it. Give it more of this.

More HCl also leads to fat loss. *The Journal of Clinical Diagnostic Research* reported that drinking sixteen ounces of water a half hour before breakfast, lunch, and dinner burned fat and prompted significant body composition changes in a group of fifty overweight girls.[3] So not only did the girls in the study lose weight, but they burned fat and changed the shape of their bodies—all from drinking water! Have a tall glass of room-temperature water before your meals. You will notice how hungry you become a half hour later— that is the HCL in your stomach saying, "I am ready for food!" You will love how good this feels, and how fit it makes your body!

However, you do not want to overdrink water. Water, like anything else, needs to be digested. A good rule of thumb is this: "Chew your water; drink your food." This means chew every bite of food at least thirty-two times (once for every tooth) or until it is thoroughly mixed with saliva and "liquid" enough to swallow. The point is that your food should be thoroughly broken down and emulsified before you swallow it. Do the same thing with water. Swish every sip in your mouth instead of just guzzling it. That way, combining with your saliva, water has a better chance of actually getting to and being utilized by your deep tissues before being excreted.

For a super boost to your digestion and agni, try copper water. The molecular copper particles, which are transferred from the copper cup, act as scraping agents that sweep away ama and enhance liver, gallbladder, and intestinal function. Copper water is warming to the body, so reduce the amount you consume in the summertime (instead try silver or gold water—see the recipe on page 144.)

 ## COPPER WATER

Buy a pure copper cup (available at Indian groceries).

Fill it with pure water and leave it overnight.

Drink this copper-infused water the next morning for an incredible digestive boost. Within thirty to sixty minutes you should feel your digestive juices flowing.

Flax water is also a demulcent tonic for the digestive system that you can drink instead of plain water before meals. It will buffer your stomach and digestive tract while providing the added benefits of flax and its omega-3 fatty acids. You can add a touch of maple syrup or other sweeteners to make it even more nourishing and palatable. Here is an amazing recipe to try before meals.

FLAX WATER

Bring two to four tablespoons of raw flax seeds in a quart of plain water to a boil.

Let it cool.

Drink this smooth and viscous water fifteen to thirty minutes before eating.

Avoid drinking water during and especially after meals. The pH of your stomach acid is about two (very acidic). Water's pH is over seven, not good for helping you digest that turkey dinner. Water on an empty stomach boosts digestion; on a full stomach it bogs digestion down. If you must drink with meals, sip hot water, tea, or wine—just enough to get your food down. Wine also works well with meals but should be consumed in moderation. If you've followed some of the tips above, you should not feel thirsty during meals.

> **Water on an empty stomach boosts digestion; on a full stomach it bogs digestion down.**

You should also drink water by itself. Coffee is not water. Neither is wine, tea, or milk. Yes, these are liquids, but most actually make you thirstier rather than relieving thirst. Your liver has to process alcohol and other toxins, and if it's already overloaded by stress and poor dietary habits, you are simply adding to its troubles. Sports drinks, vitamin water, and other sugary drinks are no help either, and actually make you fat. Did you know that to benefit from a sports drink, a typical person needs to exercise continuously for more than two hours? And did you know that the people who routinely run dozens of miles each day, such as the Tarahumara of Mexico, only do so by drinking—you guessed it—water? By drinking pure water the right way, you will turn your body into the fat-burning, toxin-excreting machine it was designed to be.

By getting enough water you will feel less of a need to drink alcohol, coffee, and iced soda drinks, which, in turn, will help your liver and metabolism function better. We often turn to these crutches to ease digestion. Because of their constituents, wine or cola may help the stomach digest greasy heavy foods. But their detriments often outweigh the benefits. When your own inner furnace is fully stoked you will never need to depend on anything else to get the most zest out of food, sex, or life itself!

Replace Gatorade with Ayurade

If you are active or chronically dehydrated, try making your own sports drink with this recipe below. This electrolyte balancer is better for you than what's on the market, and it is easy to make at home. Rock salt or, better yet, black salt, is available from Indian and Asian markets.

◈ AYURADE RECIPE

To a quart of water, add fresh lime juice, a pinch of rock (or black) salt, and maple syrup to taste.

Adjust the ingredients as you see fit.

Coffee: Do's and Don'ts

Remember my client Jane? She was concerned this new healthy life-style would require relinquishing her morning ritual.

"This all sounds great, Simon, but you know I love my morning cup of Joe. What do I do about coffee?" Jane casts a yearning look my way. Surely I wouldn't take away one of her precious treasures. No, I wouldn't dare.

"For a long time," I tell her, "ayurveda was practiced by the elite—the kings and queens of the world."

"What does this have to do with coffee?" her silent look tells me as she awaits my verdict with some trepidation.

"And the reason was simple: the health of the ruler reflected the health of the kingdom. If a king was sick, irritable, or hung over, any bad decisions he made could affect the welfare of hundreds, maybe thousands, of people; it was literally a question of life or death. That's why the court physicians had to be skilled at keeping their benefactors healthy and happy, even after late-night binges of food, sex, and other extravagances."

Jane starts to smile—a smile of hope that her own little indulgence might somehow be neutralized by ayurvedic magic.

"In some ways, the goal of ayurveda is for us to relish the pleasures of the world while minimizing their side effects—to have your cake and eat it too. So, of course, there are remedies and tricks for enjoying the good things in life without falling victim to their inevitable consequences."

Jane quietly but gleefully claps her hands together, perhaps thanking those quondam kings for paving the way to her morning Starbucks.

I break the mood with this final caveat, a sermon on karma: "One thing to remember is that, like Newton's third law, for every indulgence there must be a penance of the same intensity and duration. Kings and queens who desired durable vitality were willing (presumably) to pay this price for their continued enjoyment, and subjected themselves to enemas, sweat boxes, purgation, oil in practically every orifice, even bloodletting and other therapies to get them back in the game. You should be ready to do the same thing."

One of the reasons coffee is a megabillion-dollar industry is because we don't get enough bitter taste in our diet. "Bitter is better for the liver," says Dr. Lad, and not enough bitter greens and herbs make it onto our plates, which is why our bodies crave bitter substances like coffee and even tobacco to keep them balanced.

Coffee is also a diuretic, and it helps to push food through the GI tract by stimulating peristalsis. This makes us feel good because toxic sludge is also temporarily expelled, though, in the long term, coffee creates more ama than it clears, and it is not effective at cleansing the body at a deep level. Therefore, it is best to treat coffee as medicine and take it in small amounts when you need a little bitter pick-me-up. Traditionally, coffee was sipped after meals as a digestive aid, and that is still the best way to drink it—not on an empty stomach. For regular coffee drinkers, consider supplementing with other bitter substances in your diet, such as kutki, neem, or milk thistle, and eating more bitter leafy greens, like dandelion and kale. This will reduce your need for coffee. Cafix and Pero are also alternatives you can try if you want to reduce your caffeine intake and coffee's side effects.

You may also try making cold-press coffee.

◈ COLD-PRESS COFFEE

Add room temperature water to freshly ground beans in a French press and let it sit overnight. Fewer toxins and less acidity make it to your mouth when the beans remain unheated.

If you like it hot, simply heat up the pressed coffee, leaving the beans and residue in the presser.

Another way to avert some of coffee's deleterious side effects is to spice it up by mixing cardamom, cinnamon, clove, nutmeg, and other herbs, thereby warming up this cold and bitter drink. This is the traditional ayurvedic recipe for taking the edge off black tea, which, with a little milk added, turns into chai. Warming herbs make anything they're added to more digestible and easier on your system, though they do not entirely eliminate its side effects.

Perhaps the best way to curb coffee's jitters is to mix ghee into freshly brewed coffee and blend it together. The result is a creamy, latte-style drink that not only tastes great, but is better for you than coffee alone. The ghee helps to minimize coffee's side effects and bring out its benefits, especially when used along with warming spices. Instead of a crash as the caffeine wears off, there is more of a slow descent, which for many is almost unnoticeable. The Tibetans have butter tea; we can have coffee-ghee!

Keep in mind that you should consult with an ayurvedic health practitioner before drinking ghee or taking any medication—ayurvedic or otherwise. You should not drink ghee if you get nauseated from it, have high cholesterol, suffer from diabetes, have a sensitive liver, or are obese. For red-haired and fair-skinned persons, especially those with freckles, drinking ghee is not advised.

Me and Bobby McGhee: The Benefits of Ghee

Ayurveda is crazy about ghee, and what's not to love? It's a true superfood. Ghee feeds the healthy flora in our gut while keeping our intestinal lining nourished. It has a super-high flashpoint (485°F), which makes it great for cooking (other oils, like flax or olive, have much lower flashpoints). Perhaps most important, it's an herbal delivery system that carries medicine to our deeper tissues. There are hundreds of ayurvedic preparations made with ghee (called *ghrita* in Sanskrit). In fact, the classical text Astanga Hrdayam says that ghee is capable of giving a thousand effects by a thousand different kinds of processing. Some examples of these include:

Tikta ghrita: for detoxification, for alleviating skin problems and fever, and for cleansing the blood

Maha kalyanaka ghrita: for addressing mental and psychological issues

Shatavari ghrita: to promote lactation, to regulate menstruation, and to promote overall female reproductive health

Triphala ghrita: for cleansing and detoxification

Brahmi ghrita: for enhancing intelligence and memory

Licorice ghrita: for promoting the voice and lungs

Ashwagandha ghrita: to combat the effects of aging and to counteract sexual debility

Chitrakadi ghrita: to enhance digestion

Ayurveda traditionally used four types of oil for healing: ghee, vegetable oils, animal fat, and marrow. Ghee is primarily used for internal oleation, while the others can be used both internally and externally. The materialist philosopher Charvaka contended, "As long as we're alive we might as well be happy. Even if you have to go into debt, drink ghee." For poor peasants in ancient India ghee was a luxury, but its importance to health and vitality cannot be overstated.

Drinking ghee is a way to heal your "inner skin," just as oil massage nurtures your outer skin. When your outer skin is dry, you can bet your inner skin—the lining of your intestinal wall— will also be dry. If you've ever seen a cracked piece of leather you know that it is not good for much—leather needs to be oiled regularly to keep it flexible and strong. The same is true of your living skin: dry mucous membranes are precursors to allergies, colds, and flu. A dry intestinal lining does not allow good bacteria to flourish, instead inviting bad bacteria and excess mucus to take over, which leads to a host of health problems.

Taking a shot (one to two tablespoons) of ghee two to three times a week in the morning is vital if you live in a dry climate or suffer from internal dryness. Use plain or medicated ghee, chased with ginger tea or, if you drink coffee, blended with your morning java. Take on an empty stomach and wait at least an hour before having food. In fact, if you're not hungry, don't eat. Let the ghee do its job of lubricating your insides and stimulating bile from your liver. When you do eat, have a low-fat, high-fiber breakfast to bind the extra bile that has been secreted and ferry it out of your gut. Bile contains recycled red blood cells and other toxins, and should be encouraged to flow and leave the body. Having a low-fat, high-fiber meal after drinking ghee also reduces strain on your liver and any possible nausea.

 MAKING GHEE

Ghee is clarified butter.

To make it, put unsalted butter, preferably organic and from grass-fed cows, in a saucepan and warm it slowly until it melts.

Reduce the heat to low or medium low and wait. The ghee will bubble and churn as the moisture evaporates from it, leaving white cholesterol clumps on the bottom or the surface.

When it ceases to bubble, quickly remove the pan from the fire; ghee burns easily (though some people love the taste of burned ghee!).

Allow it to cool and strain it through a metal or cheesecloth strainer into a glass jar. The ghee will keep at room temperature as long as no contaminants get into it.

◈ *MAKING MEDICATED GHEE*

Add one part herbs (licorice, asparagus root, ashwagandha, or *bala*) to sixteen parts water.

Bring to a boil and let simmer on very low heat without covering, stirring occasionally.

After this mixture has reduced to one fourth its original volume, strain out the herbs. This may take several hours

Add the strained tea to an equal amount of ghee, and cook them together over a low flame until all the water evaporates. You will know when the water is gone when the liquid stops bubbling.

What's left is medicated ghee.

FASTING

Humans are built to fast. Sleep is a fast from wakeful awareness, just as night is a fast from day. Fasting is the engine that drives nature's cycles, both within and outside our bodies. Even breathing is a cycle of fasting and feasting—gorging on oxygen and then doing without. The better we become at fasting, the longer we live. This includes fasting from air by practicing breath work, as well as fasting from sensual gratification and sex, all of which build strength and immunity. The reason many popular diets work is because of the fasting principle, from Atkins (a fast from carbohydrates) to vegetarianism and veganism (which constitute fasts from animal products to varying degrees). Understanding nature's cycles will not only make you healthy, it can help you balance your inner world. A famous quote from the Yoga Sutras states that "Yoga is the cessation of the fluctuations of the mind stuff." The "mind stuff" cited here includes physical sensations as well as mental chatter. When we fast, we give the GI tract a break, which allows our bodies to detoxify and rest. You cannot have *citta vrtti nirodhah*— peace of mind—if your belly is full. That's why yogis emphasize a light diet as well as purification practices like enema and pranayama to keep the gastrointestinal tract clear and vritti-free. While we cannot all live a yogic lifestyle, we can incorporate some of ayurveda's best practices into our daily lives. The foremost of these is fasting.

Fasting once a month, or even once a week, promotes clarity—not just in the body, but in the mind as well. When our stomachs are not busy churning away at the latest greasy meal, our attention becomes more settled, our awareness keener. We begin to see the quiet beauty in nature in ways that may have eluded us before. The fall of a leaf, the language of animals, and nature's rhythms all become clearer as we connect to a deeper part of ourselves. Inspiration comes like a sweet breath moving through us, filling us with intimations of our immortality. This is the Spirit, and its subtlety is difficult to perceive. Only when we have silenced our minds can we glimpse this most elusive of realities.

You can fast on the day that's most convenient for you: Saturday or Sunday works for most people.* Or you can choose a day with special meaning, like the day of your birth or your planetary period.† During fasting, you typically don't have the same energy you normally do, which is why you should devote the day to rest, allowing your body to catch up from your busy week and heal itself. Aside from resting, consider taking easy walks in nature, playing or listening to music, or engaging in any light, inspirational activity. This allows your body, mind, and soul to reset and get ready for the week or month to come.

This periodic self-reset through fasting is known to boost longevity—actually slowing down the aging process—as well as improve memory and brain function, regulate blood sugar levels,‡ and bolster other physical markers. For people who are not used to it, fasting

---

*Saturday is a special day for fasting because it is governed by the planet Saturn, which rules penance and humility.

†Your planetary period is your life cycle, which appears in your Vedic life map. Consult a Vedic astrologer for information about your Vedic life map.

‡If you are diabetic or have another health condition that prevents you from periodic fasting, consult your physician about your options.

can be incorporated in a number of ways. Let's say you've chosen Saturday to fast. You can do one of the following:

+ Fast for twenty-four hours, from Friday's dinner to Saturday's dinner.
+ Fast the entire day Saturday, from Friday's dinner to Sunday breakfast.
+ Fast from sunrise to sunset: do not eat on Saturday until after the sun has completely set. Sunset times can be found in your local newspaper, or by looking outside!

The third option is usually the most popular (especially during the shorter winter days), but you can fast any way you like. Fasting is part of many spiritual traditions and for good reason: it promotes health and spiritual awareness. Even the Three Square Meals diet plan is a fast since it banishes snacking.

BREATHE FOR LIFE

Along with diet and lifestyle, ayurveda recommends pranayama, or yogic breathing, as a tool to kindle agni, balance your hormones, and burn mental ama. Mental ama is the residue of unprocessed thoughts and feelings in the brain. In ayurveda, emotions and thoughts are considered material things. Science seems to agree, with research results showing that thoughts and emotions ride on the molecules of our bodies and are affected by diet, lifestyle, and, yes, our breath.*

Eastern medicine believes that where there is no life force, or prana, there is no life, and disease and pain are the result. Doing pranayama invites prana to flow through the body freely. To preserve your mental and emotional well-being and prevent mental decline, begin a practice of yogic breathing today. It not only adds years to your life, but life to your years.*

---

*See the book *Molecules of Emotion* by Candace Pert for more on this topic.

There are different forms of pranayama, the most essential of which are described in this book.* We looked at a simple technique, called ujjayi pranayama, in the exercise section (see page 92). Now I will introduce you to some common and not so common breathing exercises that will help you avoid Alzheimer's disease, improve your cholesterol profile, eliminate aches and pains, and cure depression. In *Balance Your Hormones, Balance Your Life*, Dr. Claudia Welch credits pranayama for helping her clients when even diet and lifestyle couldn't. Pranayama is one of the most powerful tools for self-transformation because our breath is the bridge between the mind and body. Fifteen to thirty minutes of yogic breathing every day can save your life and your relationships.

> **Fifteen to thirty minutes
> of yogic breathing every day
> can save your life and your relationships.**

Prana ayama literally means "breath extension." It encompasses dozens of exercises, some held secret for thousands of years and others better known. The simplest is diaphragmatic breathing. This entails taking air into the lower lobes of the lungs, where 60 percent of oxygen receptors are located. Lower lobe diaphragmatic breathing produces a calm, fat-burning state by activating the parasympathetic nervous system. By contrast, shallow upper-lung breathing activates the sympathetic nervous system and the stress response.†

---

*These and other forms of pranayama not discussed here can be viewed online at www.spirittype.com/breathing.

†For information on stress, how to avoid it, and why to relieve it, refer to *Why Zebras Don't Get Ulcers,* a thorough review of the science of stress; *Balance Your Hormones, Balance Your Life,* the modern woman's guide to alternate ways of balancing your hormones; and *Body, Mind, and Sport,* the contemporary athlete's bible for using the breath to guide your workout.

DEEP BELLY BREATHING

Sit up straight or lie on your back.

Place your hands on your belly and take a few deep breaths. As you breathe, feel the air going down to your belly button, pushing your hands out.

Practice this for a few minutes. When belly breathing has become easy and comfortable, try putting your hands on the side of your rib cage, low, by your kidneys.

Now try pushing your lower rib cage out, using your breath as you inhale. You should feel your hands move a little bit, not as much as on your belly. Practice filling your lungs this way in addition to deep belly breathing; it will activate your deep, calm center, which is not only great for physical rejuvenation, but for peace of mind as well.

Practice this until it feels natural. With enough practice you'll be breathing this way all day long. When you've got the hang of deep belly breathing, move to the next pranayama exercise, alternate-nostril breathing.

ALTERNATE-NOSTRIL BREATHING

Make the *vishnu mudra* with your hand (see figure 4.1).

Holding your right nostril closed with your thumb, inhale through the left nostril. Try picturing a sea of tiny blue shining particles moving with the air, vibrant, alive, and full of consciousness. This is visualizing light as a particle; you can also inhale pure light as a wave of shimmering consciousness. In either case, as you breathe in let this cosmic prana (or chi, vital energy) merge with your third eye.

Pause for a second, holding both nostrils shut using your thumb and ring finger, and let the air swirl around your skull, doing what it needs to do—cleansing, building, or recycling old thoughts and emotions.

Then, keeping your left nostril closed, release your thumb from the right. Let the air out of your right nostril and with it let go of all negative or used-up mental processes. You can picture some of the prana particles releasing from the top of your head as well, moving up and out at the same time as your nostril breath, contributing to the cosmic consciousness. This helps to build higher awareness and makes this practice a bridge between physical, emotional, and spiritual healing.

Repeat this, inhaling through the right nostril.

Never force the breath to the point where you feel light-headed, irritable, or uncomfortable. Your face should be completely relaxed, with no tension in any of your facial muscles. Try making a light smile as you do this; it helps.

Do this as quietly as you can. Prana is subtle; it rides on the air like a

Figure 4.1. The vishnu mudra: thumb, ring finger, and pinky raised, index and middle fingers down.

beach ball on the surface of a river. It is independent of the river. Focus on the ball, not the water—the prana, not the breath.

Practice for at least five and up to twenty-five minutes every day.

In the beginning, focus on making the exhale quiet, while keeping the inhale normal or even forceful. Let the outward breath flow gently out without a sound, like a turtle breathing.

When this becomes easy, try it the other way, making your inhale quiet.

Ideally, you should not be able to hear yourself inhale or exhale. Experiment and let your body tell you what is right for you.

Alternate-nostril breathing is perhaps the simplest and most effective technique you can use for physical, mental, and emotional health. Practicing the visualizations recommended above can also turn this pranayama into instant meditation.

The yogic secret of meditation is that you don't have to try to empty your mind; let your practice do it for you. One of the reasons beginners drop out of meditation is that simply sitting can be painful and boring. But starting with a light physical warm-up, like yoga, dance, or t'ai chi, then proceeding to pranayama can help you slip into meditation much more easily than just trying to sit. The alternate-nostril techniques described here, and the methods such as the phantom breath on page 58 will help you achieve pure awareness with hardly any effort or boredom. You can pump oxygen into a dead body but that will not bring it to life. Prana is not oxygen; it is cosmic consciousness. Learning to work with it means becoming as silent as possible.

PUNCH YOUR KARMA

If you've lived with ama for a long time, it has probably penetrated into your deeper tissues, disrupting cellular function and accelerating aging. The ama-destroying plan in this chapter will keep new toxins from forming and slowly begin eliminating deeper sludge, but if you want a jump start to dislodge it at the cellular level, do *pancha karma*—ayurvedic detox—at least once a year. Pancha karma (PK) refers to five main therapies. However, in practice, PK deploys multiple modalities to rid the body of morbid toxicity and return it to youthful vitality, including diet, lifestyle, massage, a customized herbal regimen, steam therapy, *shirodhara* (a steady stream of oil poured on the third eye), enema, and other techniques specific to your mind/body type. Think of it as the deepest spa therapy you've ever had.

PK is best done under the guidance of specialists in a qualified pancha karma clinic, but you can do a simple version of this at home. Dr. John Douillard's *Colorado Cleanse* details a well-researched and tested home program that works. Dr. Vasant Lad also specifies how to perform a classic home PK in his book *The Complete Book of Ayurvedic Home Remedies.* Both books are must-haves if you want a deeper understanding of the body's dharma.

If you do home PK, do it during spring and fall, six months apart. A full PK lasts two to four weeks. Those who engage in a full PK regimen often report feeling younger, more vital, and more energized on a deep, cellular level. Make time for a two-week or even one-month home or clinic PK retreat at least once a year and your body will thank you for it.

Most of your daily routine is centered around what you do in the morning. For the rest of the day, simply follow the ama-busting tips in this chapter and you are set. There are additional practices to incorporate once you have adjusted to the schedule, which are specified in the "Oil Is Love" sections throughout this book. But for ease of use, begin with one or a few recommendations and slowly add more until you feel comfortable with your routine. Some people may not like putting oil in their noses; others may thrive on it. Everyone is different, but the core routine explained in these chapters outlines the essentials you need to do to become a healthy, happy lover!

Oil Is Love—Love "Nose" No Bounds

For Immunity, Allergies, and Carefree Travel

Nasya, or nasal application of oil, is very popular in ayurveda, and for good reason. Kids and adults tend to get sick during fall and winter because as the weather gets drier our nasal membranes also dry out, and the body responds by overproducing mucus in an effort to compensate. This excess mucus, in turn, becomes the breeding ground for bacteria, making us more vulnerable to catching colds and flu.

An easy way to prevent this is to lubricate your nasal passages regularly. There are several ways to do this, the most common of which is to use simple ghee (clarified butter), sesame or coconut oil, or a medicated oil specifically designed for this purpose, like Super Nasya Oil, available at www.ayurveda.com. Most people who try Super Nasya Oil once become hooked on it and take it with them whenever they travel.

How Does It Work?

The way to the brain is through the nose. Unlike *karna purana* (oleation of the ears), which acts more indirectly, nasya is a direct gateway to the brain and the rest of the nervous system. Whatever is inhaled through the nose is absorbed via contact with the upper palate and the cribriform plate. (This is one reason cocaine and other snuffed powders produce rapid effects in the body.) Medicated oils or powders carry their medicine to the body quickly to produce the desired effect when administered by way of nasya.

Nasya therapy comes in three forms:

Shamana, palliation, which is good for Pitta types with inflammation, allergies, or irritation.

Virechana, purgation, which is good for Kapha conditions, where mucus and detritus need to be expelled to clear congestion

Brimhana, nourishing, good for Vata types because it builds the body and nervous system and supports stress relief.

How Do I Do It?

Nasya can be done in many ways. In a clinical ayurvedic setting, doctors may administer herbal juices, oils, medicated milk, dry powder, or even the juices of foods like onion and ginger through the nose. For daily use at home, however, complex nasya therapy is not recommended, and requires a doctor's supervision. For home use, try the following two methods:

Method 1. Lie with your head just off the edge of your bed, tilted back so that your nostrils are almost parallel to the ceiling. You can do this lying on the floor, but it requires craning your neck back quite a bit and may be uncomfortable. Take a dropper-full of oil or warm ghee and put three to five drops inside each nostril. Five drops is the maximum. Sniff this up so that it reaches your upper palate and imagine it going into your brain. Close your nostrils with your fingers and move your septum gently from side to side. Stay in this position for a minute or so, then sit up. Expel any excess oil by blowing your nose (gently!) into a tissue. Some of the oil may result in a postnasal drip; this is normal. The important thing is that it has had a chance to come in contact with and lubricate your entire nasal passage.

Method 2. The second method is simpler because it does not require you to lie down, though it does not lubricate as thoroughly as the first. You may have to repeat this once or twice a day, whereas doing method 1 above typically requires no reapplication.

Dip your clean pinky finger into a jar of ghee and put it inside your nose, moving it around to ensure that every part is lubricated. Repeat with your other hand for the other side, making sure you don't corrupt your ghee by double dipping. (Ghee can last a very long time as long as it's kept away from moisture and contaminants, such as food. Always use a clean spoon or finger when taking ghee from its container.) Close your nostrils and move them around. If necessary, expel excess oil or ghee by blowing your nose gently in a tissue.

Note: Typically, pungent oils like garlic or diluted clove oil are preferred for ear oleation (karna purana), while for nasya cooling oils like coconut or Super Nasya are better. Generally speaking, it is better to keep the brain cool and the ears warm.

The Airport Expedient

Here's a little story about improvised ayurvedic therapies from a frequent flier:

"Because nasya and karna purana are so useful for diminishing jet lag during travel, I always make it a point to do these before I fly (especially during the cold and dry winter months). However, it is not always possible to remember everything, and one day I found myself at the airport without any ghee or oil and with dry, complaining nasal passages. I immediately thought, 'Where can I get some ghee?' and quickly made my way to the nearest fast-food place. There I picked up a small square of prepackaged butter and held it in my hand to warm it up as I headed for the bathroom. Unfolding the little butter pat, I proceeded to give myself a quick nasya using my little finger. I'm not sure what my bathroom compatriots thought about this, but if they saw me, they said nothing. Within minutes I felt amazing—as if a burden had been lifted—and made the rest of my journey without getting sick, even while people were coughing and sneezing all around me!"

5

From House to Home

Using Vastu Shastra to Create a
Home to Match Your Desires

Many of us in the West do not know how to be satisfied with enough. We buy a three-bedroom home today, but in a few years we need one with four bedrooms. We don't know how to make a house a home or a spouse our own—how to make our spaces (and our spouses!) valuable and sexy, which is why we trade them in after a few years for an upgrade.

In traditional cultures it is almost a sin to sell your family home, especially if it has brought you prosperity and shelter over your lifetime. Homes and husbands are the pillars of stability in traditional societies, and to lose these is thought to bring calamity to a family.

Vastu shastra, the ancient Vedic science of placement (akin to the Chinese science of feng shui), can teach us how to breathe life into our living spaces. In vastu, each corner has a purpose, and learning to fill it intentionally can create a home that even your wealthiest neighbors will envy. The intelligent use of space makes a little apartment feel like a cozy palace, though how to do this takes a bit of learning. This chapter will introduce you to the basics, as well as some secrets that even advanced vastu practitioners may appreciate.

In Hindu mythology, the Vedic patron of the home, called Vastu deva, was born from forces of darkness and light. This myth illustrates how every home can become a hell or a heaven for its inhabitants, a place of sanctuary or a battleground. Sometimes perfectly compatible couples move into perfectly incompatible homes, and the arguments begin. A look at their floor plan can reveal the hidden causes of this domestic *dosha*, or affliction.*

DOMESTIC DEFECTS

Disease can take many forms, and holistic physicians like Dr. Vasant Lad can create a healing environment for patients by meeting them at every level of suffering—physical, psychological, and spiritual—including distress caused by personal relationships and their living situation. One cannot be a holistic practitioner—someone who treats the whole person—by focusing exclusively on the body. Understanding the art and science of vastu shastra can help us identify problems in the home and work environment and offer solutions for fixing them.

This is not completely new in the West either. Over the last forty years we have passed laws to protect us from lead paint and asbestos, nuclear and industrial waste, and other vastu defects. Vastu takes this understanding a step further, however, by examining the subtle doshas in the environment, just as ayurveda treats the doshas in the body.

For example, a toilet in the northeast corner of a house is highly undesirable, flushing away prosperity, spirituality, and progeny. The northeast direction is considered auspicious for prosperity and prog-

---

Dosha literally means "that which causes pain/suffering." In the context of biology the goal is to keep the doshas balanced—when out of balance they bring pain and suffering. By extension, a person's perfect doshic balance is unique. This idea will be explored in the next chapter through the dosha types.

eny as well as spirituality, and cluttering it with junk or putting a toilet there blocks the flow of these in your home. When you have clutter in the northeast corner of your home, you will have to work harder to earn money and create serenity in your life.

The opposite is also true: a mediocre couple can become the epitome of conjugal bliss when a good environment supports their union. Moving into a space with good vastu can increase your likelihood of comfort and success by properly aligning you with the geometric and magnetic forces that create positive energy in the home. Vastu shastra states that the geometrical alignment of your home and the rooms inside it can exert an influence on your health, prosperity, and relationships. Let's take a look at how this works.

Figure 5.1 on page 118 shows the optimal layout of rooms in a home. The northeast is best for prayer, meditation, and study. Because it also relates to the Water element, water fixtures like fountains are good here, but not toilets. A river or a well in the northeast of your house or property promotes prosperity, as long as the water is alive and flowing and is not a foul, stagnant pond. The east makes a good space for the living room and bathroom, while the southeast is best for the kitchen. That is because the southeast is ruled by the Fire element and putting stoves, ovens, and technology-laden equipment there will satisfy agni deva, the god of fire. This includes automobiles, so the southeast and the northwest are the best places for a garage. The dictates of good vastu hold that bathrooms, swimming pools, or other water fixtures in the southeast quadrant of your home or property will dampen the fire in your home, which can result in poor digestion, metabolic problems, even a lack of passion in your relationships. Thus, we can add an extra rule to the steps discussed in chapter 4: honor the southeast and its deity, agni. Doing this may be as simple as keeping a salt lamp or candles there, along with red-colored items, or even depictions of the Sanskrit bija mantra *ram* drawn in red saffron ink. All of these

NW	N		NE
	OFFICE **GUEST BEDROOM** **STAIRCASE** study/library garage exercise room room for pets basement meditation/prayer kitchen	**TREASURY** (where you keep valuables) **STUDY/LIBRARY** office	**MEDITATION OR** **PRAYER ROOM** basement study/library living/dining room **no bathroom** **no staircase** **no guest bedroom** **no kitchen** **no storage/heavy** **fixtures**
W	**CHILDREN'S** **ROOM** study	**SPIRIT SPACE** *Empty* **no bathroom** **no staircase**	**BATHROOM** **LIVING/DINING** **ROOM** **E**
	BEDROOM storage dressing room **no basement** **no living/dining** **room**	**STORAGE** living/dining room bedroom bathroom	**KITCHEN** **STAIRCASE** garage basement meditation/prayer living/dining room storage **no bathroom**
SW	S		SE

Figure 5.1. Optimal layout of rooms in a home. Rooms in uppercase are the best in the direction indicated. Rooms shown in normal type are also okay well for that direction. Actively avoid rooms in bold for indicated direction.

invite agni into the area, especially if it is deficient. You can do the same in the part of your house where your kitchen is situated (if it's not in the southeast).

To continue, the south is fine for storage or a dining room, and bathrooms are okay here as well. Southwest is the optimal direction for your bedroom, while the west is good for children's rooms and studies. Putting your bedroom in the southwest ensures that you get a good night's sleep, due to the heaviness of the Earth element there. The northwest is ruled by Air, and makes a fine place for an office (where you do lots of talking). Because the Air element is also prana—the life breath—it's a good place to exercise and move. Plants and livestock, should you have any, are well-suited to the northwest too, though houseplants, depending on their type, can pretty much do well anywhere.

The Skinny on Plants

You can place plants in areas of the house corresponding to their color—red for the south and southeast, brown or yellow for the southwest, violet for the west, white or green for the northwest (any plant does well in this direction), green for the north, blue for the northeast, and yellow or red for the east.

One vastu upaya (remedial measure) says that aloe vera plants should always live in your bedroom because they absorb negative energy and are suited to the southwest direction in general. If you have aloe, keep it where you sleep or in the southwest part of your property (if these are not identical). This direction is associated with the troublesome Rahu and Ketu—the nodes of the moon—who, when provoked, invite mischief in the form of unwanted elements, thefts, and illegal activities. In this context, *provocation* refers to letting the southwest part of your house become dilapidated, cluttered, or unprotected. One should always keep the southwest well-protected with walls, gates, and "heavy" fixtures.

Vastu shastra holds that the guest bedroom in the northwest is ideal, since guests will not overstay their welcome: the Air element keeps them moving! The NNW direction is also ideal for a lover's nook—a place to kindle passion for lovemaking and romance. Finally, north is the best direction for a library or office, and the optimal place to put the safe where you store your valuables. Just make sure that it is out of sight. Here's a true story to illustrate this point.

> "We lived in a small apartment with huge north-facing windows in a lower-income, troubled neighborhood. Knowing the north was ideal for my valuables, I routinely kept my computer (my most valuable possession after my car) there on my desk, alongside my wife's laptop, as I worked every day from home. I also regularly pulled the shades up to allow the sun to shine through. Well, one day we got home and our computers were gone! We had been robbed. In the Middle East it is said that you keep your most precious possessions—your jewels and your wife—out of sight. It slowly dawned on me that we had done just the opposite. With the drapes open, we never noticed the staircase just outside the window, from which people could see everything we had. Every day, as they went up and down the stairs, they got a clear view of our most valuable possessions! That is a lesson I'll never forget— keep your valuables hidden and don't flaunt your wealth!"

THE PLACE OF SPIRIT

The center of any room, home, or property is called the *brahmasthana*— the "place of spirit"—and is appropriately ruled by the Space element. This "spirit space" should remain empty; don't violate it by placing or building heavy or cluttered items on it, like sofas or staircases. It makes a good place for an airy living room or courtyard.

Cities were traditionally built around a town square, the sacred center of a community that contained a church, a park, or both. In this way, nature and God were represented as the center around which social life was conducted. Today, from New York City to Santa Fe, thriving cities with this kind of center continue to attract wealth, stability, and good fortune, and so can your home if you build or arrange it using the tools of vastu shastra.

Interestingly enough, many modern American cities still embody the brahmasthana ethic in the unlikely guise of the sports stadium. For secular societies the downtown baseball park serves as a focal point, bringing families and friends together in nature for a shared common purpose. But as more and more of these parks are moved to the suburbs in favor of high-rise buildings, the prosperity they invite also follows them there, and our downtowns become more cluttered and depressed, while our suburbs become more and more prosperous.

The Brahmasthana Within

Just as vastu shastra dictates we keep the center of our homes empty, ayurveda does the same for our bodies. Human beings also come with an empty center—our GI tracts. In the previous chapters we emphasized the need to give these time to rest and replenish, encouraging practices like fasting and the Three Square Meals plan. This is nothing but vastu applied to our physiology. When our own center is clean and uncluttered, the rest of the body obtains "prosperity" in the form of health and longevity.

Yoga philosophy states that "yoga is the cessation of the fluctuations of the mind-stuff." It is impossible to curb these fluctuations when our stomachs are full. Our digestive organs, including the villi and microvilli in our intestines, work in a wavelike manner to push food through the system. These waves are called vrittis in Sanskrit, and the cessation of all vrittis is the purported goal of yoga. As a result, yogis routinely fast, and fasting is a staple of practically every religion on the planet. Jesus fasted, Buddha fasted, Mohammed fasted, Moses fasted. Fasting is a core religious ritual because it brings us closer to God—our own brahmasthana, or sacred space. Even the wise Benjamin Franklin said, "The best of all medicines is resting and fasting." Keep your space uncluttered and its center empty, and you will invite God into your body and home.

LIGHT AND HEAVY

The concept of light and heavy is a simple organizing principle for home arrangement and design. Here's how it works:

+ The south and the west of a lot, house, or room should be "heavy," while the north and the east should be "light." That means that in a house or even within a room, heavy things like dressers, beds, and couches should be in the south and the west, while the north and the east remain airy and uncluttered. On a lot this means that buildings (the house, the shed) should be in the southwest while the yard, parking lot, and open space should be in the north and east. Building your house on the northeast corner of your lot is bad news and will block prosperity and happiness in the long run as will building your house on an east to west slope. West sloping down to east, however, augurs prosperity and stability.

+ The middle of a room, house, or lot should also be light, as this is the spirit space. This also reflects the principles of artistic design. Take a look at your vacation photos and see which ones are keepers—the ones where your face is in the middle of the picture, pushing everything else aside, or those that create depth and movement by leaving the center empty and framing the subject off to the side? A painting or a photograph, like a house, employs the same design principles because these are rules of nature and, like the dharma type, they operate whether we are aware of them or not.

*Figure 5.2. In the painting "School of Athens," Raphael placed Plato
and Aristotle directly in the brahmasthana as the centerpiece
of the composition, while also making it airy and light
by showing the sky behind them.*

If we divide a picture into nine quadrants, we can apply the same elements of good vastu that we used to make a house a home (see figures 5.3–5.6, pages 124–25):

+ Make the northeast watery, uncluttered, or spiritual and inspirational.
+ Keep the center free or put nature or God there. It can showcase spiritual, uplifting, or inspirational themes.
+ Make the southwest heavy.
+ Optional: Emphasize the four focal points around the center by putting important subject matter there.

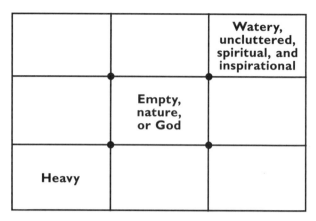

		Watery, uncluttered, spiritual, and inspirational
	Empty, nature, or God	
Heavy		

Figure 5.3. Good vastu in a picture. Dots around the central square represent placement for important subject matter.

A painting or a photograph, like a house, employs the same design principles because these are rules of nature and, like the dharma type, they operate whether we are aware of them or not.

Figure 5.4. Here is an example of bad vastu in a picture: the center is cluttered, the entire north edge is heavy, and the south is light (free from clutter, activity, shadow).

Figure 5.5. Here are the same trees, but with better vastu. Notice that the northeast opens up and the southwest becomes heavy. Though the center is still cluttered, this is an improvement over the first picture.

Figure 5.6. Use light and heavy guidelines for cropping pictures to bring out their subject matter and create depth and movement. Here is the same image, cropped to make the south and west heavier and to emphasize the open east.

The essential design principle is this: Don't clutter your center space, be it your kitchen, house, or your photo masterpieces. Keep it light and obstruction-free so people do not have to walk around it to get where they're going. For example, kitchen islands can be helpful if they are well-placed off-center, but they obstruct when they're too large and are placed squarely in the middle of a kitchen, forcing people to walk around them to get to the cupboards and refrigerator.

VASTU REMEDIES

Vastu would not be complete if it didn't offer *upayas*—remedial measures to mitigate potential issues in your home space. Some vastu defects, however, are tough to remedy, like a staircase in the brahmasthana or a kitchen in the northeast. In such cases it is often advisable to move, if at all possible, since such a home will compromise your health, relationships, and prosperity. However, vastu understands that no home is perfect, and offers remedies to deal with such domestic defects as a northeast toilet or a house with missing corners. Below are quick tips on how to work with some of these. Ultimately it is best to contact a vastu professional in your area for proper guidance.

"A home in which a man or a woman does not respect their spouse can never be remedied." This primary adage of vastu shastra is good to remember before beginning any remedial measure. If you are a jerk, improving your vastu will only make you a better-organized jerk. Another Sanskrit aphorism says that there is no remedy for a fool. Remedies are designed for the sick who want to be healthy, and will not work if you do not apply a concerted effort to bettering yourself. You have to be willing to work on yourself and your home at the same time.

If your bathroom happens to occupy the southeast or northeast corner, or even the brahmasthana, try putting a mirror on the outside of the bathroom door, facing out. A full-length mirror is not only great for checking yourself out, it creates the illusion of depth and space where these qualities should exist (instead of a bathroom).

Mirrors also work when placed above a stove that is not in the right place. Stoves and other hot things, like fireplaces, automobiles, and technological devices, should ideally be in the southeast corner of your house or lot. However, if this is not possible, try putting a small, red-framed mirror above the stove to honor the Fire element.

A home in which the brahmasthana (center area) is heavy—occupied by a staircase, bedroom, or heavy walls and fixtures—will create a sense of heaviness in the hearts of its occupants, causing depression, conflict, and lack of love. The center is the heart of your home, and if it is cluttered, your relationships will be too. Your ability to give and receive love may become compromised, and you may even develop circulatory or heart/lung problems. While there is no perfect remedy for such afflictions, you can try placing bells or wind chimes in that area. Sound relates to the Space element, and ringing these bells every time you move around here can create space, just as mirrors create space on your bathroom doors. You can also try putting four amethyst stones at the bottom and the top of the staircase, framing the top and bottom stairs.

For a home or a lot with missing corners, you have two options. First, take copper wire and run it along the missing space to complete the corner (see figure 5.7). Bury this wire underground so your

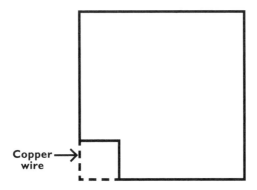

Figure 5.7. Completing a corner with a copper wire

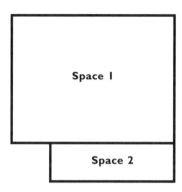

*Figure. 5.8. Apportioning a separate space for
the section of your home without a corner*

neighbors cannot see it. This forms a square or rectangle, one of the most stable shapes in vastu. You should not live in a home whose shape deviates significantly from a basic square or rectangle.

Next, you can apportion the space inside your home in such a way that it creates two independent living spaces. In this way, the missing corner is no longer a factor, as each space becomes an independent rectangle (see figure 5.8).

Mirrors also work on the outside of your home, deflecting negative energy. If there is water (a swimming pool, a well, or a pond) in the southeast or southwest of your home—which is bad for reproductive health, metabolism, and digestion—try placing a convex mirror on the outside wall facing the water. Make sure it is convex and not concave; a concave mirror will invite negative energy into the house.

Finally, for the above and most other vastu doshas, consider installing a vastu yantra. This is a specially formulated geometrical sculpture, usually made of precious metals and designed to ward off negative energy in the home. The best vastu yantras are made of gold and lined with precious gems, so they are not cheap.

The effect of vastu defects is long term and can take months or even years to accumulate. Therefore, do not despair, but remediate now.

DR. LAD'S
LOVE RITUALS FOR THE HOME

Ayurveda is the science of life that has brought a revolution to Western medicine, because not only does it treat the body and mind but it addresses our emotions and even our environment. It recognizes that though our body may be hale, if we are sad or lacking in love we cannot be truly healthy. Ayurvedic physician Dr. Vasant Lad, B.A.M.Sc., is renowned for incorporating vastu shastra (sacred architecture) and *jyotisha* (Vedic astrology), together with his medical training, to bring holistic understanding and healing to all levels of a patient's experience. If you are looking for a partner, the following are some of his recommendations and tools to attract and keep Mr. or Ms. Right.

> "The almighty god is universal. That totality is around you and within you. When you do ritual you are invoking the universality in front of you. And in that invocation the god or deity comes in front of you but you cannot see them with your physical eyes. It is just a massive energy field that manifests. Symbolically you can have a little statue of Ganesha or Durga or Shiva or your preferred deity, so that when you invoke the god to come and stay in the statue then god gets a form. Consciousness has no form, awareness has no form, but thoughts, feelings, and prayer can be concentrated so that the formless obtains a form. Therefore, we are offering these rituals to the form so we can reach the formless. Then whatever you wish, your wish will be fulfilled by the rituals. That is the magic of ritual—to fulfill your prayers."
>
> DR. VASANT LAD, B.A.M.SC.

Bangle Ritual

This technique is for women only. Hang six green bangles on each arm of a hat rack and place it in front of a full-length mirror. You can get these bracelets at Indian markets or wherever you would buy a sari. Keep it this way until you meet the right man. Put this in your bedroom, if possible, out of sight of normal traffic in your home. This simple remedy can help bring love to your life and often works when nothing else will.

Mantra and Yantra Ritual

Our next ritual involves mantra and yantra. *Mantra* literally means "that which protects the mind" or "that which transcends the mind." The mantra we will use is *"om kleem namah."*

◈ MAKING A KLEEM YANTRA
AND PRACTICING THE MANTRA

To make this yantra, you will need a yellow silk cloth and homemade red saffron or red turmeric ink.

To make the ink, simply soak red saffron in a little bit of water. Or you can mix kumkum (red turmeric powder) with water to create a liquid ink. Don't make it too thick or cakey; you want it to work just like a red Sharpie.

Lightly trace out a downward-facing triangle with a pencil on the yellow silk cloth and draw the Sanskrit letter *klim,* क्रीं.

When you're ready, follow up with the red saffron ink to finish the design.

To invite love into your life, every day recite the mantra "om kleem namah" 108 times while concentrating on the letter in the middle. It is best to begin on a Friday.

Practicing this ritual on an ongoing basis, even after you've achieved the longed-for result, will ensure that you receive more and more of the desired energy in your home.

For any ritual that involves a mantra or an invocation of the Divine, make sure you are showered and your mouth is clean. At the very least, brush your teeth and wash your face and feet before sitting down to do prayers or rituals. This applies to any spiritual tradition.

Flute Ritual

Another way to ensure love and intimacy in your home is to fasten two flutes on the wall above your headboard creating a 45 degree angle, like an upside-down V. Make sure their mouths are touching (kissing!) and weave a red silk ribbon around them to indicate the flow of love between two partners. This will ensure passion and devotion in your love life. Two flutes can also be affixed above the door to your house (on the inside) in the same tented configuration. These make a nice decoration as well as ensuring harmony in the home.

Other Tips for Maximizing Your Home Space

If you have leaky faucets, fix them. Leaky faucets create both urinary and financial problems. In men, this can lead to prostate issues (dribbling from the urethra) as well as financial distress. Remember, leaky faucet = leaky wallet! To help with finances, hanging a giant key to the right of the front door inside your house is highly desirable. The bigger the better. Also a frog statue with a coin in its mouth placed in the north part of your house invites prosperity.

For best results, consider contacting a professional vastu practitioner in your area. Make sure that the practitioner you choose has fine credentials and referrals. Vastu is not a regulated field and you want to get the most for your investment, so you can transform your house into a home.

Toilet Vastu

Just like a sagging roof devalues a house, so does poor posture diminish you in the eyes of the world. Practicing yoga asanas and postural exercises helps us improve our biological vastu, the structure of our bodies, which are the dwelling places of the soul. Proper posture also applies to how we sit on the toilet.

For thousands of years humans have squatted to eliminate. Only in the last century have we begun to sit and this has led to an explosion of colorectal problems, from hemorrhoids to colitis. Luckily, modern inventions like toilet stools help to alleviate the problems caused by modern toilets by orienting us for optimal elimination.

These devices fit easily in our bathrooms and are yet another way to apply vastu, yoga, and ayurveda into our lives. Squatting to eliminate also provides continued practice of that most natural of hip-opening postures, the squat.*

*Refer to www.apanastool.com for information on toilet stools.

6

Physical Dharma and
the Doshas

Lifestyle Practices to Optimize Your Sex Appeal

In this chapter we will look at ayurveda's most well-known contribution to healing—the mind/body type—as well as some daily routines that can aid you in keeping your mind and body healthy and vibrant. According to ayurveda there are three fundamental doshas, or defects, that must remain balanced in order for health to flourish. The specific ratio of doshas in you constitutes your mind/body type. These three doshas—Vata (Air), Pitta (Fire), and Kapha (Water)—can combine in numerous ways to form your distinct constitution. Your mind-body constitution is especially useful for living according to the dharma of the body.

You can have a primary and a secondary type and most people are, in fact, dual-doshic: Kapha/Vata or Pitta/Kapha, for example. To determine your mind-body constitution follow the "Guidelines for Determining Your Constitution" on page 134.* Tables 6.1 to 6.3 on pages 135–137 specify the main attributes of the three doshas and

---

*Courtesy of the Ayurvedic Institute. A great test can also be found at www.ayurvedadosha.org.

GUIDELINES FOR DETERMINING YOUR CONSTITUTION

Instructions: To determine your constitution it is best to fill out the chart twice. First, base your choices on what is most consistent over a long period of your life (your prakruti), then fill it out a second time responding to how you have been feeling more recently (your vikruti). Sometimes it helps to have a friend ask you the questions and fill in the chart for you, as they may have insight (and impartiality) to offer. After finishing the chart each time, add up the number of marks under vata, pitta and kapha.

This will help you discover your own ratio of doshas in your prakruti and vikruti. Most people will have one dosha predominant, a few will have two doshas approximately equal and even fewer will have all three doshas in equal proportion. For instance, if your vikruti shows more pitta than your prakruti, you will want to follow a pitta-soothing regimen to try and bring your vikruti back into balance with your prakruti. If your prakruti and vikruti seem about the same, then you would choose the regimen of your strongest dosha.

OBSERVATIONS	V	P	K	VATA	PITTA	KAPHA
Body size	☐	☐	☐	Slim	Medium	Large
Body weight	☐	☐	☐	Low	Medium	Overweight
Chin	☐	☐	☐	Thin, angular	Tapering	Rounded, double
Cheeks	☐	☐	☐	Wrinkled, sunken	Smooth flat	Rounded, plump
Eyes	☐	☐	☐	Small, sunken, dry, active, black, brown, nervous	Sharp, bright, gray, green, yellow/red, sensitive to light	Big, beautiful, blue, calm, loving
Nose	☐	☐	☐	Uneven shape, deviated septum	Long pointed, red nose-tip	Short rounded, button nose
Lips	☐	☐	☐	Dry, cracked, black/brown tinge	Red, inflamed, yellowish	Smooth, oily, pale, whitish
Teeth	☐	☐	☐	Stick out, big, roomy, thin gums	Medium, soft, tender gums	Healthy, white, strong gums
Skin	☐	☐	☐	Thin, dry, cold, rough, dark	Smooth, oily, warm, rosy	Thick, oily, cool, white, pale
Hair	☐	☐	☐	Dry brown, black, knotted, brittle, scarce	Straight, oily, blond, gray, red, bald	Thick, curly, oily, wavy, luxuriant
Nails	☐	☐	☐	Dry, rough, brittle, break easily	Sharp, flexible, pink, lustrous	Thick, oily, smooth, polished
Neck	☐	☐	☐	Thin, tall	Medium	Big, folded
Chest	☐	☐	☐	Flat, sunken	Moderate	Expanded, round
Belly	☐	☐	☐	Thin, flat, sunken	Moderate	Big, pot-bellied
Belly-button	☐	☐	☐	Small, irregular, herniated	Oval, superficial	Big, deep, round, stretched
Hips	☐	☐	☐	Slender, thin	Moderate	Heavy, big
Joints	☐	☐	☐	Cold, cracking	Moderate	Large, lubricated
Appetite	☐	☐	☐	Irregular, scanty	Strong, unbearable	Slow but steady
Digestion	☐	☐	☐	Irregular, forms gas	Quick, causes burning	Prolonged, forms mucous
Taste	☐	☐	☐	Sweet, sour, salty	Sweet, bitter, astringent	Bitter, pungent, astringent
Thirst	☐	☐	☐	Changeable	Surplus	Sparse
Elimination	☐	☐	☐	Constipation	Loose	Thick, oily, sluggish
Physical Activity	☐	☐	☐	Hyperactive	Moderate	Slow
Mental Activity	☐	☐	☐	Hyperactive	Moderate	Dull, slow
Emotions	☐	☐	☐	Anxiety, fear, uncertainty	Anger, hate, jealousy	Calm, greedy, attachment
Faith	☐	☐	☐	Variable	Extremist	Consistent
Intellect	☐	☐	☐	Quick but faulty response	Accurate response	Slow, exact
Recollection	☐	☐	☐	Recent good, remote poor	Distinct	Slow and sustained
Dreams	☐	☐	☐	Quick, active, many, fearful	Fiery, war, violence	Lakes, snow, romantic
Sleep	☐	☐	☐	Scanty, broken up, sleeplessness	Little but sound	Deep, prolonged
Speech	☐	☐	☐	Rapid, unclear	Sharp, penetrating	Slow, monotonous
Financial	☐	☐	☐	Poor, spends on trifles	Spends money on luxuries	Rich, good money preserver
TOTAL						

©1994, 2002 excerpted from *Ayurvedic Cooking for Self-Healing* by Usha and Dr. Lad.
The Ayurvedic Institute • P.O. Box 23445 • Albuquerque, NM 87192-1445 · (505) 291-9698 · www.ayurveda.com

how they manifest in the physical, mental, and behavioral spheres. Vatas need moisture, warmth, and stability in their environment, their food, and their relationships. They need to be treated like a flower; kept in a regulated environment, watered regularly, and appreciated for their gifts. Pittas are Fire, so they need to be cooled and sweetened—by diet, lifestyle, and relationships. They need cool water (not alcohol!), cool breezes (not hot summer days at noon), and cool, sweet friends who can take a licking from their Pitta flames and brush it off. An ayurvedic aphorism says, "Treat Kapha like an enemy." You may need to kick, prod, and insult Kaphas just to get them off the couch. They require spiciness in their food, environment, and relationships to motivate and stimulate their interests.

TABLE 6.1. QUALITIES OF VATA

QUALITIES	MANIFESTATIONS
Dry	Dry skin, hair, colon and joints, manifesting as constipation, cracking of the joints, dry mouth, tendency to dehydration, and arthritic conditions
Light	Ectomorph—possessing a light frame; tendency to being underweight and have scanty sleep; sleeps better with heavy blankets in a big, heavy bed
Cold	Cold hands and feet; poor circulation; hates cold and loves warmth; stiff muscles, arthritic joints; appreciates conviviality and nurturing in others; dislikes cold, abrupt people
Rough	Rough nails; irregular-shaped limbs and teeth; cracked skin
Subtle	Suffers from anxiety, insecurity, and fear; the subtle quality also manifests as tics, twitching, tremors, and goose bumps
Mobile	*cancala*—changeable and restless; loves to travel, walk and talk fast, multitask, and generally be in motion; craves excitement but lacks stability; fickle faith; can go through many friends
Clear	Manifests as rapid insight, inspiration, and clairvoyance, but also as loneliness and forgetfulness
Astringent Taste	Proneness to burping, hiccoughs, and choking sensation in the throat; requires sweet, salty, and sour tastes to balance

TABLE 6.2. PITTA QUALITIES

QUALITIES	MANIFESTATIONS
Hot	Strong metabolism and heat in the body including any and all inflammatory conditions; tendency to irritability and anger; strong appetite; early receding or graying hair; judgmental quality, especially if overheated; since Fire rules sight, Pittas are also focused, driven, and goal-oriented
Sharp	Sharp mind; sharp chin or heart-shaped face; grey or blue piercing eyes; sharp teeth
Oily/Liquid	Oily skin and hair; tendency to loose stools and diarrhea; prone to acne, heartburn, and skin eruptions; prone to migraines and inflammation especially after oily (fried), spicy, and salty food; excessive sweat and urine
Spreading	Pitta spreads quickly in the form of rashes, acne, and inflammation; Pittas like to spread their fame and be recognized for their accomplishments
Light/Bright	Does not tolerate bright light and heat; fair skin and shiny eyes
Fleshy smell	Body odor and foul-smelling breath, urine, and feces, especially when unbalanced
Yellow/red	Overproduction of bile in the liver may lead to jaundice or yellowish skin; prone to freckles, flushed cheeks and nose, and redness in the eyes

Many Westerners are now familiar with these constitutional types, thanks to ayurveda's increasing popularity, but how to manage them still remains a mystery. Below are some useful strategies for dealing with your main doshic type. If you are Pitta with some Vata secondary, for example, for this exercise consider yourself a Pitta.*

---

*There are exceptions, however. Though you may be a Pitta by birth, if your Vata is high due to extra stress, travel, or living in a dry, cold environment, you need to treat Vata until it is under control, then return to caring for your primary dosha.

TABLE 6.3. KAPHA QUALITIES

QUALITIES	MANIFESTATIONS
Heavy	Endomorphic body type—a heavy body frame and tendency to being overweight; a deep, heavy voice
Slow	Kaphas move and talk slowly; tendency to sluggish digestion; slow to change and/or grasp new concepts
Cool	Cool skin; prone to colds, allergies, and coughs
Oily	Oily skin; luxurious hair; well-lubricated joints and organs
Smooth/Soft	Smooth, hairless skin; gentle and calm nature; sweet speech; compassionate and laid-back nature
Dense	Dense body and head hair; thick insulation of fat between organs and under skin
Static	Does not like change; loves sleep and rest
Vicsous	Sticky quality leads to excess mucus and congestion, attachment, and greed, but also indicates loyalty, devotion, and a love of hugging
Cloudy	In early morning, the Kapha's mind is cloudy and foggy; often needs coffee to start the day
Sweet Taste	Craves sweet, but needs pungent, bitter, and astringent tastes in diet

VATA

If you or your loved one is primarily a Vata type, meaning that you are ruled by the Air element, you require warmth, grounding, water, and gentle care. Like flowers, Vata types do not respond well to harsh treatment, be it physical or psychological. Vatas do not do well in extremes of cold or heat either; Alaska is a poor choice for a Vata-predominant person. Tropical climates are best for this type, as plants tend to thrive in the warmth and moisture provided there. Vatas require grounding because they are constantly on the go, which is why they also feel good sleeping under heavy blankets or comforters to weigh them down. Gardening and getting in touch with the earth is also highly pleasurable for them.

Vata types should eliminate or reduce their intake of coffee and stimulants, as these have deleterious long-term effects on their nervous and endocrine systems. At the very least, drink coffee mixed with ghee, as recommended in chapter 4. Also, more than any other type, Vatas need to keep themselves hydrated—externally and internally. Oil self-massage should be a daily ritual for Vata types, especially during the cold winter months. Drink sixteen ounces of water every morning before breakfast and fifteen to thirty minutes before every meal. This is nonnegotiable: do it to survive if you're a Vata-predominant type, or else, like a wilted flower, you will shrivel up and dry out.

PITTA

Pittas may be sharp and dangerous. They are judgmental and critical when unbalanced. Therefore, tread lightly with them. Even when they're wrong, help them see the truth, as Pittas must be *shown* not *told*. "Treat Pitta like a spouse—always say yes" is an adage to remember here. Being ruled by the Fire element, they need to see the truth to set themselves straight. If a Pitta says two plus two equals five, then say, "Yes, dear. Now let's check, just to make sure." When Pittas realize their mistakes, they correct themselves, and are as critical of their own behavior as they are of others'. That is why you want to approach Pittas with innocence and love. The sight of a baby or a cute kitten can melt a Pitta's heart and turn her raging fire into a gentle flame. Pittas tend to run hot, which makes them sweat, so cleanliness is important for this type: showers, deodorants, and clean clothes are mandatory, as are regular meals, since they get irritable or hypoglycemic without food. Pitta types do exceptionally well on the Three Square Meals diet, which helps to regulate their blood sugar levels.

KAPHA

Kaphas are phlegmatic, big-boned, grounded, and heavy types. They suffer from excess mucus, slow digestion, laziness, pallor, wheezing, and water accumulation when out of balance. As a result, they may be hard to move, both psychologically and physically. They may need a kick in the rear to get them going. Like a drill sergeant, you need to be firm with a Kapha or he will never respect you. Spicy foods also help to melt Kaphas' inner cold quality and stimulate good digestion. Kaphas are tough and have great endurance, which is why they also do well in any extreme environment, the opposite of the gentle Vata type. Do not send them to Hawaii; tundras and deserts are better suited to their hardy constitution. Kaphas also handle coffee and other stimulants better than any other type.

DOSHA COMPATIBILITY

In relationships, Kaphas make the best spouses, as they can handle the sometimes neurotic nature of the Vata and endure the sharp criticism of the Pitta. When they come together with other Kaphas, the relationship might lack stimulation, however, resulting in a sedentary life. That is why two Kaphas together should have kids or busy careers in order to keep themselves balanced. Two balanced Kaphas can live well together, sharing love and raising a family. But two unbalanced Kaphas can become sedentary and prone to maladies of excess—obesity, diabetes, and heart disease.

Pittas in an interpersonal relationship want to rule the roost. They are good at seeing what's wrong and can become overly critical, which is why they tend to be the most solitary of the three doshas. Their Fire element can overwhelm a gentle Vata and they may burn out with other Pittas; of all three types they do the best alone, or paired with a hearty Kapha type. When balanced, however, Pittas make successful and conscientious spouses, as long as you know who's the boss!

Vatas are communicators, and they value inspiration and movement in relationships. When balanced, they can be fun and stimulating. When unbalanced, excitement turns into overstimulation and pointless change. Therefore, Vatas do well to pair up with Kaphas to ground them. Balanced Pittas can also help to bring focus to Vatas, but the light quality they both share (see pages 135 and 136) can create superficial relationships that never go deeper than looks or mundane conversation. Vata/Pitta couples need to take time to discuss their deeper feelings and do grounding activities together, like gardening, hiking, and otherwise exploring the depths of their relationship.

QUALITIES OF THE DOSHA TYPES

Qualities like light, sharp, heavy, and hot, introduced above, are the secret to understanding the mind/body types. If you can learn at least three qualities of your mind/body type, you are well on your way to understanding how to maintain your health and deal with changes in your environment. That is because the opposite of each quality brings balance, while like increases like. For example, Vata is dry, and eating dry foods, like rice cakes, or living in dry climates, even being around "dry" or boring people can increase Vata. On the other hand, introducing the oily or "wet" quality to your diet and lifestyle balances Vata. Soups and broths, oil massage, and a tropical climate bring down and balance this dosha. Sipping miso soup while relaxing with good company on your porch in Hawaii is heaven for a Vata constitution! Remember, in ayurveda like increases like, and opposites detract.

In ayurveda, like increases like, and opposites detract.

Ayurvedic Remedies for
Specific Disorders

Scalp and dandruff: Mix the juice of half or a quarter lime with one egg white. Apply to your scalp and let it sit there for twenty to thirty minutes, or until it dries completely. Wash normally. The egg white will nourish your scalp and remove flaking. Do this once a week or as needed to remove dandruff and condition your scalp. You can include a little of the yolk to condition the hair as well.

Coconut oil mixed with camphor also helps to clear the scalp. Simply warm a cup of coconut oil with a quarter teaspoon (or one small piece) of edible camphor. Let it cool and dissolve. Apply to the scalp before bedtime.

Herpes: Though herpes cannot be cured, it can be controlled. Whether genital or oral, herpes responds well to the ayurvedic compound mahasudarshan, which is a mix of over twenty bitter herbs. It is normally used to bring down fever and purify the blood. Half a teaspoon taken with water three times a day immediately when you begin to see symptoms will help prevent or lessen the duration of breakouts. For maintenance and to prevent breakouts, half a teaspoon a day is more than sufficient.

Cold: There are many remedies for cold sufferers. The aforementioned mahasudarshan, mixed with another ayurvedic compound, *sitopaladi,* is a great way to stay healthy during the cold and flu season. Take half a teaspoon once or twice daily with water for prophylactic use, or more as needed.

One of the best remedies for an oncoming cold or flu is garlic oil in the ears. Many people swear by this remedy (see pages 289–91). For colds, it is especially vital to keep your nose and ears lubricated, as this controls mucus production and maintains immunity in your ears/nose/throat.

Insomnia: Try drinking a glass of warm garlic milk at bedtime. To make it, put a clove of chopped garlic in a cup of milk. Bring to a boil and let cool. You can add sugar to sweeten it. Also, rubbing bhringraj oil on the soles of the feet and on your scalp is a wonderful way to calm the nervous system. A few drops of castor oil in the eyes just before bedtime also helps.

Asthma: Add ten drops of mahanarayan oil to one cup of licorice tea. Sip this slowly. Within ten minutes you will see relief.

Dry, tired eyes and fading vision: If you work on the computer or watch too much TV, or if your eyes are inflamed and dry, try putting one or two drops of castor oil in your eyes at night, just as you would do with normal eye drops. Castor oil is much more viscous than eye drops, so only do this before bedtime; never try to drive with castor oil in your eyes. You will also notice that castor oil in the eyes works as a sleep aid.

Receding gums: Try adding one-quarter teaspoon baking soda to your toothpaste when you brush, two to three times a week. This not only whitens your teeth, it will help to neutralize acidity in your mouth and kill bacteria. Also try kavala, or oil pulling: swish sesame oil with a drop or two of tea tree oil added to it, for fifteen minutes every day. This will help kill bacteria and promote healthy gums.

GO FOR THE GOLD:
THE DOSHAS AND METALS

For centuries ayurveda has treated gold not only as a valuable metal but as a precious healing substance that potentiates other medicines as well.* Proprietary techniques for turning gold into medicine are still used to this day. In India, a baby's gums are rubbed with fine gold powder, mixed with honey, to promote intelligence, immunity, and long life. Pandit Jawaharlal Nehru's cook is said to have prepared his meals by putting a gold coin in his rice as it boiled. This way, some of the microscopic gold particles were infused into his food. Many a king and queen throughout history drank from golden chalices. While gold is toxic if consumed directly—it is a heavy metal, after all—taking it in special ayurvedic preparations, as a colloidal suspension, or boiling pure gold as described below can be a safe and effective way to boost your metabolism, improve eyesight, and confer overall immunity and luster to the body. Even drinking from a gold or silver cup, like the royalty of yore, confers gold's effects.

Silver is antiseptic and antibacterial, and useful in inflammatory conditions. It cools the body and is best used during the summer, or with high heat (Pitta-related) disorders, such as acne, infection, indigestion, and others. Nano silver is currently even used in clothing and packaging for its antibacterial properties. And we have already looked at the benefits of copper (see page 73).

Gold works best for Vatas, silver for Pittas, and copper for Kaphas. If you're a Pitta or it is the summer season, substitute silver for gold in the recipe below. If you're a Kapha type, you can try drinking from a copper cup. Leave water in a pure copper cup

---

*Today, scientists are studying the use of nano-gold particles for their ability to destroy cancer and purify water as well as other medical uses. See www.youtube.com/watch?t=238&v=QorK2X7GsVU, for more on this.

overnight and drink the water the next morning to scrape away ama, kindle agni, and tone the intestinal tract. You can get the effect of gold or silver by drinking from a cup made of these metals as well, but such artifacts are not commonly available today, which is why the recipes below are more practical.

HOW TO MAKE GOLD (OR SILVER) WATER

Take a quarter, a half, or a full ounce of twenty-four-karat gold, or a piece of twenty-four-carat gold jewelry. The gold must be absolutely pure. If you are using fourteen-karat or even eighteen-karat gold, do not follow this recipe. In India, rings are often made from pure gold, and can be used for this purpose. (For silver water, substitute pure silver.)

Put sixteen ounces of water in a tea kettle or pot.

Tie the ring with a piece of string and suspend it in the water so it is not touching the sides of the pan. (I use a tea kettle for this and suspend the string from its cover.) If you are using a gold coin, do the same thing: tie it with string and suspend it from the top of the kettle so it floats in the water without touching the sides.

Bring the kettle to a boil and let it simmer for as long as it takes the water to reduce to about half. That is, let the water boil out until you have eight ounces left.

Let it cool and transfer it to a glass bottle. Now your gold water is ready.

You can drink one to two teaspoonfuls up to three times daily, depending on your constitution. Be careful! Drinking more can produce coffee-like symptoms, even though it does not contain caffeine, since gold promotes energy and vitality.

As with all medication, seek the advice of a medical professional before taking any new medicine.

In addition to being a heart and eye tonic, gold is also an aphrodisiac, and is known to promote *ojas,* the refined and highly desirable essence of digested nutrition. Ojas is the luster and attractiveness classically attributed to kings and saints, and what contemporary cultural royalty, like Britney Spears, Brad Pitt, and Marilyn Monroe, possessed when they first came on the public scene. Physiologically, ojas translates into the radiance of a healthy immune system, and, according to evolutionary biology, humans are wired to perceive vibrant health and immunity as highly attractive qualities. Perhaps this is why we are drawn to celebrities, and to people with good ojas in our own lives. Many of us know someone who has natural charm, rarely gets sick, and is generally well-liked in his social circle. This is a sign of good ojas, and gold helps us to build it by kindling agni and burning ama. For more on how to preserve ojas, refer to chapter 8.

OTHER EXOTIC DRINK RECIPES FOR YOUR HEALTH

You may be a master mixologist behind the bar, but you probably haven't tried these five salubrious concoctions. Mind you, these are not just for entertainment purposes; they pack a health punch as well!

Flax water: This deceptively simple, homemade concoction is a well-kept secret with a whole host of health benefits. Flax water's nourishment of your inner skin—the lining of your intestines—is the first step in combating dryness and irritation of your outer skin. It also promotes healthy microflora and deep hydration and even improves eyesight. Flax water is good for all three doshas. (See page 97 for the recipe.)

Yoga-soda: You've heard of cola, but have you ever had a buttermilk soda? If not, you can make a quick and healthy version at home. This is nothing but a variation on the takram recipe on page 95.

✦ *HOW TO MAKE YOGA-SODA*

Take a cup of organic buttermilk from pasture-raised cows (available at your fine food retailer—or, better yet—made at home) and mix it with a cup of water.

Add your choice of sweetener: maple syrup, cane sugar, agave nectar, or even xylitol will do.

Finally, mix in one-quarter to one-half teaspoon of baking soda. Stir in a sprig of mint and enjoy!

Yoga-soda can be made with yogurt if you don't have buttermilk, and should be served cold for best taste. It is not only yummy (it's a popular canned drink in the Middle East), it is also great for your liver and digestion if you make it fresh at home. Yogurt mixed with baking soda and a little turmeric is also detoxifying to the liver and even works as a hangover remedy, helping to counteract the side effects of heavy drinking. This is great for Pittas and Vatas.

DAILY MASSAGE AND OLEATION

One daily practice that is essential for Vata types but useful for everyone is to take time to massage yourself with warm, organic oil. The ayurvedic author Vagbhata says the foremost treatment for Vata is oleation, or oil massage. In our fast-paced, fast-food world, oleation and regulated eating are the two best ways to relieve stress and improve health, even if you are not a Vata body type. This is especially true in drier climates and in the dry winter months. You can get away without oleating during humid summers, but be sure to make it part of your daily routine in winter.

> In our fast-paced, fast-food world, oleation and regulated eating are the two best ways to relieve stress and improve health.

In the twentieth century, Dr. Hans Selye discovered the effects of stress by experimenting on rats. Ayurveda has recognized stress for over five thousand years, and over that time developed ways to deal with it that are real-world proven and more elegant than anything Western medicine offers. All this, without the rats. According to ayurveda, stress is the opposite of love, which is why oleation, *snehana*, also means "giving love." Oil massage is literally an act of love, anointing the body with nourishment and protection. Stress and anxiety are physiologically contrary to relaxation and compassion, and the antidote to stress is creating a state of relaxed openness.

Let's take a look at how to do external oleation, using the oils appropriate for each body type (see table 6.4). Keep in mind that medicated oils have the added benefit of delivering herbs deep into the tissues.

TABLE 6.4. OIL FOR YOUR DOSHA

	VATA	**PITTA**	**KAPHA**
Oil	Any oil works for Vata types, especially untoasted sesame or herbal vata oil	Coconut, sunflower, or herbal pitta oil	Corn, olive, sesame, mustard, or herbal kapha oil
Typical frequency	Daily	2–3x/week	1–2x/week

Do not put any oil on your skin that you wouldn't eat. That means no mineral oil, Vaseline, or oils with synthetic ingredients or perfumes. (Though their base oils are perfectly edible, ayurvedic medicated oils, like pitta or kapha oil, are highly potent, and should also not be ingested.)

Oil self-massage should be part of your everyday routine in the fall and winter, when vata is high, regardless of your body type, and at least once a week during spring and summer, when kapha and pitta are predominant.

Oil Is Love—Abhyanga: Self-Massage with Oil

If oil is love, as the ayurvedic tradition tells us, then applying oil to your skin is an act of love. In addition to good diet and exercise, daily oil massage is one of the best things you can do for your mental, emotional, and physical health. In India babies are massaged regularly with oil to promote their immunity and give them the benefit of touch. Touch is the gateway to emotion, and it is vital to our survival: "We can live without seeing or hearing—in fact, without any of our other senses. But babies born without effective nerve connections between skin and brain can fail to thrive and may even die."[*]

When you receive love, you are more likely to reciprocate it. From the same article cited above: "Studies of a variety of cultures show a correspondence between high rates of physical affection in childhood and low rates of adult physical violence."[†]

To truly love someone else, you have to love yourself. Daily oil massage is an act of love and self-healing. No one is born perfect, and very few of us had ideal childhoods. For many of us, traumas have left scars on our hearts and minds, not to mention our bodies. Through daily oil massage we can begin to heal these inner and outer scars and restore our youthful glow and vitality.

How Does It Work?

The skin is our largest organ, richer in hormones and growth factors than any other body part, including the brain. Stimulating the skin through daily massage puts this storehouse of healing chemistry to work. Through processes not yet clear to science, regular touch and massage stimulate multiple hormonal and neurochemical changes. Ayurveda takes it a step further by adding oil for increased nourishment, immunity, and overall detoxification.

---

[*]Joel Swerdlow, "Unmasking Skin," *National Geographic* http://science.national-geographic.com/science/health-and-human-body/human-body/unmasking-skin/.
[†]Ibid.

The ayurvedic mantra "Oil destroys vata" means that oil calms the nervous system and produces relaxation and love, the opposite of anxiety and stress. Not long ago NFL players discovered that wearing a thin, tight layer of clothing under their uniforms helped them perform better and recover from games more quickly. The clothing brand Under Armour capitalized on this and created a multimillion-dollar empire by manufacturing skintight clothes for athletes to boost performance, energy, and even confidence levels. Thousands of years ago, ayurveda recommended that we all don our own "under armor" before venturing onto the battlefield of life.

Finally, as perhaps the ultimate benefit for a rapidly aging society, oil slows the aging process when used on the skin, both inside and out. Our inner skin is the GI tract—the stomach, the intestines, and the colon. Like oil on a dry leather saddle, internal oleation rejuvenates the body from within and external oleation does the same for the outer layer (see "The Benefits of Ghee," beginning on page 101). This one-two punch combats aging and promotes longevity, according to ayurvedic tradition.

How Do I Do It?

Warm four to five ounces of oil and apply it to your head and body. Do not use a microwave; instead, put a bottle of oil in hot water for a few minutes and let it absorb the heat. The oil should be warm, not hot. (In the summer you can skip this step.)

Begin by applying oil on your head. The head and feet are the most important body parts for oil massage. Take time to massage your neck and face, working oil into and around your ears. Next apply the oil vigorously all over your body, using long strokes on your long bones and circular, clockwise strokes on your joints. Do this clockwise motion on your belly, massaging along the path of your colon (this helps stimulate peristalsis). Rub your sides and kidneys to create friction and heat. If you have bhringraj oil, rub it generously on your scalp and feet, but be careful when you get in the shower since you will be slippery.

Let the oil sit on your body for at least ten minutes before washing it off. Take a warm bath or shower and try not to use soap except on the armpits and genitals, and while shampooing your hair. You can also use a wet washcloth to rub the oil in while showering. This is a great way to exfoliate the skin while delivering the oil to its deeper layers. Or you can rub a round, plastic pocket comb on your scalp and skin to get it nice and red, stimulating circulation and movement of lymph. Just beneath your skin there are layers of lymphatic tissue. One of the greatest benefits of massage is the movement of this lymph, which can become stagnant over time. (Lymph is also present behind the lining of your intestines, which is why we take triphala and other herbs to move it.)

After exfoliating with the washcloth or pocket comb, consider applying a second thin layer of oil while still in the shower. Your skin will be wet, making it easy to spread. When you're done, towel dry yourself by patting your skin, not rubbing, so you leave a bit of oil residue for nourishment and protection.

Make Your Own Bath Scrub

My favorite way to apply oil is through a salt or sugar scrub. The key here is to apply it to wet skin and massage vigorously. I turn off the water while I do this because I like to get a good, intense massage in to wake up my entire body.

In a plastic container, add equal amounts of fine sea salt and sugar and fill with sesame, sunflower, or olive oil according to your body type (Vata, Pitta, and Kapha, respectively). The oil should be just level with the salt-sugar mix. You can add a tablespoon of freshly ground cardamom seeds for an invigorating and healing aroma.

Mix this well, and apply after you get wet in the shower. Rub it vigorously all over your wet skin and rinse. This scrub acts like the washcloth-and-oil technique described above to nourish and exfoliate.

Stronger Detox Scrub

For a more intense detox scrub, try making a combination of half baking soda, half fine sea salt. This mix will move lymph and help to pull toxins from your body, not to mention that your skin feels like silk afterwards—an amazing sensation!

After wetting your skin with warm water, allowing your pores to open, turn off the water and apply this to your whole body. Really scrub it in until your skin is pink; this is a sign of lymph circulation in the deeper layers. You should build up a light sweat when doing this, as abhyanga is a form of passive exercise. This way you are encouraging the release of excess toxins through your skin.

Continue as described above, rinsing with warm water. Or you can draw a bath and soak for fifteen minutes. You will really feel the detox and nourishing effects of the salt–oil–baking soda triple threat!

Oiling up during a hot shower is a great way to warm up your body, especially during cold winter months. The warm-up doesn't happen only through exercise: heating your muscles with vigorous massage, sauna, or hot tubs does the same job as fifteen minutes of light cardio (without the cardio benefits, of course). Performing self-massage before a warm or hot shower is enough to prepare your muscles and tendons for your daily exercise routine. Unless you do extremely vigorous exercise in the morning, showering *after* exercise is not recommended. This is because ayurveda considers the sweat you exude doing yoga or light calisthenics beneficial to the skin and the microbes that live on it. This also applies to sweat produced during gentle lovemaking. Perspiration formed during heavy exercise or vigorous sex is a different matter, however: excess heat from these activities needs to be removed, so bathing after heavy exertion is recommended to cool the body.

REGULATED EATING FOR
THE MIND/BODY TYPES

Having a regular eating schedule calms Vata and reduces stress, the first steps to healing most disorders. Following a scheduled eating plan is part of such a routine, except, instead of imposing mealtimes on your body, let your body tell you when it's hungry. Our guts are thinking centers, just like our brains, and they make many crucial decisions without our being aware of them.[1] When our guts are overworked and underappreciated they get "dumbed down," unable to think or do their other jobs because they're too busy digesting. The gut is responsible for many functions besides transporting food, including regulating mood and behavior. Ninety-five percent of serotonin is produced in the gut, and 75 percent of our immune system is centered there, making it more than a simple food processor. In ayurveda, as in modern science, the gut has direct links to bone density and osteoporosis as well as to other diseases, such as depression, autoimmune disorders, and even Alzheimer's disease.

So what's the point of all this? We need to appreciate our second brain and take care of it like the one between our shoulders, by giving it time to rest and rebuild. Regulated eating is the way to do that. "You can oleate all day long, but without a regular diet vata will never come under control," says Nomi Gallo, instructor at the Ayurvedic Institute. This is another nod to the idea that one should think freely and live in regimented ways, rather than living freely and thinking in regimented ways, to paraphrase Pandit Rajmani Tigunait's *Seven Systems of Indian Philosophy*. The best way to regulate ourselves is to follow the Three Square Meals plan (see page 76).

And why is Vata important? Because our fast-paced world is especially stressful and Vata-vitiating. As noted with Jane in chapter 1, this stress translates to every area of our lives, including less tolerance in our relationships, compromised immunity, weight gain, and even a lack of a sense of purpose. Therefore, even if you're not a Vata type, practicing these techniques will help you align with the dharma of your body and, in the words of Dr. Robert Svoboda, live with nature before nature comes to live with you.

AFTER YOU EAT, DO SOME LSD

No, not the drug: LSD stands for "left side down." Lying on your left side for fifteen minutes after your biggest meal has great benefits. By lying quietly after eating, you allow your digestion to work without the stress of driving, talking, reading, or doing other tasks that divert the blood supply to other body centers. You want to focus on digesting, not crunching numbers, after a good meal. This also increases the satisfaction you get from food, which means you'll crave less later on. Satisfaction generates "good" hormones that boost sex drive and mood, improve muscle tone, and enhance sleep patterns. Don't create stress after you eat by rushing around, reading, or trying to focus too hard on one thing. Relaxing means simply that: not doing anything (though taking a short walk is okay). Traditional cultures sometimes spread their meals over two hours to ensure a relaxed social atmosphere and family bonding.

By lying on your left side, you allow food to pass through the duodenum to the small intestine unimpeded. In addition, this position helps to open your right solar *nadi*, or energy channel (see figure 6.1 on page 155). When the solar channel is open, which you'll know because you will be breathing primarily through your right nostril, digestion is encouraged. When you sleep at night, however, you want the left (lunar) nadi open—that is, your left nostril—because this promotes sleep and quiet relaxation. LSD is not about falling asleep; its purpose is to help you digest your meal. If napping happens, great; your body probably needs it. Just make sure to keep it short—fifteen to thirty minutes—or you will wake up groggy.

If you can't find a place to lie down, lean to the left. Leaning in your seat or on the couch for five to fifteen minutes creates the same effect and lets your body unwind. If you cannot do LSD or want to be more active, try the alternative: walk a hundred steps after meals. This ancient adage is well-known in many traditions because it works. In his book *The 4-Hour Body*, Timothy Ferriss experiments with brief bursts of exercise, like squats or lunges, just after meals to jump-start digestion and metabolism.[2] By moving your body after meals you promote peristalsis, the downward movement of food through the GI tract. One caveat is that you must do this in a relaxed, nourishing way: creating stress with movement or exercise will only shut down your digestion, not jump-start it.

BEDTIME AND SLEEP POSITIONS

Go to bed no later than 9:30 p.m. in the winter, 11 p.m. during summer. If you can't, expect to be hungry. The midnight-snack phenomenon is real, and you ignore it at your peril. Evening is the best time for sex and romance. Use the evening as a winding-down time, rather than doing work or other intense activity before turning in. In chapter 11 we will discuss the optimal times to make love and why evening is most suitable for sex and leisure (a fact not lost on the entertainment industry!).

The best positions for a good night's sleep are on your right side for Pittas, on the left side for Kaphas, and on your back or right side for Vatas. When in doubt, sleep on your right. It was good enough for the Buddha, so it's certainly good enough for you!

THE THREE PILLARS

Sushruta, perhaps the most illustrious surgeon in history, defined health as follows: "Health is balance of the body's three humors,

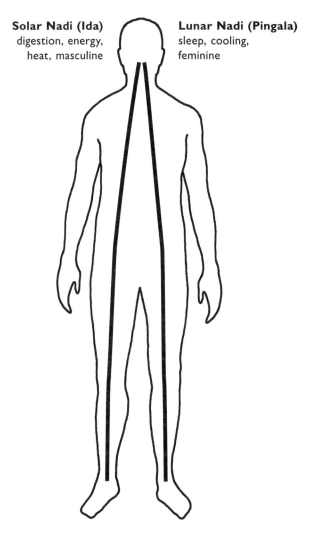

Figure 6.1. Solar and lunar nadis, or energy channels

metabolic activity, bodily systems and tissues, healthy excretion of wastes in the form of urine, feces, and sweat, as well as a calm and clear mind, senses, and personality."

To achieve a calm and clear body, mind, and senses, follow the recommendations in part one. If you cannot incorporate all these tips and daily routines in your life, stick to these three simple steps.

1. **Clear ama:** For fresh breath, good digestion, and a clear GI tract, take triphala daily. Triphala is a miracle compound that detoxifies and nourishes the body at the same time. Few substances can claim this.

2. **Eat well:** Follow the Three Square Meals plan to ensure that your body not only gets what it needs from your food, but has the time and energy to absorb and assimilate it.

3. **Practice pranayama:** Incorporate pranayama into your day to clear the senses and invigorate your spirit. Pranayama, like regular exercise, can spell the difference between dullness and depression on the one hand and clarity and emotional buoyancy on the other.

These three pillars are simple and require minimal changes in your life. Make them the foundation of your day. Soon these practices will become automatic, and conscious breathing, eating, and taking your triphala will seem as normal as brushing your teeth!

PART TWO

Sex

✦

*Putting Science
and Spirit behind the Act*

7

The Laws of Attraction

Woman as Laborer and Man as Warrior

In this chapter we'll look at biological imperatives in sex and relationships, as well as how to move beyond these. Some of the content in this chapter may sound fatalistic, but the only way to transcend limitation is to first understand it. Our bodies have specific dharmas and nature wires us to play them out, whether we are aware of them or not.

The archetypal polarity of Male and Female is embodied in the dharma type model. The seed of Warriors lies dormant in all men, just as the seed of Laborers underlies all women's dharma types. At a basic level, all men are Warriors and all women are laborers. Males, no matter what their individual dharma type, share the basic role of hunter, protector, and provider. Women tend to share the role of homemaker, and serve as the glue that holds a community together. Without women, men would probably still be in caves. Women also bear the burden of birthing, nurturing, and caring for children. Physiologically, they receive and process a man's energy, cleaning and purifying it. Women have faith, devotion, love, and pair-bonding instincts that also link them to the Laborer dharma type. On the other hand, men generally have drive, aggression, and risk-taking behavior that naturally identify them as Warrior types.

In times of stress, when basic survival is at stake, men and women tend to revert to these roles.

In societies where people are allowed to flourish, where threats from the environment are minimized, they naturally stratify into the five dharma categories, and pour the full measure of their personalities into the mythic mold of their particular dharma type. But a basic remnant of our evolutionary past remains that classes men and women into Warrior and Laborer archetypes, respectively. That is why a significant portion of male initiations include Warrior tests and challenges and why traditional female training involves Laborer skills, such as cooking, tending the home, and nurturing and rearing children.

Rituals like the vision quest were common in ancient societies, where boys were left on their own in nature, guided by their instincts and training. Such trials, though supervised by elders working behind the scenes to minimize the risks, still contained the potential for harm or even death, infusing them with a sense of real danger. The rituals where a child leaves as a boy and returns as a man are still practiced in traditional societies around the globe because such training builds confidence: a boy who survives a brush with death will remember and draw on that experience for life. Lacking these trials in modern Western culture, boys tend to gravitate toward sports, fraternity initiations, fast driving, or even drug and alcohol abuse—activities that engender the same sense of risk and potential reward. And though women may not go on comparable quests, their rituals are no less important or difficult.

INITIATIONS

We undergo many transitions in life. Initiations are a way to mark those transitions by honoring the past and celebrating the future; by shedding an old identity and embracing a new one. Here are some examples of traditional initiations, still performed in many societies today.

> "No matter how they vary and evolve . . . these life-cycle rites point to an understanding that life is not experienced seamlessly, and that individuals take on different identities at different ages and stages of life. [Making] these individual transitions public and visible through ritual, each person [is] made stronger by the presence and support of others."
>
> ELLEN COON, "RITES OF PASSAGE—NEPAL STYLE"

Birth

Welcoming a child into the world is a huge step for any family. Making this time special by greeting the newborn soul and introducing it to its family via an intermediary, such as a priest or a shaman, is common in many cultures. Sometimes midwives perform this function, which is as important for the baby as it is for the community. Children change the dynamic within a family, usually bringing blessing and prosperity, but sometimes hardships and even ruin. This first initiation is therefore vital as a way to ensure that the energy and personality of the baby are congruent with that of the family into which it is born.

This ritual usually involves bathing the baby and anointing it with oil. Then the baby is massaged and dressed, presented first to God and then to the father (who is often absent at birth and may have had little interaction with the baby up to that point) and the rest of the family. In Indian households, this is also a baby's first anointing with *kajjal* (eye salve) and red sandalwood for protection and health.

Naming Ceremony

Naming a child is an often overlooked ceremony in Western culture, belying its importance. Your name is the sound you will hear most in your life, and it should resonate with who you are. Vedic tradition believes that every sound is a mantra, and hearing the wrong sound over and over can disrupt your life. Even poorly chosen nicknames can create dissonance: consider the late Princess Diana's moniker. Hearing "Lady Di, Lady Di, Lady Di" over and over is not a positive, life-affirming mantra. Therefore it is supremely important to pick the right sounds for your name. Luckily, there are several ways to do that, though some involve knowing details of the Vedic horoscope.

Based on the moon's degree in your birth chart, there are specific sounds that can be used to begin the baby's name (see table 11.2, page 317, for more on this). For example, if the sound is *keh*, then the name Kendra or Kendrick will work. If you're not sure what your moon's degree is, it is best to consult a trained Vedic astrologer.

Keep in mind that this moon star syllable is the same thing as your primordial sound—a concept popularized by Dr. Deepak Chopra that works on the identical principle: namely, that the sound you hear most, if it is in alignment with your deepest self, will integrate your personality and bring relaxation and spiritual awakening.

Or the child may be given a spiritual name after the family tradition. For example, in a Christian family the parents may pick their favorite biblical character, like Peter. Or in Hindu households, where Shiva is worshipped, one of Shiva's many names may be conferred on the baby to carry on that spiritual lineage

Ultimately, having the child named by the family guru is probably the best way to go, especially if that person also has a working knowledge of the astrological principles outlined above. Otherwise, the name may be picked by a family elder. Elders who have been ritually consecrated as wisdomkeepers are eligible to name children, based on their life experience and connection to Spirit.

First Feeding

A baby's first taste of solid food is a special occasion, as it begins a lifetime of eating. To commemorate it, many families offer sweets or rice to God in some form (like Ganesha) while saying a prayer for the child's welfare. Then they present that blessed food to the child, usually with a gold or silver spoon, to symbolize prosperity and health and to encourage a life of good eating habits. As we discussed in part 1, gold and silver have healing properties, and you can harness these by drinking gold water or using a silver tongue scraper or simply by eating with actual silverware—forks, knives, and spoons made of real silver. There is a reason why the expression "born with a silver spoon in your mouth" correlates to wealth. It also relates to health, though that part of its meaning may now be lost to us.

Future Profession

A peculiar and entertaining ritual in India that goes along with first feeding is the test of a child's future tendencies. To do this, family members present various objects to the baby, and the ones the child reaches for first indicate his future profession. Some examples include a book or a pen for scholarship, money for wealth and business, a clump of earth for property ownership, and a mala for spiritual life. If the baby grabs for food, she will be healthy. Keys may symbolize that all doors in life will open for the child.

First Studies

This all-important ritual is performed at the beginning of study, usually when youngsters start learning their ABCs. One tradition states that it should begin when a boy is four years and four months old and when a girl is five years and four months old. Another says it can start when a child can touch her left ear with her right hand passed over her head. This initiation is usually led by a teacher or a guru. Holding a child's hand, the preceptor traces the child's first letter or letters (A or OM) on a chalkboard or in a plate of rice. Invoking the goddess of speech and learning, Sarasvati, the teacher helps the child pronounce these letters several times. Before and afterward, offerings of food and/or money are given to the teacher, or a donation may be made to a local school or another educational institution. The act of giving for educational purposes positively links you to the muse of education, and positive beginnings herald desirable outcomes, according to the principles of ritual and astrology.

> **Positive beginnings herald desirable outcomes, according to the principles of ritual and astrology.**

Initiation into Spiritual Life

This can happen anytime between ages five and thirteen. In Western societies, where this ritual is not typically observed, spiritual initiations may happen at any time, even during adult life. This is when children, typically boys, are initiated into their dharma type, their specific spiritual duties, and the rites that will allow them to eventually perform the funeral rites for their parents. It is a big deal and involves self-sacrifice on the part of the child to prove himself worthy. It may be accompanied by shaving of the head, fasting, and other humbling gestures that essentially segregate him from worldly life. At the age when youngsters begin to build ego and vanity, these rites strip them down to remind them of who they really are—a spirit having a physical experience, not the other way around.

Entry into Adulthood

Some of the rites for young boys and girls entering adulthood are described elsewhere in this book. Typically, for young girls, the adulthood ritual begins at menarche—first menstruation. This is when girls are generally taken out of sight of the community for a number of days and only allowed to confer with other girls and women—friends and elders—who coach them in the specifics of being a woman. They may then reemerge into the community wearing clothes, makeup, or adornments that mark their new status in full view of their society. Such coming-out ceremonies are common across different cultures, and serve to announce the rebirth of a girl's identity from child to sexually mature woman.

It is more difficult to time when a young boy is ready to step into manhood because physical signs like menstruation are not present in males; this task is often undertaken by male elders who determine when a boy is ready. For boys, initiation entails a disappearance from society, similar to the one described for young girls, but for them the journey is outward, whereas for girls it's inward. For boys this may be a nature quest, a hunt, or the exploration of some unknown space, like a cave or a forest. But instead of being supported and nurtured, like his female counterparts, a boy is typically presented with challenges to test his mental and physical strength and fortitude. If he survives these (and his elders do everything to ensure that he does), he reemerges with a new identity and strength of purpose. He is now a man, and he hunts with the men. He becomes part of the fraternity of adult males, and this helps to shape his identity until his next major initiation: marriage.

> "Be lenient with a son the first five years, and very strict the next ten; but when he has attained his sixteenth year, treat him like a friend."
>
> CHANAKYA, NITI SHASTRA

Marriage

Traditionally, marriage is viewed as a once-in-a-lifetime event, just like entry into adulthood and birth. There is little justification for divorce, so it is of the utmost importance to get the first marriage right. The details of how to pick a good day for this most auspicious event, as well as how to match couples together, are revealed elsewhere in this book (see, especially, chapter 12).

Conception and Pregnancy

In India and other traditional societies, prescriptions and proscriptions abound when it comes to mating and conception. Among them are the following.

In cultures that prized male progeny, doctors were pressed to provide ways for couples to tilt the balance in favor of their desired gender. Ayurveda's classical texts give techniques for influencing the gender of a child. Here is a simple one: if you want a boy, insemination should occur on an odd-numbered day. For a girl, it should happen on an even-numbered day. Days are counted from the onset of menstruation, which is considered day one. Thus, if a woman began menstruating January 6 (day one) and insemination occurred on January 20 (day fifteen), then there will be higher likelihood of having a boy because day fifteen is an odd-numbered day.

Tantra provides another example: to influence the sex of a child during copulation, both partners should breathe through the left nostril to produce a girl or the right nostril for a boy. This is said to open the female and male nadis in the body at the time of ejaculation. A nadi is an energy channel that runs through the subtle body and is controlled by the breath. (Lying on your left side after meals also works on this principle, since lying on your left opens up the right nadi, which in turn encourages metabolism and digestion.) Special techniques like this, however, need to be learned from qualified teachers before they can be applied effectively.

According to yoga philosophy, sex at the junctures of day and night (sunrise and sunset) is thought to be harmful and depleting to both a couple and the child produced from their union. Sunrise and sunset are sacred, spiritual moments, during which *sattva*, purity, is prevalent in the atmosphere, and it is better to observe these moments with silence or prayer rather than sex and activity. It is a time for meditation, not copulation; therefore, keep the thirty minutes before and after sunrise and sunset sacred. Early night is optimal for romance as it represents rajas, the quality of passion.

According to Vedic astrology, in addition to keeping the right nostril open and mating on an odd day, couples desirous of male offspring might also consider what *nakshatra* (asterism) the moon is in.* A male nakshatra increases the odds for a male child and a female nakshatra for a female child. Astrology also contains techniques to help couples increase their odds of conception or to avoid conception, as the case may be. According to one principle, a woman is fertile when the moon is in the same phase as it was the moment she was born. This period, which lasts about twenty-four hours, is especially fertile for her if it coincides with her ovulation cycle. However, women have been known to conceive during this moon period even at times when they were not supposed to be ovulating. Thus, couples desiring children and those who do not want children should be aware of this possibly fertile time.†

There are other methods for influencing the health of one's offspring. According to ayurveda, a baby is the result of what its parents ate up to three months before conception. Eating chilies or oily food or drinking alcohol before sex will transfer the quality of excess pitta into the child. Pitta corresponds to the Fire and Water elements. Likewise, eating dry, cold, and light foods, like granola, or having sex during periods of stress, dehydration, or even in an airplane, can cause a vitiated Vata mind/body constitution in a child produced from such a union. And having ice cream, pizza, or heavy foods before sexual activity will result in a baby with exaggerated Kapha qualities.

---

*Nakshatras are unique to Vedic astrology. They are twenty-seven (sometimes twenty-eight) asterisms (small signs) with specific meanings and mythologies. For example, when someone asks you your sign in India, they are referring to your moon nakshatra, not your sun sign, as in Western astrology.

†This is called the Dr. Jonas method. For more information about it, visit www.iconceive.com.

> **The Vedic sciences help us to take control of our lives by revealing the unseen causes of everyday reality, even those invisible to the subtlest tools of modern science.**

The techniques described above for determining the sex of a child and aiding conception have been shown effective, though the reasons are not readily apparent. However, we should not dismiss them just because we are unable to determine how they work. A layperson does not know why a virus makes her sick, but a trained doctor understands the mechanisms by which it happens. Just because something is invisible does not mean that it cannot affect our body, mind, and spirit. The Vedic sciences help us take control of our lives by revealing the unseen causes of everyday reality, even those invisible to the subtlest tools of modern science.

Old Age

Initiations into retirement are just as important as those into adulthood, which is why some cultures honor their elders by ritually initiating them into privileged elder status. In this way they take on the role of wisdomkeepers for their clan, a safe refuge for youngsters in need of guidance. They also symbolize the spiritual life, because they are closer to death and the beyond. This is one reason to revere our elders; they are closer to God and sources of blessing.

Retirement doesn't have to be a gold watch and a hasty farewell—it should be a happy transition into the autumn and winter of life, during which we embrace new obligations and let go of the old.

Death

This final initiation, which we still observe in every religious tradition, is a soul's final transition, its departure from this world. Death rituals come in many shapes and sizes, all with the professed purpose of helping to speed the remaining identity—that which has survived the body—onto its next home. This is also a transition for the living members left behind, a ritual that gives them the space to grieve, celebrate, and make peace with the departed soul.

Other Initiation Rituals

There are many other rituals that can consecrate your life, including a child's first outing, piercing of the ears, and other local customs. It is important to remember that these are meant to enhance our life experience, not drag it down in superstition. Use rituals and initiations to honor the past, celebrate the present and welcome the future. Do not use them to segregate or create divisions, for that ultimately brings misfortune to everyone involved.

WHAT WOMEN WANT: TESTS OF QUALITY

Biologically, women's bodies are wired to look for *quality* and men's for *quantity*. A woman seeks the best possible mate, while men seek as many mates as possible. A woman's body judges quality by continually testing and confusing men and evaluating their responses. As long as a man meets the quality standards of a woman, her body generates a desire to be with him. This is what we can call *attraction, chemistry,* or *biological love*. When a man fails to meet these standards, a woman's body disengages from him, and her feelings cool. She may continue to give him tests to prove and redeem himself, but if a man cannot consistently meet her standards, her body may begin to search elsewhere for a mate with better qualifications.

None of this happens on the conscious level. Women's bodies have evolved advanced mechanisms that bypass the conscious mind and work mostly in the background to confuse both women themselves and the men they are with. This is because women run a far greater risk in entering relationships. Men can father a child and simply walk away, but women have to go through nine months of pregnancy, during which they are vulnerable and unable to fully care for themselves. Then, after giving birth, they must care for their children for years on end. As a result, their bodies have developed powerful defenses that test the strength and stability of potential fathers. If a man is deemed wanting in his genetic makeup or in his ability to provide for his mate, a woman's body will automatically reject him as a suitor by turning her off to him.

In large part, nature controls who we respond to by wiring men and women to react positively to certain qualities and negatively to others. For example, in general, women prefer a man who demonstrates strength, power, and control—Warrior qualities. Such control may mean financial, physical, intellectual, or other forms of excellence that evince quality in him. Men can fake having true quality for a while by using seduction techniques or other forms of manipulation, but the only way to demonstrate quality over the long term is to fulfill his life's purpose. Like the Warrior he is at his core, every man must strike out and make his mark in the world, even if in the smallest of ways. In chapter 2 we discussed the value of purpose. There is nothing more attractive to a woman than a man with a purpose, even if he hasn't fully realized it yet. There is nothing as unattractive as a man who is confused, ineffectual, and whose life is in disarray. A man in touch with his destiny radiates an aura that attracts the opposite (and the same) sex. Likewise, a woman who knows how to love, who is in touch with her Laborer qualities and her life's purpose, also stirs a man deeply, without any conscious effort on her part.

But a woman can't just ask if a man is worthy of her. She finds this information by presenting him with challenges. Based on his skill in handling her tests or challenges, he is placed in one of three categories—potential lover, potential provider, or neither—and her body responds by generating the appropriate emotion. Again, most of these mechanisms are predicated upon biological instinct, not conscious choice, and it is natural for a woman to be the selector and judge the quality of a man, and for a man to display himself for her approval. This constitutes the mating dance that has been going on for millennia in practically every animal species on the planet.

The proof lies in our very biology. Women's bodies and emotions are notoriously difficult to understand, even to women themselves. From taking off her clothes to finding her clitoris and bringing a woman to orgasm, men face enormous challenges. Furthermore, what makes one woman sexually aroused may do nothing for another. Men have to continually learn and relearn what makes a woman tick. The best way for a man to pass a woman's tests is to authentically display the qualities of his dharma type.

HOW MEN GENERATE ATTRACTION

So how does a man use this knowledge to generate attraction? The answer is simple: find your quality. The reason you did the BE FIT exercises in chapter 3 was to help you find your uniqueness and superiority—areas where you excel and are unlike anyone else. Understand your dharma type and play up its qualities. Are you a Warrior? Show a potential partner what a powerful mission you have protecting those who can't protect themselves. If you don't have such a mission, find one. It can be teaching guitar to inner-city orphans or donating goats to village families in Africa. Women are interested in a man who wants to make the world a better place. Also show her your courage, decisiveness, and adventurous spirit by going to places that highlight these traits. From rock climbing to strip poker, show her your mastery in everything you do.

Are you an Educator? Show her your class, culture, and intelligence—not in a self-absorbed way that glorifies you, but by truly adding to her wisdom. Show her your ideas and how they set you apart. Let her see others admire you for those ideas—accolades are a powerful aphrodisiac. Having a mission and wanting to make the world a better place are basic Warrior traits that all men—no matter what their dharma type—can cultivate, since they all carry the seed of the Warrior type. Evolve Warrior traits that will help you stand up for and respect yourself: don't let your compassion make you spineless; instead let it be a sign of your inner strength.

Are you a Laborer? Show her how good you are with your hands. Your practical sense has no equal; you can make things that other dharma types only dream about. Let her see your skill. Play up scent, but use a light touch with cologne or essential oils; don't overdo it. Be plain and direct, and overwhelm her defenses with your genuineness and attentiveness. Have self-respect—you're a catch, and show her that you respect her too, but without buying gifts or flattering her, at least at first. Your attention and presence are your gifts. A rose on top of it all will then melt her heart.

Are you an Outsider? Wow her by being unpredictable, offbeat, and exciting. There is nothing as fascinating to a woman as a man with an air of mystery. You were born unique, so flaunt your uniqueness. Bear in mind, however, that too much unpredictability can make you look unstable. Demonstrate your ability to wear many hats by taking her to places she's never been. Go Mongolian dining then spelunking. You love your freedom: demonstrate it by keeping her guessing about what will happen next. Combine that with inner emotional consistency and you become a riddle she's dying to solve.

Are you a Merchant? Then fun and enthusiasm are your distinctive charms. Use your wit and connections to show her the best time of her life. Show her that you can have fun regardless of where you are. Be up to date on fashion, music, and other details of pop culture to engage in fun conversation. Use money wisely: show her you know its value and what to do with it.

HOW MEN ARE TESTED

Basically, a woman looks for two things in a man: genetic superiority and/or stability.

Genetic superiority is a matter of short-term compatibility, created by personal chemistry—a man's physical proportions, smell, taste, personality, wealth, humor, popularity, social standing, and other attractive features. It qualifies a man as a potential lover and a candidate to father her child. Women's bodies react to genetic superiority by creating powerful sexual attraction. Their tests for this may be different from the ones they give men to find out if they are good long-term partners or providers. Here, women are not necessarily looking for relationship material, but the best choice physically to pass on genetic material. For men to ace these tests they must present an overwhelming display of quality, whatever that may be. Men who can bypass, or at least temporarily short-circuit, women's defenses are usually seen as genetically superior and potential candidates to father children. Men who cannot do this but who do show stability and other positive qualities, like nurturing and friendship, fall into the next category. They enter what's commonly called the friends zone, the place where sex is withheld but affection is still possible.

Stability is where women test men to judge their ability to stay over the long haul, provide for a family, and care for their offspring. These tests begin with the first meeting and continue for the duration of a relationship. Again, they are unconscious trials set up by her biology to ensure that a man is suitable not just to father, but to rear her children. When a man displays provider qualities, like routinely buying gifts and dinners, compromising and discussing instead of arguing with her, and putting her needs before his own, women's bodies perceive this as long-term courting behavior and tend to withhold sex and continue testing, until either marriage or a long-term relationship is established or the courting relationship ends. A lover is a short-term candidate to whom a woman responds sexually. A provider is a long-term candidate to whom a woman usually responds by withholding sex. Knowing in which bracket he wants to be is crucial for a man, and his elders teach him how to maximize his effectiveness with techniques to cultivate and demonstrate either genetic superiority or stability—or both. If he wants only sex, he must focus on his genetic superiority. If he is seeking a life mate, he must emphasize his stability. The most successful men embody both sets of traits, and are capable of passing any test women's bodies throw at them.

> **Men continue to grow by facing and learning from testing by the women in their lives.**

These tests are not all bad for men. Men continue to grow by facing and learning from real-world testing by the women in their lives. These tests help men to become their most authentic selves by weeding out their inauthentic behavior. Women have evolved an acute sensitivity to authenticity and can determine if men are living their highest life. By continuing to test them throughout a relationship, women help men evolve. There is no greater cause for a Warrior than a just battle. At some level all men are Warriors, and the toughest battles they face are usually at home, in the intimate arena of interpersonal relationships. A man's potential for greatest growth comes from learning to live with a partner.

Men negotiate a woman's tests by harnessing the power of their authenticity to break down her defenses and access the real "her" inside. Women generally respond to charm, wit, intelligence, confidence, expertise, mystery, adventure, social status, and similar attractive qualities in men. Whatever the overpowering trait, it needs to be displayed with enough energy and consistency to show a woman that it is real, and to overcome her resistance.

In India, the *shiva lingam* is the symbol of cosmic conscious-ness. It is a smooth, phallus-shaped stone that remains implaca-ble in the face of the offerings and oblations poured over it. This ability to remain unperturbed, to see humor even in her strongest tests, and to be cool under fire demonstrates a man's detachment from his reactive desires, control over his mind, and command of his world.

Yet only another man can teach a boy how to cultivate such self-assurance. While women can offer advice and insight, this crucial training cannot be transmitted by a woman, since it is primarily concerned with the fundamentals of being a man. Boys raised by single mothers face a particular challenge in this area; these boys need to seek out the wisdom of male elders to train them to become well-integrated men. Otherwise, they are at a disadvantage when it comes to surmounting the cultural, emotional, and physical chal-lenges presented by women in their society.

Thus, a woman can only test a man, but she cannot show him how to pass those tests. She may not even have the answers to them herself; she only knows when a man gets it right. The tiny tumblers and locks in her biology turn when a man gives the correct answer. This is the deeper meaning of what turns her on. When a man pushes the right buttons, the mechanism of attraction responds. In this respect the conscious mind functions as a controller, a safety mechanism to keep a woman from doing something stupid that will cost her suffering in the long run. However, it is mostly the body that runs the show.

Positive examples of testing by women include holding men accountable, keeping them true to their word, and not letting them backslide into immature conduct. Some negative examples of testing by women include changes of mood and behavior, com-plaining, and nagging. However, nagging can be an opportunity for one or both partners to step up and embody their true nature.

Nagging, or repeated urging and complaining, is a way for a woman to get a man to become better than he is. Yet it usually ends up breaking him down, and eventually compromises the relationship itself. Women must recognize this and change their approach if they want to keep their relationships intact and get what they need from men. Men, on the other hand, must take the opportunity not only to meet but to exceed a woman's expectations by doing something strong, unexpected, and caring. Instead of just taking out the garbage, why not clean the entire house before your wife comes home from work? This is the seed of romance, and how love and desire are kindled. One bold stroke wipes away the persistent torment of nagging and sets a man up for the next test, when it all begins anew. But such is the playing field of interpersonal relationships

Once established in a solid relationship a woman may not see fit to continue testing, or at least not with the same intensity and frequency as she did during the first stages of the relationship. However, some positive tension still generally characterizes interpersonal relationships. Attraction is built around polarity, that magnetic charge between man and woman that is another word for *tension*. When all the positive tension goes out of a relationship, so do the sparks. We must contrast this with negative tension, which is created by real fighting, disparagement, unchallenged nagging, and the like. Positive tension is built around play fighting, play teasing, and play nagging. Teasing a woman is one of the fastest ways to build attraction, if it is done in the spirit of humor and play. Belittling and disparaging her, by contrast, is the quickest way to foster dysfunction in a relationship. Play-nagging a man is sexy; constantly harping on what he's doing wrong is not. Couples who grasp the nuances of positive tension understand one of the most important components of keeping relationships fresh and exciting. Of course, no amount of excitement can replace real love in a union, but love flourishes in an atmosphere of play and tension, just as a tree grows from the interplay of sunlight and rain. Without these, the mightiest redwood remains an acorn, a seed of potential greatness waiting to be nurtured into maturity.

> **Love grows around the dynamic forces created by play and tension, just as a tree grows from the interplay of sunlight and rain.**

GIRL-WOMEN AND BOY-MEN

Boys and girls must learn the prerequisites of their gender before fulfilling their dharma type. That is one of the qualities that separates men from boys, women from girls. Pouting is cute when a girl is nine, but sad when she's thirty-nine. Immaturity is endearing in a young boy, but not in a middle-aged man. When the only tool that boy-men and girl-women have is the proverbial hammer, they treat everything like a nail: using adolescent strategies to deal with situations that require nuance, sophistication, and wisdom. For a woman, increasing a man's desire does not entail raising her hemline, but raising her love and awareness. For a man, getting and keeping a woman does not mean following her around with flowers, but giving her a reason to be with him.

> **For a woman, increasing a man's desire does not entail raising her hemline, but raising her love and awareness. For a man, getting and keeping a woman does not mean following her around, but giving her a reason to be with him.**

Modern girl-women have been mistakenly taught to think that by whining, attracting attention, or injecting enough sexuality in their relationships, they can get whatever they want. Unfortunately, this is often true, as excessive sex or nagging can weaken and eventually break down a man, forcing him to consent to anything. The flip side is that women end up with a man who is broken and likely to act out by cheating, lying, or being reckless in an attempt to redeem his masculinity. In the end, both partners lose and the relationship falters. Better to start with mature strategies than to repeat these destructive cycles.

Boy-men jeopardize their relationships by enacting later in life the same strategies that may have worked for them when they were little, such as bullying or running away to resolve problems. Their refusal to mature into responsible men also includes a lack of basic self-care regimens like bathing, washing dishes, and keeping a clean and clutter-free living space. Many boy-men never learn essential self-grooming and often wonder why adult women avoid them.

A prerequisite to being a man is mastery of your personal space, including your physical body and immediate surroundings. Body odor, mismatched clothes, or a neglected living situation demonstrate to a woman that you lack basic self-respect or perhaps never learned these skills from your parents, and are not likely to be a good partner. It also signals an inability to integrate into society, and is a major turn off.

WOMEN AND FAMILY

Women typically have stronger limbic bonds to their children than men do, which is why fathers walk out on their families more frequently than mothers do. Like Laborers, women are designed to create family and strengthen community. In general, their pair-bonding instinct is stronger than a man's. Raising a family is a full-time job, which is why, though it's not remunerated in the same way as other professions, homemaker is the career many women undertake. Sacred societies recognize this career not only as a valid form of personal expression but as a necessary component of social harmony, just as important as banker, soldier, or teacher. Because Laborers are the foundation of society, without homemakers there is no possibility for others to pursue careers, because there would be no family, no well-integrated children, and no stable society.

Therefore, women in sacred societies are the foundation of healthy communities. The term *homemaker* takes on the connotation of *community builder*. A mother becomes a go-to person, a confidante, and a source of comfort for her village. When a mother cooks a meal there is always something left over for neighbors, friends, or the indigent. Except in cases of extreme poverty, there is always more food than necessary for the survival of the family unit. A well-integrated Laborer with the tools to develop her craft will always display that craft in abundance. In a productive society this means that even the less fortunate, the mendicants, and the outcasts will have a place at a matron's table. This is why the cow is sacred in Vedic societies, because it gives milk not only to its calves but to any animal that needs it. It is indiscriminate in its giving, like a real mother, like a true Laborer type.

> **The cow is sacred in Vedic societies because it gives milk not only to its calves, but to any animal that needs it.**
> **It is indiscriminate in its giving, like a real mother, like a true Laborer type.**

A special role for homemakers is nourishing Educators and those in Educator periods, as well as those in the Autumn season of their lives.* In this role, a matron symbolizes the great divine Mother—embodied Nature herself. When a woman taps into her infinite potential for creativity, she accesses nature's ability to provide and nourish the world, just as Sarasvati nourishes our minds, Lakshmi our bodies, and Kali our souls.† In return, that matron is doubly

---

*The circle of duty and priority is explained in detail in *The Five Dharma Types*.
†These Vedic embodiments of nature personify a woman's ability to enrich humankind on the intellectual (Sarasvati), physical (Lakshmi), and spiritual levels (Kali).

blessed—first by the act of sharing, and second, by the intended or unintended blessing of the holy person whose quest for enlightenment she is furthering. As a result, women have the power to heal and to bless because they are receptacles of blessings themselves. Women who have raised a family and created life from within their bellies and nourished children from their breasts are indeed blessed creatures.

WOMEN AND SOCIAL TRENDS

Another quality shared by women and the Laborer type is sensitivity to public opinion. Women are more sensitive to fashion, social trends, and the movements of popular culture. Laborers value public opinion and are usually conservative and consensus minded. One permutation of this quality is that women are sexually attracted to males well liked by the public, whether they are actors, athletes, or just popular men in their spheres of influence. In general, being attractive to others is a sign of social value—a highly attractive trait. Biologically, it signals that offspring of this kind of man would share the same popularity, and therefore have a greater likelihood of survival.

This makes women's bodies crave such a man, engendering biological urges that are sometimes overpowering. Male celebrities are all too familiar with women throwing themselves—their bodies—at them with the implicit (even explicit) mantra, "I wanna have your baby!" Men, for their part, like the Warriors buried in their DNA, strive and compete for that popularity, even to the point of risking their lives, because they know it will allow them to mate with the most desirable females.

Ultimately, our higher faculties can check such behavior and control our urges, but it doesn't mean we don't have them. A glance at the spectacles that surround celebrities in our culture is enough to demonstrate the powerful influence of social status on human biology, whether we choose to act on it or not.

WOMEN AND SEX

Women are also teachers in matters of sex. Laborer types represent the proletariat, that part of society that the Romans who coined this term deemed useful chiefly for their ability to breed. *Proles-tari* means "valuable for their offspring," a rather demeaning and oppressive way to view a class of people, especially when lumped into a hierarchical system that does not value the contributions of each class equally. But originally such labels had their origin in a deep respect for nature and the feminine power to bring forth new life.

Women are valuable to society for giving the gift of life. Without women or Laborers, humankind would become extinct. But rather than acclaiming them, this simple yet profound truth has been used to demean Laborers and women alike through the last five thousand years of history that Vedic wisdom calls the Dark Age of human civilization. These last five thousand years or so have witnessed a separation of matter and spirit, and exaltation of the material over the spiritual. The survival of the fittest and dog-eat-dog paradigms have infiltrated science, religion, and society as a whole.

But sacred societies have always recognized that women rule the roost during the Laborer or Spring period of life, when children grow from infancy to young adulthood, for women are the primary caregivers during this time. As Warriors, men are more instrumental during the next phase, Summer, when young adults begin to assert their personalities in the world.

THE BURDENS WOMEN BEAR

Having a wife and children to protect, a man fulfills his role as a Warrior; having a husband and kids to love, care for, and provide for, a woman fulfills her role as a Laborer. Yet a woman's role in relationships is more complex than a man's. Another reason that women are selectors in nature becomes clear when we look at the burdens they bear in relationships. A woman not only has to care for her children, but she must also purify, civilize, and empower her mate. As guardians of shakti, positive energy, women not only raise families and build communities, they also elevate and acculturate their spouses. Like the mythic Vedic goddesses Lakshmi, Sarasvati, and Kali, who bring prosperity, culture, and spiritual energy to humankind, a woman functions as a triune goddess in her marriage. In order to do this, she needs to have a partner who is equal to her.

The Sanskrit term for wife is *bharya*, literally "she who bears the burden." As sexual receptacles for energy, women are affected by the quality of their partners and the sex they have together. Because the woman receives a man's seed, she must ensure that he is physically, emotionally, and spiritually qualified to inseminate her. A woman does not want a man with problems she can't handle, especially if she is busy raising his children. As we have already seen, women want a man who's in control of himself and his environment.

> Like the mythic Vedic goddesses Lakshmi, Sarasvati, and Kali, who bring prosperity, culture, and spiritual energy to humankind, a woman functions as a triune goddess in her marriage.

Because men do not have the monthly purification cycle that women possess, they often purge through sex. Men release frustration, anger, and repressed emotions by releasing semen, by themselves or with a partner, and this serves to keep them civil and socialized for a while. A woman must therefore ask herself—whether consciously or unconsciously—"Do I want to be a receptacle for this man's energy? Do I want to help him purify himself in the hope that he will offer me something useful in return?"

To answer these questions, women's bodies evolved the sophisticated testing mechanisms discussed above, whereby potential mates are selected according to hardwired criteria that must be met if a woman is to allow a man access to sex. A child created from an imperfect union presents more challenges than one conceived in love, in harmony with nature's rhythms. As an example, consider that while a glass of wine is helpful for digestion, relaxation, and romance, having drunk sex does not foster the optimal well-being of a child produced from such a union. That is because intoxication is tamasic, and tamas equates to dullness, darkness, and ignorance.

When a man is tamasic—that is, burdened with tamas—either due to his eating habits (tamasic food), diurnal rhythms (tamasic activities), or temperament (tamasic thoughts), he brings his partner down by association.* Of course, the same holds true for tamasic women, though since they are receptacles of energy they are more affected by their spouses than are men. Knowing this, the Vedic sages categorized everything in the world according to the three basic gunas, or qualities, in nature—sattva, rajas, and tamas—and encouraged us to follow appropriate lifestyles to harness them. When used properly, each guna has its place, even tamas, which is necessary for us to sleep. But too much of this quality promotes dullness (the kind you get when you oversleep) and ignorance of dharma. In relationships it begins when men and women forget how to express their masculinity and femininity, respectively, and ends in broken marriages and divorce.

---

*Tamasic food includes leftovers; spoiled, frozen, or canned food; meat; liquor; and fermented foods. Tamasic activities include sleeping in, frequenting bars and clubs, smoking, and gambling. Tamasic thoughts and emotions include depression, greed, dullness, and overall ignorance.

EMBODYING OUR PRIMAL ARCHETYPES

Before we evolve into spiritual beings, we must evolve into men and women. Before we can step into the more complex destiny of our dharma type, we must first embody our primal sexual archetypes: male/female. If we fail to evolve into mature men and women, this can create gaps in our experience of the world. Though not essential for spiritual enlightenment, sidestepping this process may create obstacles to achieving that goal: many students cannot move forward in their spiritual lives because of sexual hang-ups or because they never received basic training in how to be a man or a woman. In such cases, gurus and teachers have to fill the lacunae in their students' awareness, which can take precious years away from their spiritual progress. Even gurus can fall prey to inappropriate uses of sexuality, such is the power of this most basic instinct.

A house built on sand cannot endure, and a personality structure assembled on poor foundations cannot support the turrets and spires that reach for heaven. People lacking the foundation of their male/female archetype cannot withstand the weight of their dharma type. A man cannot be himself until he knows how to be a Warrior; a woman cannot know what it is to be a woman if she cannot be a Laborer. Sexual hang-ups do not just relate to the act of intercourse, but to the basic fact of being a man or woman inherent in our existence as a person in a gendered body.

> **People lacking the foundation of their male/female archetype cannot withstand the weight of their dharma type.**

As we noted, adolescent boys and girls ideally evolve into men and women through a process of instruction and initiation by their elders. In societies where this structure is nonexistent or poorly defined, men and women tend to enact the symptoms of stunted growth through immature and inappropriate behavior well into their adult years.

LEAN BACK, STEP IN: THE WARRIOR'S ROLE

So how does an evolved man behave? Kerry Riley, in *Tantric Secrets for Men*, says that women look for "a man with spine and an open heart." To demonstrate these, you have to consider how integrated Warriors face challenges, standing tall to assess them, leaning back to consider their options, then moving in to resolve them. *Lean back and step in* is the mantra for the Warrior type, and for every man who wants to embody his masculinity.

What does this mean? *Lean back* means to relax and observe, knowing you're in control. Warriors who know themselves don't need to lean in to get meaning from their partner, their boss, or anyone else. When people lean toward others, they give away energy; by contrast, leaning back collects it. But that is only the first step. The second step is taking action. If you only lean back, you become aloof, uninvolved, uncaring. By stepping in you demonstrate that you care, that you are engaged with reality.

In the face of a woman yelling at him, in the face of interpersonal problems, household chores, or work obligations, the evolved man stands firm, leans back while listening to his beloved, and steps forward to address her concerns. A Warrior never runs, unless all other options have been exhausted. Heading for the door to go to the bar, be with your friends, or just take a walk is never the first step. It is always a sign of weakness, of immaturity. By leaning back you allow space for a woman to be heard and demonstrate that you're listening. You create a safe atmosphere for the problem to come to the surface. And by stepping in you show your commitment to address the problem and resolve it. It is not so important that you know what to say: your actions communicate what words can't. A woman doesn't want you to fix her; she wants your presence and attention. Stepping in to face her creates intimacy, a powerful force that strengthens relationships.

By being present, facing her squarely with feet forward (do not turn to the side or let your feet point in another direction; that signals that you're not really listening), you show her that you are willing to stand up for yourself and fight for the relationship. And this may be just the beginning: if the situation is bad, she is likely to intensify her testing in the form of yelling, crying, or otherwise trying to break you down to see if you will stand firm. That is to be expected. The only way to pass the tests is to be genuine and continue stepping into the argument. This does not mean showing force or physical intimidation; just the opposite. Warriors evolve into Educators, which means they become calm and peaceful, like the eye of a hurricane, even when everything around them is spinning out of control. The image of a martial arts master poised in quiet contemplation is a good visual for the true Warrior and masculine man who knows when to fight and when to negotiate.

Show her that you are willing to do what it takes to resolve the problem. If she's being irrational, you can give her space by saying, "I will give you a few minutes to settle down because we're not really having a discussion anymore. I'll be back in thirty minutes so we can talk further." This way if you leave, you're not running, you're leaving with a purpose, which is to heal your relationship.

This kind of chivalry, like opening doors or walking on the traffic side of the sidewalk, shows with your body language what you could never convey with words—that you are there for her when she needs you. Remember, the Warrior's role is to protect others, and being reliable and present are among the best ways to demonstrate your Warrior quality.

EMBRACE AND SUPPORT: THE LABORER'S ROLE

One image of the male/female dynamic is that of the tree and the vine. The first embodies the male principle—a stiff, strong

Warrior, reaching straight for the sky. The second is the sinuous and beautiful vine that wraps her arms and legs around the tree, making it stand out, giving it purpose and value, and supporting its growth. Nature and the feminine principle are curvy; the masculine principle is straight and direct. One role of mature shakti and the Laborer type is to recognize the growth potential in any living creature, including a woman's partner, family, and coworkers, and to bring this potential to the surface, to bring out and encourage the best in people. This is a sign of real devotion and mature femininity.

Laborers and women create value. Studies routinely show that married men live longer, make more money, are healthier, and have higher social standing than their single-guy counterparts. This is in large part because their wives transfer this shakti—the ability to embrace and support—to them, though women may have careers of their own. If this happens naturally, imagine what you could do if you cultivated that quality consciously. Ask the question, "How can I serve and support?" Not from a subservient point of view, but from the orientation that if you bring out the best in someone, your relationship with that person grows deeper and more meaningful. There is great nobility in service, which is why the Japanese respect the person who bows lowest!

> **The power of a woman's love conquers all enemies, just as a black hole consumes all energies.**

The Laborer is associated with the Earth element and its force of gravity. The more dense matter becomes, the more powerful its attractive force. Ultimately, the final expression of the Earth element and gravity itself is the formation of a black hole, the organizing principle of galaxies and star systems. The power of the Laborer's love is the organizing principle that brings family and community together and overcomes any obstacle. Warrior men may be an irresistible force, but the power of Laborer women's love is truly an immovable object, swallowing everything and transforming it into light. That is why the feminine principle is portrayed as a goddess who slays the demons of this world—hatred, jealousy, aggression—with grace and even humor. The power of her love conquers all enemies, just as a black hole consumes all energies.

The divine mother in Vedic cosmology has many faces, three of which are Lakshmi, Sarasvati, and Kali. You don't always have to create value with your physical presence (Lakshmi); you can do it with wisdom and words (Sarasvati); or power, leadership, and intention (Kali). The form of the goddess you take in relation to a man, your children, and your society depends on the situation and your personality. Allowing yourself to be the goddess you are is the first step to embodying your femininity. Recognize that you are inherently valuable by virtue of your gender and that you transfer value to whomever you share feelings and time with. Understand the precious treasure that you are custodian of, your femininity, and use it wisely; it can and does change the world.

One recommendation on how to do this comes from Vedic scriptures: if you can see everyone younger than you as a son or daughter, everyone your age as a brother or sister, and everyone older as a parent, you are on the path to the real feminine. Or, you can see everyone—even the elderly—as your children, because no one cares more for another human being than a mother.

ROLE-PLAYING IN THE BEDROOM

Sex is one of the easiest and most natural ways for a couple to get in touch with their basic Warrior-Laborer archetypes. But what if a woman is a Warrior dharma type? How does she translate this into the bedroom?

> **A violent man is not a Warrior, but a boy in a man's body
> who cannot control himself.**

Understanding your role leads to happiness. In some part of a woman's life she has to feel her Laborer side come out, just as a man must let his Warrior shine. How and where we do this is up to us, but the bedroom is the most natural place. Even the most mild-mannered man becomes a penetrator during sex, and the toughest of women the penetrated. Men have a need to penetrate and conquer and with no other outlets this can take the form of playing violent video games until midnight, playing golf on the weekend, or getting into fights or engaging in other unruly behavior. A violent man is not a Warrior, but a boy in a man's body who cannot control himself.

Some men go in the other direction and zone out on TV, beer, pot, or just by becoming emotionally unavailable. These are not evolved Warrior behaviors, but coping mechanisms for repressed Warrior energy.

Spicing Up the Missionary Position

Missionary (with the man on top) is the most natural position for sex, and the most common. However, it can become dull if it becomes routine. Here are some ways to spice up this classic to create wild orgasms for the woman and deep satisfaction for the man.

Starting from the missionary position, the man can place one or both hands under a woman's buttocks (she may need to lift her hips up slightly to let his hand ease beneath her). This tilts the man down and pulls her hips up toward him, connecting her clitoris with his pubic bone. The woman can place her heels on his calves, bringing them even closer together. Thrusting is limited here, but the intimacy created by this position, and the angle of the penis inside her, can stimulate points that regular missionary cannot reach and create powerful orgasms.

A more exotic variation goes like this: From the missionary, the man comes up into a kneeling position. Bringing the woman's legs up, he crosses them and places them on his shoulders (if possible). Crossing her legs while he's inside her creates tightness and penetrates deep while stimulating her G-spot. He can then push down on the back of her legs as he thrusts. This is highly arousing and can lead into other positions like the one detailed above.

WITHHOLDING SEX

Men equate sex with love; women equate love with intimacy. By withholding intimacy, closeness, and attention from their mates, men deny them love and support. By withholding sex from their mates, women deny them love and nurturing. When men work long hours and plop down in front of the TV without acknowledging their partners, they do themselves and their relationships a disservice. By putting things like the ball game above their beloved, they cut off the flow of intimacy, which signals to a woman that they do not love her anymore. This is not usually what men mean to convey, but it is the message a woman receives.

As a result, women reply by withholding sex, consciously or not. Because they are not feeling loved and nurtured by the man's genuine attention and presence, they do not warm up to him as fast, and their sexual passions cool. After marriage or in long-term relationships, men expect sex as a matter of course. But this expectation devalues their partners. Women and Laborers are associated with the Earth element and the Sanskrit word *artha*, which denotes wealth, meaning, and value. According to the Brihat Samhita, a woman's shakti is the most valuable force in the universe. Men should consider how hard they worked for sex early in the relationship to earn this shakti.

They gave their partner massages, sang her songs, and took her dancing, all ways of lavishing attention on and valuing her. There is no
reason this should stop after the relationship is established. Warriors
are ruled by the Fire element and fire relates to sight. A woman needs
to feel seen by the man in her life to feel loved.

> **Presence, not presents, is the greatest gift a man can give to
> foster intimacy and a fulfilling sex life.**

But for women, refusing sex is not the answer. Because sex is so
often tantamount to love for a man, refusing to give him sex is con-
strued as withholding love, and when a woman withholds love, her
relationship is headed for failure. Instead, show him how to turn you
on and earn sex from you by honoring your value. Most women know
what would make them feel special, and it's usually not material gifts.
Presence, not presents, is the greatest gift a man can give to foster
intimacy and a fulfilling sex life.

THE COSMIC PAIR

From the standpoint of evolutionary biology, females choose males
who are strong and capable of taking care of their offspring. From
the view of spiritual biology, women seek men who can transcend
their base instincts and demonstrate emotional and psychological
self-control. A man may be strong enough to conquer rivals for a
woman's affection but not evolved enough to conquer his own pet-
tiness, anger, or jealousy, and may thereby fail to keep a woman. The
energy women share with men is the hardest energy for them to control, because women embody nature itself. That is why a man must
learn to dwell in the only force that transcends nature: consciousness.

While primordial woman embodies nature—Shakti, the energy
of manifest creation—primordial man represents Shiva, pure con-

sciousness, the seed-giving Father, the indestructible, immutable backbone of the universe. Shiva and Shakti, consciousness and energy, are two aspects of God that represent the Unmanifest and the Manifest Divine. Shiva is silent, eternal, unmoving, while Shakti dances with the orders of creation.

The Cosmic Pair

Shakti	Shiva
Nature	Consciousness
Changeable	Eternal
Female Divine	Male Divine

Here, irresistible force meets immovable object. Is it any wonder that the ancients devised the moon and sun to represent these archetypes? One constantly transmutes her form, the other is fixed and solid, a source of strength and life. The sun gives the moon his light, expecting nothing in return. The moon adorns herself in that light, donning a different gown as she walks every night through the mansions of the sky. They complement each other as rulers of the night and day: hers, the domain of plants, nature, dreams, and fantasy; his, the harsh light of reality. The spiritual metaphors of sun and moon, day and night, extend to describe the universe itself in the understanding of our ancestors.

The sun stands for Reality, Spirit, the Divine. The changeable moon represents the paradox of manifest reality. Bound by time, though never ending; physically immanent, though ultimately unreal, she is called *maya*, illusion, like a chair that looks solid, though at the molecular level it is 99 percent empty space. She is the womb, he the seed-giving Father: they are both immortal, beginningless, and primordial. The Mother is beloved, the Father respected. Both are necessary for our survival. Both exist as archetypes we can look up to, since so very few of us had ideal parents of our own.

THE ROLE OF GRANDPARENTS

One reason families break up and children are raised without fathers is that men feel their Warrior purpose threatened by the impending need to raise a family. A man's mission must come before everything else if he is to fulfill the basic requirements of his Warrior masculinity. When he has no help in shouldering the burden of raising children, he may opt to leave. As a result, many children grow up with emotionally or physically unavailable fathers. Unfortunately, this feeds a vicious cycle in which those children, when they're grown, may abandon their own family responsibilities. Yet knowing why men leave is useless if we cannot offer a solution. That solution lies beyond the basic husband/wife dynamic to include grandparents and other family members in the rearing of children.

In traditional communities, extended families usually live together as large units. It is not uncommon for three generations to cohabit under one roof, or in the same family compound. Today, the Western emphasis on independence is ripping families apart. The mistaken notion that independence is a mark of maturity is a major reason for high divorce rates and many relationship difficulties. Our elders, in the Autumn of their lives, have no greater purpose than to enrich the next generation with their wisdom. It is only later, in the Winter of life, that they may opt for isolation and asceticism.

> **The mistaken notion that independence is a mark of maturity is a major reason for high divorce rates and many relationship difficulties.**

Because they have had a chance to lead their lives to the fullest (having had help in raising their own kids); because they possess greater wisdom, patience, and experience; and because it is their role to impart these qualities to future generations, grandparents are ideally suited to help raise grandkids, and to give their own children the freedom to fulfill their individual destinies. Just because a man and a woman have a baby does not mean that their personal evolution is over. In fact, it is just beginning: the process of raising a family should never stand in the way of fulfilling one's personal, worldly, and spiritual dharmas. Romance does not end with the birth of kids. That is why grandparents are crucial to an integral family unit.

Family elders are uniquely suited to share their lessons with the next generation. Having up to four grandparents, as well as aunts and uncles, presents diverse opportunities for children to grow up more well rounded than when they are raised by one or two parents alone. For grandparents, Autumn season is the perfect time to give back, to become jewels of wisdom and compassion to their grandkids. Elders who have the resources to enjoy their lives may rightly feel they have earned their freedom.

> **Romance does not end with the birth of kids. That is why grandparents are crucial to an integral family unit.**

Hard work over forty years to earn a retirement check indeed merits the rewards of freedom and leisure. But that does not mean that these should be squandered. The time to go bungee-jumping is early in one's life; the time to impart wisdom and experience is during the later years. That is not to say that older people cannot have fun. Giving back to their families and feeling not only needed but indispensable are enormously gratifying and do not have to take up their entire schedule. People in the Autumn phase of life may enjoy themselves with travel and leisure when they like, as long as they remain rooted in the family tree and continue to adorn and nourish it with their wisdom.

SEX AND SPIRIT

In the material world, the biological realities of sex, food, and sleep rule our lives. Obtaining food, shelter, and a partner for procreation are the major drives of the human animal, no different in the twenty-first century than they were ten thousand years ago. We work to procure the basic elements of our survival and competition is common, since material resources are limited: the laws of natural selection work just as well in the urban jungle as in the jungles of the wild. The strongest survive and the weakest perish, or at least make do with a lesser-quality existence. These laws are nowhere more apparent than in the body's drives to reproduce and in human sexual relations.

Human sexual behavior is driven by attraction. Eben Pagan, aka David DeAngelo, coined the phrase *attraction isn't a choice*.[1] Attraction is a biological response to potentially valuable qualities in a mate. A woman's body seeks out strength, status, and virility in a man, among other things, while a man's biology is drawn toward physical beauty and signs of fertility in his female partners. As long as the partner provides these, men and women are content to stay in relationships; when these are lacking the human body begins to search for alternatives in other partners, no matter what the domestic situation or how long a couple has been together. These drives are unconscious; you cannot choose who you are attracted to, it just happens. . . . Or does it?

The mechanics of attraction are just as instinctual and predictable in humans as in all animals. When its needs for attraction are not being met, the body may convince the conscious mind that a relationship "is just not going well and needs to end." It becomes restless to find a magic spark with someone else. That magic spark, or chemistry, is nothing more than our biology attracting what we need in the biology of another. Whether it is a strong male who will take care of her kids, for a woman, or a fertile female who will produce children, for a man, humans share these basic drives with other creatures in the animal kingdom. What they don't share with animals is the spiritual side of relationships.

Humans have attempted to spiritualize relationships through institutions like marriage for eons. Marriage brings God into the equation to help couples overcome the natural biological drives that lead to infidelity. Marriage is an agreement whereby both parties pledge to transcend their biological needs in the name of a higher ideal. That higher ideal is the spiritual union that is sanctified by the marriage vow. Unfortunately, most people are unaware of the powerful forces hardwired in their bodies, and fall victim to the influence of those forces. But a man who is in touch with his body's programming, who fulfills his dharma, and who understands the constant testing of women is better equipped to draw on his innate skills in the face of adversity, and thereby keep a marriage together.

In the same way, when a woman understands the power of her femininity, her shakti, and the immense treasure she is guardian of, she can build up a man, rather than destroy him, and strengthen the glue that holds them together, because the only outcome of destroying her partner is to abandon the relationship and find a new one. This is the most notable quality of a fully evolved woman: she works to keep the crucible of a relationship intact and to strengthen the family bond, rather than weaken it. Evolved women have a power of attraction, of cohesion, that is almost overwhelming. They possess a gravity that keeps all elements of their world harmoniously spinning about them. They are a smart glue that bonds anything they wish to them, but does not stick to things that they do not want. Girls, by contrast, lack this "smart bond" quality. They are a runny, undefined substance that sticks everywhere indiscriminately. They have not developed the awesome gravity of their shakti, but instead fly errantly through the universe in search of a planetary system to call their own.

> **When a woman understands the power of her femininity, her shakti, and the immense treasure she is guardian of, she can build up a man, rather than destroy him.**

Women are the treasure keepers. They hold the secrets of the kingdom. A man's challenge is to find and unlock that treasure. This is the inner meaning of the dragon myths of yore, where a hero rides to slay the beast and claim its treasures. The drama unfolds simultaneously on the physical, emotional, and spiritual levels. Dragons represent the tests men must face to prove their worth. These include the female body itself, which is a wonder to make sense of, as well as the emotional and mental challenges posed by her femininity. The cave is the physical womb, where a man must "die"* in order to create new life, but also the crucible of their relationship, where each of us gives of ourselves in order to create something higher. The treasure within is the secret shakti that a woman is privy to, often unbeknownst to her conscious self, and that a man can access too if he knows how.

These themes are the basis of tantric sexuality. In tantra, as in the dragon myths of legend, the sex act is often an external allegory to an internal, alchemical event. Tantra is no more a license to unrestricted sex than the epic of *Beowulf* is a sanction to slaughter and plunder. Central to each myth is the ritualized journey that has as its end the enrichment of the world. And one doesn't have to be a tantric or a Taoist master to reap the benefits of this alchemy. Anyone who has been in love and worked to maintain a

---

*It is no wonder that the term for orgasm/ejaculation in French is *la petite morte*—"the little death." Ayurveda and traditional Chinese medicine would even consider this phrase to be literally true, inasmuch as it depicts the outflow of a man's very life essence.

relationship knows its benefits: married people make more money, live longer, and experience less depression than singles. And these are just the tip of the iceberg. Once couples have refined themselves, having whetted the keen edge of their spirit upon each other, no enemy can withstand their collective force and no hardship can rip them asunder. This is because love transcends biology; it is the spiritual substance of the marriage vow, and what makes the struggle to overcome the physical limits of our animal selves worthwhile.

Love is the matrix wherein the paradox of opposites becomes a dance, more artful than any conceived-of human thought, subtler than the microcosm of subatomic life, and more inscrutable than the cosmic mysteries of the stars and heavens. The love bond between two people, like the unfathomable black hole at the center of our galaxy, becomes the powerful organizing principle of culture and society.

GURU-DISCIPLE

There are no secular solutions to issues that are essentially spiritual. There is no political, psychological, or societal remedy for the one deficiency that is at the core of our delusion: self-ignorance. That is why spirituality, and its organized cousin, religion, have been and will continue to be the greatest self-help methods in the world—because they factor into the equation our spiritual component.

According to Vedic traditions, *avidya*, ignorance, is the primal human failing from which springs all secondary evils, such as pride, fear, lust, jealousy, and the like. The job of dispelling ignorance falls to the gurus and elders, the wisdomkeepers of our culture, which is why it is so important to have rituals set up to recognize these elders in our society. It is up to them to initiate future generations, train them, and transmit knowledge to them, starting at a young age and all the way through to adulthood. The dharma types are central to this aim, as they cut across religious and social boundaries to a person's essence.

The most important thing one can do in learning to become an evolved and fulfilled man or woman is to find a teacher, a mentor, a guru. Seminars, schools, and lectures serve that purpose in the Western world today. But in India, the Vedic tradition of the guru-disciple relationship is very much still alive. At the appropriate age, boys are sent away to study with their gurus for up to twelve years at a time. In this way they are initiated into maturity and spiritual masculinity. There is no way for those who don't know how to do this to initiate themselves. There is no way to cross the gap from boy to man without the example of an older man to guide the way. There is no way for those who do not have the light to make a fire themselves. The spark must be transmitted, person to person, in order for the world to know light. The age we live in is called the Dark Age not because we lack technology to light the night, but because we lack the wisdom to illuminate the inner spaces of the soul.

This section began with an invocation of oral traditions and sacred knowledge. It must end with the note that all sacred knowledge is hidden from the eyes of the uninitiated. That does not mean that all of us have to undergo initiations and rituals. It may simply entail sitting at the feet of mentors who gradually open up the wisdom of the world to us. It is only then that we can become teachers ourselves, for only one who has seen the light can testify to others of its splendor.

> The age we live in is called the Dark Age not because we lack technology to light the night, but because we lack the wisdom to illuminate the inner spaces of the soul.

When we understand the principles of nature, we can use them to enhance our lives rather than denying our vitality, as we do when we adopt unskilled attitudes toward sex and life. This is the purpose of the science of life—ayurveda—and other sacred traditions that have withstood the test of time: to unite us with the laws of nature for lasting satisfaction in the material world and the subtler realms of the spirit. Just as physics and mathematics are complementary disciplines, ayurveda, vastu shastra, jyotisha, and the dharma types are sister sciences, because these all hearken back to the Vedas, the great progenitors of wisdom on the Indian subcontinent. Yet wisdom does not just belong to India. The word *veda* comes from *vid*, which means to know. Thus, veda is knowledge in any tradition, be it the Ifa customs of Nigeria or the Kabbalistic wisdom of the Middle East. Veda is available to all of us at any time, provided our minds are cultured and ready to receive it.

Oil Is Love—
Castor Oil for Female Health

Castor oil can work miracles for women suffering from abdominal pain, premenstrual syndrome (PMS), fibrous or tender breasts, or uterine stagnation. Warm castor oil packs on the abdomen encourage healthy, pain-free periods; reduce congestion; alleviate discomfort associated with endometriosis; and improve reproductive health.

How Does It Work?

Castor oil has been used safely for thousands of years, both internally as a laxative and externally for massage, especially as a lymph mover. Castor oil has the special properties of producing a slow, sustained heat when applied externally, but it has a cooling effect when used internally. It is an ingredient in ayurvedic arthritis and pain formulas, and is effective externally for painful areas, lumps, cysts, and tumors.* Castor oil is used to treat extreme dryness of the skin, and one to two drops can even be put into the eyes before bed to treat dry eyes, styes, conjunctivitis and for overall eye health. One of its main uses is for alleviating abdominal pain and cramping.

Contraindications: Castor oil should not be used internally during pregnancy, as it may induce delivery. Castor oil packs should also not be used by pregnant women externally.

Also, though the denatured and pressed oil is harmless, the whole seed of the castor plant is exceedingly toxic, as it contains ricin, a deadly poison. Harvesting castor beans has potentially damaging effects on workers who cultivate them, and for this reason some people may choose not to use castor oil. In this case, sesame oil is a good replacement for the abdominal packs described below.

How Do I Do It?

You will need a flannel or wool cloth and a hot water bottle to make this castor oil pack. Begin by massaging warmed castor oil on your abdomen. (To warm the oil, put hot water in a container and place the bottle in it for five to ten minutes.) Next, put some oil on the flannel cloth: don't soak it; just place enough on the cloth to cover it. Place this cloth, oil side down, on your belly. It is useful to put a plastic bag over the cloth so it protects your clothes from the oil. Then, place a hot water bottle on the plastic bag. Do not use electric blankets; these are not suitable for this purpose. Finally, put a folded towel over the hot water bottle to hold in the heat. Leave it on while reading, relaxing, or even watching TV.

Hold the pack for sixty to ninety minutes every day, except during your menses. Continue after bleeding has stopped. Practice this for a total of at least thirty days. After thirty days of applica-

---

*Sebastian Pole, *Ayurvedic Medicine: The Principles of Traditional Practice* (Philadelphia: Singing Dragon, 2013).

tion you can reduce the frequency of use to two to three times a week, depending on how you feel. This method has worked wonders for women suffering from PMS symptoms and general stagnation, but you have to stick with the routine to see results. It's okay to miss a day here and there, but continue until you feel the stagnation significantly lessened. In some cases this may mean even two months of application.

Your first period may be more intense after applying castor oil packs; this is because stagnation is clearing out from the uterus. Stick with it and you will see the benefits.

Castor Oil Internally

A week to ten days before your period, you can take four teaspoons of castor oil mixed with orange juice (or any juice except grape juice) on an empty stomach to help clear out gastric congestion. Do this once a month for up to six months, but no more; otherwise you may develop a laxative dependency. Try not to eat until this has produced one or two bowel movements.*

One-half to one teaspoon of castor oil can also be mixed into shakes and food daily for its joint-protecting properties. Make sure that it's not producing a laxative effect. If it is, lower the dosage. This is a great way to keep your joints healthy and lubricated.

CCF Oil

For fibrocystic changes in the breast or for breast tenderness, massage with CCF, an equal blend of corn, castor, and flax oils. Alternatively, you can just use castor oil, but it is more viscous and may be harder to spread. Warm the oil and massage the breasts from the inside out; that is, from the sternum out to the armpits,

---

*Dr. John Douillard's Life Spa, www.lifespa.com/support-for-a-healthy-menstrual-cycle.

then below the breasts and around the nipples. This should be done before a warm shower or before bed.*

Note: Never warm oil in a microwave! Put your oil bottle in the sink and fill the sink with hot water. Or fill a vessel with hot water and leave your bottle there for five to ten minutes.

Castor oil and flannel cloth come prepackaged for this purpose from the Ayurvedic Institute (www.ayurveda.com). Hot water bottles are available at your local pharmacy.

---

*Dr. Vasant Lad, B.A.Sc., *The Complete Book of Ayurvedic Home Remedies* (New York: Harmony Books, 1998).

8

Sex in a Sacred Society

A Modern Application of
Traditional Sexual Initiations

The term *sacred society,* as I use it here, does not refer to a particular place or time in history, but to how people can organically evolve, guided by the precepts of natural law. Many current and ancient societies practice or practiced some of the principles I'll describe in this chapter. It is up to us to use in our own lives those tools we deem valuable from this chapter while leaving what's unnecessary behind.

> **"One should save money against hard times, save one's spouse at the sacrifice of riches, and invariably one should save one's soul even at the sacrifice of spouse and riches."**
>
> **CHANAKYA, NITI SHASTRA**

A society, like a person, has a dharma. There are principles that govern the evolution of culture, just as there are laws governing the growth of plants in nature. It is the role of a society to serve as a crucible for the evolution of its members by promoting their dharmas at every level, including gender and dharma type. Here we shall take a look at how such a society would encourage its members to express and grow into their sexuality.

203

A YOUNG MAN'S EDUCATION

Ideally, when young men reach maturity in a sacred society they are initiated into sexual awareness by their female elders. This becomes the first step in turning them into mature men. Around their sexual peak, they may be instructed in the art of lovemaking by women who are themselves experienced and know how to guide them.

The first stage of life is called *brahmacharya*, the Spring season that corresponds to about the first twenty years of life. During this time, boys follow a path of strict celibacy (brahmacharya) to minimize distraction from their studies. For this to happen, however, there must be little or no contact with girls, and limited sensory stimulation. *Brahmacharis* (celibates, or boys in the Spring season of life) are enjoined to follow strict rules of conduct. Here is an example, from the Code of Manu:

> The Brahmachari should take a bath daily, not use oils, salves, or perfumes; he should not wear flowers or ornaments, or participate in music and dance; he should not have shoes on his feet nor use an umbrella; he should not sleep on a cot or gamble; he should not look at women, talk to them, or even talk about them. He should be regular and simple in his diet, should not wear soft clothes, should worship gods and rishis and serve and adore his preceptor. He should not enter into disputes, nor speak ill of others; he should always speak the truth, should not insult another, and practice complete nonviolence. He should totally renounce lust, anger, and greed, sleep alone, and never allow any loss of the vital fluid.

These rules were put in place to ensure that boys in the Spring season of life retained their vitality and therefore their ability to mature physically, emotionally, and psychologically into well-integrated men. But the codes and regulations of one age cannot be literally imposed on another without an understanding of their underlying principles. The laws of Manu were made for cultures radically different from our own. Today it is more difficult for boys to abstain from sex and masturbation because it is the dharma of a Merchant society to be as visually stimulating as possible, and kids are overwhelmed with sexually charged images from the Internet, television, and the music world on a daily basis. It is all right to maintain celibacy as long as our environment supports us, but when this becomes impossible, it is better to express than to repress our sexual impulses.

Spiritual principles may be perverted into social and political customs that do not honor, but rather oppress women, and degrade the men who practice those oppressive customs. We need to maintain the sanctity of spiritual principles even as we adapt them to contemporary society. Where practicable, it is all right to abide by the letter of the law, but usually reinterpretation is in order. That is why saints and mystics continually offer ways to reform our spiritual and social systems.

> "Brahmacharya is not a virtue that can be cultivated by outward restraints. He who runs away from a necessary contact with a woman does not understand the full meaning of brahmacharya. However attractive a woman may be, her attraction will produce no effect on the man without the urge."
>
> GANDHI

In our contemporary culture, it is wiser to teach boys how to cultivate sexuality than to force them to repress it for arcane reasons. It is more advisable to train them in the proper expression of their sexual impulses than to leave them with no education, grasping at straws to figure it out for themselves. They cannot learn how to become mature, sexually aware men unless they're properly taught, and many men spend futile years of trial and error attempting to grasp the nuances of mature masculinity.

A sacred society should respect the natural cycle of the Spring season, allowing brahmacharya, abstinence, until boys are at their sexual peak, and training them in the arts of love when they are most ready and willing to learn. This prepares them for the next season, during which they become family men and householders and have to use what they have learned every day not only to survive, but to maintain lasting relationships with their spouses, children, and peers.

> **"He that's always thinking of chastity will be always thinking of women."**
>
> SIR ISAAC NEWTON

Adolescent boys in any society instinctively pick up on the need to train themselves sexually during their later Spring years. Lacking sacred institutions, they may secretly accumulate their own knowledge through pornography, masturbation, and self-generated fantasies. It is difficult to resist the modern temptations of a sexually charged culture, and masturbation is an easy outlet for unreciprocated impulses. But this need not be the case. A society that provides an outlet for young men at their hormonal peak, by pairing them with women who are themselves ready and willing to train them in the arts of lovemaking and interacting kindly and gently with the opposite sex, pays dividends in the long run for both men and women.

THE VENUSIAN ARTS

A man cannot learn how to touch a woman from reading magazines or watching movies. The Venusian arts of foreplay, romance, and lovemaking are best taught to a man by a woman, just as the martial arts should be learned from another man. Some techniques for attracting women and for performing in the bedroom can also be learned from experienced male elders. But one-on-one training and experience with a woman is invaluable, because through experience a man acquires confidence, and confidence in the bedroom can spill out to many area of a man's life. Knowing that you know how to touch a woman and bring her to ecstasy promotes a kind of self-esteem that permeates everything you do and is easily perceived by others. Men and women both sense this type of capable self-assuredness and respond to it with attraction. Men want to be you, and women want to be with you, and they often don't know why.

> **Through experience a man acquires confidence, and confidence in the bedroom spills out into almost any area of a man's life. Knowing that you know how to touch a woman and bring her to ecstasy promotes a kind of self-esteem that permeates almost everything else you do.**

By training mature young men in the Venusian arts, women do themselves and society a favor. They make men better husbands and lovers without the entanglements of misguided love. This type of training is not about love, but rather sexual desire and the interplay of men and women as sexual partners. Young men often become infatuated with older women, because this reflects nature's urge in them to be trained. When properly done, this training can lead them to become the role models society wants them to be. It is safer for adolescent boys to have an outlet for their hormonally charged instincts in a female mentor than to repress those instincts. A look at the violence perpetrated by young men with no viable expression for their passions testifies to this. In contemporary society, sexual initiation is more important than it was in previous ages, because it teaches adolescent boys proper self-expression, respect for women, and crucial relationship skills that we are sorely lacking as a society.

In addition, girls their age are safer when lust is taken out of the equation and boys can assume their natural role as protectors of the feminine, becoming the gentlemen that society and their parents want them to be, rather than the rascals and exploiters they sometimes degenerate into when no such outlets exist. How often have we seen fathers being overprotective of their teenage daughters, because they know all too well the mental states of their younger male counterparts? When a young man's needs for intimacy are met in training, he is less likely to demand sex from girls his own age. Then, it is easier to just be friends with his female peers, and social interactions become more natural and less angst ridden.

Acceptance by the opposite sex is a major motivator for teenagers—both in the hope for gain as well as the fear of loss. The desire to belong and the stress of not belonging are two key drivers of teenage psychology. When these are addressed early on, the anxiety they generate can be defused. Young people can avoid the stunted emotional growth that results when a preponderance of energy and time are invested in being accepted. Young men are freed from desire, and young women no longer have to beat away their unwanted advances. Fathers can also put away their baseball bats and rely on adolescent males to be the chivalrous young men they are meant to be.

This practice allows girls to remain chaste, releasing them from the nuisance of managing the charged emotional states of their male counterparts. Women so often find themselves emotionally babysitting men; this is not what they want to do. Most women are looking for men with a grasp of the world, not boys in men's bodies. But this is what they get when men are not allowed to evolve into exemplary embodiments of their gender. Besides the freedoms of life and liberty, the privilege to mature sexually is a basic right fulfilled by few. That is because the instruction and structure needed to guide men and women along that path is not available in most societies, so young people are left to fend for themselves.

That is not to say that all young men must engage in this type of sex education. Like conscription into the army, this is not for everyone. Some young men may choose abstinence, or may opt for early marriage, while others may choose partners their own age for their sexual initiation. Whatever the case, it is the role of a sacred society to provide the opportunity for the training of young men in interpersonal relations by female elders, whether these young men avail themselves of it or not.

Male Masturbation

In the absence of opportunities for training in intimacy, adolescent boys often turn to masturbation, which has been around since humans first discovered sexuality. Egyptian Pharoahs were at one time required to masturbate ceremonially into the Nile, to ensure the fertility of its lands.[1] More recently, studies report that over 90 percent of men and 40 to 60 percent of women have masturbated in their life.* Other studies show medical benefits to masturbation, including relief from depression, high blood pressure, and stress, and the practice is generally recommended by the medical profession to adults and teens as a way to express sexual tension without the risk of pregnancy or sexually transmitted diseases.†

In ayurveda and other Asian traditions, however, it is not considered wise to waste one's *shukra,* for this diminishes vital energy. Masturbation and orgasm are depleting for both sexes, though more so for men, who are not advised to masturbate unless built-up sexual tension risks ill health, mental anguish, or violence. Human

---

*For a great resource on masturbation for parents and teens, visit the University of Michigan Health System website: www.med.umich.edu/yourchild/topics/masturb .htm. For more sex statistics visit the Kinsey institute website: www.kinseyinstitute .org/resources/FAQ.html.

†For more on this study see "Happy News! Masturbation Actually Has Health Benefits" at http://theconversation.com/happy-news-masturbation-actually-has-health-benefits-16539.

companionship is almost always a better alternative. But where to draw the line between what is healthy and what is depleting, between modern science and ancient wisdom, is sometimes difficult, especially in our overstimulated culture, where access to pornography and sexually charged images is as easy as the click of a mouse.

> "In masturbation there is nothing but loss. There is no reciprocity. There is merely the spending away of a certain force, and no return. The body remains, in a sense, a corpse, after the act of self-abuse. There is no change, only deadening."
>
> D. H. LAWRENCE

Understanding the nature of your dharma type comes in handy in this case. Outsiders typically need more freedom to express themselves, and masturbation is a natural part of such expression. It can be a source of stress relief for the naturally anxious Outsider, or those who find themselves in Outsider life cycles. Educators, who tend to be secretly lusty, may also need to self-gratify to keep from transgressing social boundaries or degenerating into perversion. However, like Gandhi, they may also take the road of celibacy in an attempt to control the fires of their lust.

Merchants, who may be hedonistic by nature, may experiment with masturbation as a source of pleasure, though less so than Outsiders and even Educators, since they typically have access to more sources of diversion than any other type. Finally, Warriors and Laborers should masturbate less than their fellow dharma types, because their active, physical natures provide other outlets for stress relief and require them to be physically strong and ready to work.

Masturbation teaches men little in the way of how to please a woman, and is of little use when it comes to finding the woman of their dreams and successfully partnering with her. Better to train young men in the nuances of intimacy than to nurture empty solo fantasies, which can cause problems in later life.

"Sexual energy is the reason a human is born, lack of sexual energy is the reason a human dies. Within this sexual energy is the secret not only of health but of immortality as well. In men the secret lies in conservation and retention of sexual energy. In women the secret lies in its development and activity. Lao Tzu himself states, 'The mysterious female is inexhaustible. How the Yellow Emperor achieved immortality and how Western Royal Mother achieved immortality cannot be compared. Each has its own path and seeks the other's essence to become complete.'"

WHITE TIGRESS MANUAL

In the Taoist tradition, the cult of retention is developed to its fullest. There, a man seeks ultimate control of his life energy by regulating the outflow of his semen and thereby gains "immortality." The quote above from the White Tigress Manual also notes the different sexual strategies men and women must implement on the road to immortality, for each has its own path.

RECYCLING SHUKRA AND OJAS

"Do not spill your seed on the ground" is not just a Judeo-Christian imperative. The caveats against a man's loss of his precious fluid are found in many traditions. Ojas is the end product of food, and just as ash is the essence of fire, ojas is the essence of a man or a woman.* Fire reduces fuel to its most rarefied form, and the friction and heat of sex bring out the distilled version of a man's life force,

---

*Ojas is the next stage of refinement after shukra (see sequence on page 244). That is, after food has undergone seven stages of transformation in the human body, from plasma, blood, muscle, fat, bone, and marrow to shukra, it undergoes a final stage, which is turning it into ojas. This is a partly mystical, partly physical component of living beings that confers immunity, intellect, and a palpable glow, visible in pregnant women, charismatic personalities, and saints. Ojas is nourished by natural, undefiled foods, thoughts, and activities; it is depleted by sex, stress, and poor digestion—all the more reason to master the practices in part 1 of this book.

his shukra, and with it its by-product, ojas. Shukra is the physical precursor of this most precious of living essences, and it is vital to retain it if a man wants to preserve his longevity, immunity, and clarity of thought. Ascetics and worshippers place ash from the sacred fire on their bodies to obtain the blessings of a ritual. The same may be done by men who wish to partake in the blessings of the sexual ritual and retain the protection of their essence after they have ejaculated.

This is done by placing some of their ejaculate on their nipples, tongue, perineum, and testicles in order to receive back the essence they have spent. The logic is not hard to follow: recycle the energy lost through the penis by putting it on your body. In ayurveda, the nipples are the root of *shukra vaha srotas*—the pathways of reproductive energy in men. It makes sense that putting a bit of expelled shukra back onto the nipples and testicles after sexual intercourse helps a man feed his reproductive tissues and recover faster. The tongue is a gateway to the mind. Have you ever wondered why a taste of chocolate makes us melt the moment we put it in our mouth? It hasn't had a chance to hit the stomach yet, not to mention be digested, but the receptors on the tongue immediately send signals to the brain to expect what's coming, based on the taste. Our brains react—in this case telling us to close our eyes and delight in theobromine-induced bliss. In the same way, placing some shukra on the tongue helps to recycle its energy and enables men to recover faster from sex.

Though this may not be as effective as not ejaculating in the first place, it at least speeds recovery and prevents the total loss of a man's faculties after sex. When it is impossible to raise one's energy level through spiritual practices, it is better to express that energy than to repress it. If shukra and ojas cannot be sublimated through internal alchemy, they at least can be recycled externally. On the physical level, imbibing a trace of the proteins, zinc, and other nutrients in semen also helps the body to regenerate these faster. But the physical constituent of seminal fluid is only part of the vital essence contained therein. The power to seed life is the greatest gift of nature in a man; to waste this potency is tantamount to *prajna paradha*—a crime against wisdom.

In some Taoist traditions, women are secretly trained in oral sex to receive this energy from a man's orgasm and circulate it throughout their systems. Women can also benefit from a man's ejaculate by rubbing it onto their skin after intercourse; it disappears, leaving no film or trace if spread quickly and vigorously. This practice is nourishing to the skin and the tissues below it, and helps connect a woman to her partner. Taking a man's shukra is not advised, however, if the relationship between the partners is toxic or they are not following a good diet. Men, who have no menstrual period, often

---

Building Ojas

Ojas-building foods and herbs: Dates, unfermented dairy (ice cream, milk, ghee), natural sugar, almonds, coconut, saffron, shatavari (*asparagus racemosus*), aswagandha (*withania somnifera*)

Ojas-building attitudes, emotions, and behaviors: Love, caring for others, living your dharma, meditation, laughing, pranayama, communing with nature, getting adequate sleep (early to bed and early to rise)

Much of the guidance in part one of this book is dedicated to building ojas by helping you follow your dharma, optimize your digestion, breathe for life with pranayama, and organize your day to free yourself from stress. Following the prescriptions in these chapters will build ojas, attract positive new relationships, and revitalize existing ones in your life.

---

cleanse through ejaculation. If a man is angry, abusive, or unclean, it may not be wise to recycle his energy. Taking on a man's shukra will connect you with him. The question is this: Is the man worth it?

SEXUAL DEVELOPMENT IN WOMEN

Young women expect a man to know what to do in bed, and men expect their partners to tell them what they like. Neither can happen if women haven't first discovered their bodies and what makes them feel good, and if men haven't practiced in the bedroom to gain experience. What a sorry state of affairs for young people just entering the romance game. No wonder alcohol, drugs, and other buffers play such a role in early mating rituals; they help erase or make light of the blunders we make during these first fledgling years of sexual activity.

A woman's sexual development is slower and more complex than a man's. While men are encouraged to train in their late teens, women need time to mature and allow their sexual impulses to ripen. Like a complex circuit, a woman's system needs to finish its wiring and is more likely to short if she's initiated into sex too early. This can leave psychological and emotional scars, even if the experience is positive.

Female elders mentor young women in cultivating their femininity. However, this kind of mentoring is less concerned with sexuality than with sensuality. Sex is left for later on, when young women's bodies and minds have matured. Self-exploration through masturbation, dance, yoga, and other disciplines designed to cultivate shakti and femininity is advised, and best learned from other women. This is never a role male elders play. Men stand back and allow young women to blossom and learn from their mothers and female mentors, while remaining pillars of wisdom and virtue for them. It is the job of well-integrated men to serve as role models for girls in society, to show them what proper masculinity looks like. This teaches them to help the men in their own lives—be they brothers, children, or spouses—to become all they can be. There is nothing as inspiring to a man as a shakti-awakened woman; there is nothing as deflating to a man as a woman who never learned how to build cohesive relationships.

Female Masturbation

In contrast to boys, for whom intimacy education is recommended while masturbation is discouraged, for girls finding pleasure through masturbation may be an important step into adulthood. Intercourse should take place much later—another example of the differing paths for men and women. Taking time to explore your body using the self-massage rituals described in chapter 6 (beginning on page 146) is a way for young women to awaken themselves to sexual pleasure long before engaging in any sexual contact with the opposite sex.

Some societies in India still initiate girls into sex through ritual penetration by a shiva lingam—a sacred, phallic embodiment of the Divine. This means that they belong to the Divine first, before they belong to any man. But this kind of solemnized sexual act also gives them a sense of control over their sexuality before they are penetrated by a lover. Ritualized sex with a phallic instrument is a way for women to prepare for intercourse on their own terms.

Before joining with a man, a young woman should be taught to explore her own body and reach bliss by finding her orgasm. Learning to climax is a way to center yourself in your body and connect to your sensuality without the interference of a man. Girls who become sexually aware women are better able to guide their lovers when they finally do have sex, and their experiences can be self-directed and fulfilling, rather than the random, painful interludes that often characterize early sexual experimentation. Lacking this opportunity in early life, women may take it up later, during what's called their sexual peak. But like men in their midlife crisis, this is not the time to begin exploring sexuality, but to master it. And like sex training for young men this is not mandatory—many women will prefer to be initiated into sex by their partners. However, the education and support for young women who want to discover their sensuality early should be available.

A GIRL'S EDUCATION

Starting at a young age, and continuing through their teen years and early twenties, girls in sacred societies learn how to cultivate, shape, and express energy through sacred movement. Shakti needs to dance, and traditional movement practices such as yoga, hula, kathak, and flamenco teach women to harness their passions with a purpose. They also emulate the spiral vortex shape of nature found in galaxies and in our DNA, which helps raise kundalini, the vital spiritual force, and channel it upward. Kundalini is synonymous with shakti and is expressed in the body as creativity and the ability to have children. It is expressed universally as divine radiance or love.

Whereas boys may be drawn to more competitive activities, such as sports, girls tend to benefit from non-goal-oriented communal rituals, including cooking, music, and crafts. That is not to say that girls should not participate in sports, but they should also cultivate soft yin energy in addition to vigorous yang energy. This may seem to perpetuate the myth that a woman's place is in the kitchen, but that is not so.

Cooking, weaving, and dance help generate shakti, and the lessons learned in doing them translate into every area of life, making women more powerful in anything they do. For example, consider that many young men and women today are raised on fast food. This is not only bad for their health, but for their emotional maturity as well. Even when such food is healthy, fast-food culture separates us from our bodies, because our bodies are made of food and when we don't take part in the sensual act of shaping what goes into us, we become desensitized, which negatively affects our ability to be good lovers. Why do you think that the cultures known for their food are also known for having the best lovers? It is no accident that Italy, France, and Spain enjoy such a reputation, because sensuality flows directly from the kitchen to the bedroom.

> Why do you think that the cultures known for making the best food are also known for having the best lovers? It is no accident that Italy, France, and Spain enjoy such a reputation, because sensuality flows from the kitchen into the bedroom.

Just as touch is vital for a newborn baby to survive, bonding with family and friends is crucial for building emotional and psychological maturity. Regularly cooking and dining together with your tribe teaches social connection and creates a model for healthy relationships, one our kids miss because of their addiction to fast food. Short-term convenience is useful in a pinch, but cooking as a family is more than feeding the body; it is a means of sharing love. There is more truth in the cliché "the way to a man's heart is through his stomach" than we would like to admit, because food is life, sex, and vitality, and a woman who can harness the creative energy of food has a distinct advantage when it comes to the other two.

SHAKTI

Shakti is akin to the Hebrew Shekinah: both are feminine nouns that describe the energetic manifestation of divinity. In the Judeo-Christian tradition, it is the Holy Spirit, the dove descending from heaven in biblical imagery. In the Talmud especially, Shekinah refers to the Divine Feminine. It is also one of the names of God in Hebrew, meaning "divine presence or indwelling."

The Wisdom of Solomon

Shekinah is the Supreme Spirit devoted to the good
of all people . . .

She shines bright in the bloom of ignorance; She is unfading;
She is easily seen by those who love Her, easily found
by those who look for Her, and quickly does She come
to those who seek Her help.

One who rises early, intent on finding Her, will not grow weary of
the Quest—for one day he will find Her seated in his own heart.

To set all one's thoughts on Her is true wisdom, and to be ever
aware of Her is the sure way to perfect peace. For Shekinah
Herself goes about in search of those who are worthy of Her.

With every step She comes to guide them; in every thought She
comes to meet them . . . The true beginning of spiritual life is the
desire to know Shekinah.

A desire to know Her brings one to love Her. Loving Her enables
one to follow Her will. Following Her will is the sure path of
immortality. And immortality is oneness with God.

So the desire to know Shekinah leads to God and His Kingdom—a
never-fading Kingdom.

With all your thrones and scepters you may rule the
world for a while, but take hold of Shekinah and you will
rule the world forever.

ANONYMOUS, BUT ATTRIBUTED TO KING SOLOMON

Jesus was frequently equated with shakti, the Holy Spirit, both
by Paul and by John in the Christian scriptures. In this sense he is
the true feminist of the scriptures, for no one can heal or perform
miracles but by abiding in, generating, and transmitting shakti. This
is perhaps the reason that conspiracy theorists to this day conjecture
about his relationship with the women in his life and ministry.

Shakti, like Shekinah, is the shining, dazzling, radiant presence of God, though it is more than just an esoteric concept. Shakti is life energy, without which there would be no manifest existence. It is present everywhere, in everything, and it is especially visible in the generative power of nature. Living things depend on reproduction for their survival. Sex is the engine that drives creation and creativity, and women (the female principle) are keepers of its secret.

A woman's purpose is to understand her shakti, and girls are wise to grasp this early on. On the physical level, this is synonymous with the biological impulses of sexuality and procreation. On the emotional level it relates to faith, passion, compassion, and devotion. And on the spiritual level it refers to love. Thus, women are the teachers of men in these domains, and no man can demonstrate real love, devotion, and virility unless he is initiated into these practices by a woman. This may come by way of the female principle inside him (his own anima, acccording to Carl Jung) or by an actual, physical initiation by a woman. This is part of the reason for the training period suggested earlier for young men. In Kabbalistic circles and the shakta and tantra lineages of India, it is not uncommon for women to initiate men into the secrets of shakti, which is why some claim that Jesus had deeper connections to the females in his ministry than is suggested by the mainstream Gospels.

Abstinence and the Veil

Societies modeled on sacred principles generally support young men and celibates in their commitment to abstinence. One symbol of such practices still in use is the hijab, the veil worn by Muslim women, a nod to the power of a woman's shakti and the spiritual sanctity of the male vow not to violate it.

From before biblical times the wearing of veils has been associated with goodness, nobility, and spirituality in women. Modern Western women still embrace this custom by donning veils for their most momentous life occasions, like funerals and weddings. The lifting of the veil by the groom represents a woman's opening to her husband, both spiritually and sexually. Some contemporary cultures view the unveiling of women to the masses as perverse and sacrilegious.

TEACHING GIRLS TO CULTIVATE A SPIRITUAL PRACTICE

Learning to organize and express energy in functional ways is key to success for young girls, be it in a household, a relationship, or in communion with the Divine. The physical, social, and spiritual are three spheres of integration (see figure 8.1) every human being must develop, and women who do become the glue and the civilizing force in society.

The first is the organization of personal space, so important for day-to-day life. Ayurveda teaches how to care for the space of your

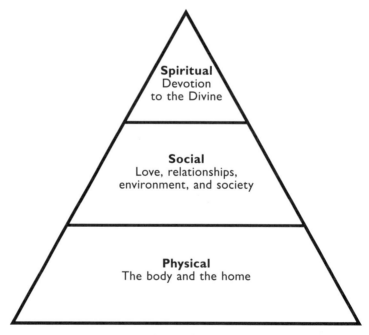

Figure 8.1. Three spheres of integration that every human being must develop

body, and vastu shastra offers powerful analogous techniques for optimizing space, be it in a room, a household, or an entire city. Girls who learn the living lore of traditions like this have significant advantages over their peers, who only rely on instinct or what they learned from their own mothers who were themselves never properly instructed. The Vedic tradition possesses well-founded *kalas*, sacred arts and crafts that turn what we consider everyday activities, like cooking or weaving, into art and magic. As with all sacred traditions, it takes the instruction of a mentor to initiate girls into these kalas.*

> The ability to attract and maintain stable, life-affirming partnerships is a quality of the mature woman, and the inability to do so is a sign of immaturity or incomplete education in women.

But it is not only Vedic lore that weaves the various skills girls require into an overarching culture. The Hawaiian tradition of hula combines dance, song, weaving, storytelling, even cooking and painting together into a community affair. To be a hula dancer is to be a holder of space for your culture and its history. It also means that you learn handicrafts, like making drums or leis, and become a responsible, ethical member of your tribe.

Once girls learn how to handle their personal space, they are taught how to express love and devotion. This encompasses relationships in their community and social circles. The ability to attract and maintain stable, life-affirming partnerships is a quality of the mature woman, and the inability to do so is a sign of immaturity or

---

*In Indian society there are sixty-four kalas, skills that develop sensual awareness by incorporating all five elements into their practice. For example, music and recitation invoke sound and the Space element, while working with perfumes and flowers develops a relationship to scent and Earth. Cooking and making medicines invoke taste and the Water element, and visual arts correlate to sight and Fire, while poetry and sex invoke Air, which represents both touch and communication.

incomplete education in women. Finally, girls learn to organize and shape their shakti into a personal relationship with the Divine. The intent is to teach girls how to cultivate a spiritual practice. By mastering these three levels of energy organization, girls learn to relate to their environment, to significant others, and to their spiritual selves.

WHEN THINGS GO AWRY

The perils of girls initiated into sex too early, voluntarily or, worse yet, involuntarily, are too many to name. They are evident in the life stories of many of our TV starlets and pop-music queens. An unripe fruit plucked too soon becomes a dry and sour reminder of this crime against nature. Because young girls have not completed their sexual circuitry, it is difficult for them to connect intercourse with love. Instead, their bodies associate the act with physical pain and penetration. Only when a woman has been allowed to mature, and has been trained by her mentors to develop her femininity, can she associate sex with lovemaking.

Premature sex can scar a woman's mind and body and remain recorded in her cellular memory. In the worst cases, girls may turn to drugs and alcohol to numb themselves to it, or engage in self-denigrating or inappropriate sexual behavior in response to feelings of guilt and shame. They may never mature into the fullness of their shakti but instead begin to hate their bodies, or turn away from sex altogether, secretly fearing or despising men as abusers.

These are all negative defense mechanisms that women use to cope with the trauma of premature sex, molestation, or rape. But self-hatred is never a useful long-term strategy. The best approach is prevention. A sacred society's customs help protect girls by removing desire from boys their own age, and educating them in the proper expression of their sexuality. When well-trained boys grow into men, they become protectors, not exploiters, of women.

SEXUAL HEALING FOR WOMEN

Our bodies and minds have an incredible ability to regenerate. Today doctors are recognizing what was long thought impossible— that the brain can heal itself and create new pathways, even into old age. Women who have suffered abuse, or have been initiated into sex too early, can seek spiritual counseling and physical rejuvenation through natural healing modalities to overcome the trauma of these events. Pancha karma is especially useful for this purpose because its therapies target the toxins and memories stored in our deep cellular tissue. In addition, with a partner trained in the proper use of his own sexuality, women can begin to rewire body and mind to associate sex with love once again.

Reprogramming your past is a function of living holistically in the present.

Going back in time to restore oneself to wholeness is possible. Getting up early, doing pranayama, and following agni-building practices encourage the release of old painful memories and allow the body to heal. Reprogramming your past is a function of living holistically in the present. Healing means wholeness, and wholeness begins with self-knowledge. This, in turn, leads to acceptance, and acceptance begins the healing process. Acceptance of the past can heal the present, and right action ensures that this is never repeated, for the best cure is prevention. Refer to page 71 for more on the practice of going back in time and healing the past by performing exercises like pranayama during the time of day that relates to your trauma.

Contemporary Western society, though advanced in matters of economic and technological development, is stunted sexually. Billions of dollars are spent every year to treat the emotional and psychological fallout resulting from the inappropriate initiation of young men and women into sex, not to mention the billions that are poured into pornography and the sexually charged imagery we lust for to gratify our suppressed desires. Repression over time becomes perversion and perversion is a germ that spreads countless social ills.*

SAME-SEX INITIATION

Just as sacred societies foster the education of young men when it comes to heterosexual activity, they do the same for young homosexual men. The practice of pederasty has a long history, and has been variously praised and condemned over the ages. Pederasty is a mentor-student bond between an older gay man and a young gay acolyte in his late teens or early twenties. This bond includes friendship as well as social and sexual intercourse, and is initiated when a young man is mature enough to understand his sexual orientation and make consensual choices to express it. When understood in the context of a sacred society and the proper initiation of boys into manhood, it makes sense that young homosexual men would require the same type of guidance as their heterosexual counterparts, and a gay male mentor takes on the role of initiating them.

Just as young homosexual men benefit from guidance from older gay mentors, young lesbians may be educated by older female mentors who share their sexual orientation. This ensures that young gay women receive the same training as their hetero counterparts, encouraging a healthy sexuality and early integration into society.

Today, it is clear to the scientific and lay communities alike that people who are gay are as predisposed to their sexual preferences as

---

*In the United States, one-hundred thousand boys, girls, and women are trafficked into sexual slavery every year. Worldwide, that number approaches 1 million, according to CIA estimates. Misguided sex and perversion are at the root of these travesties. For information and how to help, visit the International Justice Mission at www.ijm.org, and other Warrior organizations that fight for the rights of the oppressed.

heterosexuals. Like the dharma type, sexual preference is a genetic birthright that can be suppressed and hidden, but never erased. Also like the dharma type, the same injunctions hold true for a fulfilled life: express who you are or suffer the hell of living someone else's dharma.

Historically, people who are gay have been treated as outsiders, and many *are* Outsiders, standing out by dint of their sexual preference alone. But being gay does not automatically make a person an Outsider. In societies and cultures where homosexuality is accepted, people who are gay are just as likely to be Educators, Warriors, Merchants, and Laborers.

Pederasty and the Initiation of Young Men versus Pedophilia

Pedophilia is sexual desire, expressed or not, for young, prepubescent children of either gender, before they are mentally, emotionally, or physically ready to experience sex. Pedophilia is illegal, and often coercive and predatory; it does not reflect either friendship or goodwill. We must be very clear to draw a distinction between the initiations of young men by an older male or pederasty and pedophilia: the first are natural instincts to educate young men to become proper adults; the second is a disorder or perversion of the repressed natural urges arising out of this instinct.

Just as food that is improperly digested results in ama and its symptoms—burping, gas, and digestive distress—the inappropriate assimilation of natural urges turns into toxic mental ama. When men and women are not properly initiated into their own sexuality, nor taught how to function as well-adjusted people in their community, perversions can creep into their psyche. Such poor self-awareness is only exacerbated by the lack of good mentors and the lack of support of friends and family.

We have noted that the natural rhythms of sexuality do not apply totally to the Outsider type. From frequency of sex to definitions of marriage, Outsiders are allowed to stretch, bend, even break the normal rules of propriety, with the understanding that they are also responsible for the effects of such behavior. From depletion and sexually transmitted diseases to bliss and ecstasy, Outsiders experience the effects of their actions more strongly than other types.

THE YOGA OF SEX

One method to gauge the appropriateness of any activity is to pay attention to the three gunas, the qualities present in nature at any given time. For example, sattva is the quality of purity, light, and wisdom. It is a time for study, self-reflection, and spiritually inspiring activities. To have sex during sattvic hours violates the natural ambience of such a period, and does not represent the best use of one's time. Here is a summary of the three gunas and the hours during which they are prevalent (based on a 6 a.m. sunrise and a 6 p.m. sunset; please adjust accordingly):*

> **Sattva:** 4–8 a.m./p.m.—generally speaking, about two hours before and after sunrise and sunset. (The two hours before sunset are more tamasic however.) Light, purity, stillness, understanding, spirituality, balance, truth; best for meditation, study, being in nature, communing with the Divine.
>
> **Rajas:** 8–12 a.m./p.m.—the time when most work gets done; activity, desire, passion, friction, longing, thirst, attachment; best for driving, working, making money, sex, sports, passion, eating.

---

*Some authorities differ on the diurnal rhythm of these gunas, ascribing different times to each one during the day.

Tamas: 12–4 a.m./p.m.—the time when most rest gets done; siesta time in sacred societies; dullness, darkness, frivolity, inertia, unconsciousness, illusion, sleep; best for rest, sleep, massage, routine work.

In other words daytime is naturally rajasic, nighttime is naturally tamasic, and the junctures (sunrise, sunset) are naturally sattvic. Tamas is best suited for sleep and rest, while rajas is optimal for activity, including work, sports, and sex, though the evening rajas period (8 p.m.–midnight) is preferred for sex over the morning time, as the day is better suited to getting work done. The passion and desire that characterize rajas fully bloom during these hours because the evening also blends in a fair amount of tamas to make physical exertion pleasurable.

It should be noted that these times roughly amount to four hours each, though they will be longer or shorter, depending on one's locality and the season. For example, during winter in the Northern Hemisphere, daylight hours are shorter, and sattva, rajas, and tamas may only last three hours during the day, while their duration overnight may extend to five hours. Calibrate these times for your locality and the current season. Ultimately, the best way to understand sattva, rajas, and tamas is to feel them in yourself and your surroundings. This is not so difficult once you become used to tracking their changes over the course of the day and noting how the body/mind reacts to them.

Note the stillness and the calm hush that overtakes the world during sattva time, as even the birds settle in to watch the sunset or sing with joy at the sunrise. Notice the hustle, bustle, and noise of a rajas period—from traffic and people to the busyness of nature. Notice also the dullness and heaviness present in your body during tamas time. These will become clearer as we examine another method for measuring diurnal rhythms in chapter 11.

FAKE MEN, FAKE WOMEN

Merchant dharma types like to work with shakti, and they are particularly good at developing practices for women. From the Kama Sutra and seduction to song and dance, sumptuous food, and fashion, Merchants know how to get a woman in touch with her sensuality. Merchants are also the evolution point for Laborer types. Furthermore, Merchants are ruled by the Water element, which allows them to appreciate the deep mysteries and fluctuations of the feminine mind. Merchants seem naturally in tune with the ebb and flow of human emotion, which is why they stride in lockstep with the march of fashion and popular culture.

But in marching to the beat of fashion's drum, Merchant society sometimes hurries men and women to cultivate substitutes for archetypally attractive qualities; for example, pushing women to put in breast implants and men to pump up their muscles in an attempt to enhance their femininity and masculinity, respectively. But attempts like this miss the point that masculinity and femininity are inner qualities, and fall like a house of cards when propped up only from the outside.

Merchant attitudes favor beauty, and what is attractive typically holds more value that what is not in a Merchant world. Consequently, Merchant society's members have a high regard for what makes them beautiful and hence valuable to their community as well as to the opposite sex. As a result, Western society tends to worship form over function, meaning that men and women are appreciated for certain physical attributes—real or not—rather than the essence behind them.

Large breasts in women are supposed to signal femininity because, biologically, extra fatty tissue may supply more warmth, comfort, and milk to nurture a hungry infant. But even if this were true, how can supplementing a woman's natural endowment with silicone provide these qualities? How does plastic equate with womanhood? Doesn't it make sense that if men are attracted to femininity, women should be supported in cultivating that, rather than seeking to replace it with cheap (and not so cheap) substitutes?

Needless to say, in order to thrive in Merchant society some women do go the surgical route,* and in cases when this genuinely improves their self-confidence, or even their earning power (Pamela Anderson was outspoken about this), it remains a personal choice to be considered. When done consciously, with awareness of the consequences and clarity about the motivation, artificial enhancements can be a useful crutch. But in the end it is important to remember that crutches are designed to prop us up while we develop our muscles to walk on our own.

Conversely, qualities like confidence and self-control build up any man in a woman's eyes, regardless of his physical stature. Ask yourself this: Who is more sexy—Denzel Washington or Dorian Yates, Robert Redford or Ronnie Coleman, Johnny Depp or Lou Ferrigno? The first are famous actors, the second, world-champion body builders. Chances are, most women have never even heard of the body builders.

Even penis size is less important than masculinity: weigh the world's top porn stars against the first group and you will still find that in most cases women choose Brad Pitt over Ron Jeremy. A man who can hold his center, maintaining his integrity while taking care of business in any situation, is the true masculine man, and the master of attraction.

---

*Many men also go under the knife, but the statistics relating to plastic surgery still show that women undergo these procedures far more than men do. In 2013, over 1.5 million cosmetic surgeries were performed, just 13 percent of them on men. The most common procedure among women is still breast augmentation, at over 290,000 in 2013. ("2013 Cosmetic Surgery Gender Distribution," American Society of Plastic Surgeons, www.plasticsurgery.org/Documents/news-resources/statistics/2013-statistics/cosmetic-procedures-men.pdf)

> **The flesh is but a gateway to the realm
> of the man-woman mystery.**

Admittedly, attraction for men is more basic than for women, as males are wired to react to physical assets more than females. Nonetheless, when a woman cultivates her femininity by building, organizing, and expressing shakti, she is better equipped to entice her partner than by mutilating her body in order to appear feminine.

Guys pumping up at the gym and girls hiking up their skirts to inject a magnetic charge between the sexes do not exemplify real masculinity and femininity. The flesh is but a gateway to the realm of the man-woman mystery. If we only pay attention to the bare physicality of a person, we are walking the grounds of a great estate, but never bothering to look inside and discover its treasures.

FEMINISM

In reaction to oppressive male-dominated institutions, feminism moved women to cultivate greater independence and more yang (male, forceful) energy, sometimes to the point that the primordial polarity between yin and yang, women and men, was sacrificed. By contrast, modern men's movements often travel too far in the other direction, effeminizing men without revealing their masculine secrets. Both err when taken to this extreme, and powerful attraction between the sexes becomes more difficult to achieve. But nature always tries to redress an imbalance; when yang is in excess, yin will speak up. When a woman's basic femininity is perceived to be wanting, men may demand substitutes for it by influencing women to nip and tuck and fit into the mold of a busty goddess they are "supposed" to be. This feeds a deleterious cycle against which women rebel, taking men and discarding them as a show of their "liberated" sexuality, which is actually a substitute for real femininity.

Or women may behave coldly and nudge men out of their lives, rationalizing that they do not need a man to make them happy. Both of these attitudes miss the point, which is that a balanced femininity knows how to behave in the presence and the absence of a man. While a woman does not need a man to complete her, she should know how to relate to one.

Some solutions for women include getting in touch with their bodies by doing specifically feminine activities to which men are not privy. Activities that ground women in the deep sensuality of their being can engender confidence in everything, from making love to making money. As mentioned above, taking a yoga, dance, craft-making, or cooking class can reconnect a woman to the vitality of her sensual self, which is perhaps why these have become so popular in the West. This should have nothing to do with pleasing men or doing anything for anyone but themselves. These are methods of expressing shakti, and the cultivation, organization, and expression of shakti is a woman's legacy. Whether creating a sumptuous meal or a gorgeous piece of pottery, women must find ways to express love and sensuality through practices that channel their vital creativity.

A woman's love is the most powerful, attractive force in the universe. In its basic form it results in the creation of offspring. But, at subtler levels, it can create and shape any experience she desires. Less evolved women who understand this use it to manipulate men into doing what they want for them. More evolved women can influence the movement of society in profound ways.

To evolve this kind of creativity, we must embrace spiritual traditions that invoke the Divine Feminine. These are not limited to Vedic lineages but can be found all over, including in Jewish, Native American, European, and other Asian cultures that have a long history of incorporating the feminine in their worship. In addition, seeking the company of female elders is crucial to learning to handle life in a woman's body. Female support groups are a necessary source of inspiration if women are to empower themselves with knowledge and skill in the use of their femininity. There are things that only women can teach other women—trade secrets that should never pass between the sexes. After all, women and men must keep some sense of mystery in their relationships, lest the male-female dynamic lose its polarity. One law of vastu shastra states that people require a basic minimum of space and light. Crowding, whether in an office cubicle or in a relationship, inevitably results in misery.

SPACE AND MYSTERY

Men have no need to know exactly how women cultivate femininity. From making up to making out, women should retain some of their allure in order to keep relationships vibrant. Likewise, the wisdom that male elders pass on to boys, teaching them how to drive a woman wild with irresistible masculinity, should stay within the male fold, because such secrets are essentially useless to the opposite sex. Trying to know everything about your partner dampens attraction, reducing it to the trivialities of day-to-day life. You don't need to stand over him while he's urinating; he doesn't need to see you waxing your armpits. Close the door; overfamiliarity is one of the major reasons long-term couples lose their sexual spark. Create space and give your partner the gift of missing you, if only for a minute. Your sex life will thank you.

> **Close the door; overfamiliarity is one of the major reasons long-term couples lose their sexual spark.**

Better for men to embody their authenticity and allow women to admire it. Better for women to radiate shakti than to reveal the secrets of how it was cultivated. These things are left to the elders of society to teach their young, and one of the first keys male elders teach boys are the rules of the game, the mechanics of attraction: what women look for, how they test men to find it, and how to pass those tests. Starting with a woman's biology and leading to her heart and soul, men must teach boys what it takes to spark attraction, and the difficult self-development necessary to maintain that spark for life.

THE PILL

Oral contraception has been a boon to women's rights, but as research is showing now, a potential bane to their health. Perhaps the pill's greatest contribution to women has been social, not biological. The pill gave women a way to exercise control over their bodies and offered them choice in a world where men had this in their favor. This led to a rise in feminism and a new awareness of women's rights.

However, even if the pill were harmless (which it decidedly is not), it is still a tool, a crutch, giving only the illusion of control, since you are dependent on something outside of yourself to control your body. Were the pharmacy to run out, your doctor to stop prescribing, or the politicians to ban it, you would be left relatively helpless again.

The best way for a woman to take charge of her reproductive health is through education. Learning family planning methods, getting in touch with her monthly cycle, and fully understanding her body—these are the anchors of real feminism, for they put control in a woman's own hands, rather than in the hands of the pharmaceutical company, the doctor, and the lawmakers who dictate social policy. Knowing when you're fertile, you can choose to abstain from sex or use barrier methods like condoms for protection if you don't wish to conceive.

Women on the pill have a reduced ability to detect pheromones and to smell potentially compatible partners. A woman on the pill also smells different to men, which can make it more difficult for them to find and become turned on by her natural scent, and to even authentically relate with her.

Smell is one of humanity's most important senses. It relates to the Earth element and the first chakra, and is the most basic survival level of sensation. We see this in animals, whose olfactory senses are far better developed than ours. The olfactory sense is useful for us when we smell putrid meat that may not appear otherwise contaminated, or when we are attracted to a partner because he or she just smells right. Pheromones are the subtle communicators of chemistry that separate just any potential mate from "the one." More powerful than looks in determining whether to pursue a relationship with someone is the chemical compatibility conferred by these pheromones through the sense of smell. Anything that interferes with that, such as synthetic oral contraceptives, risks skewing the attraction mechanism and destroying relationship opportunities, either by causing us to reject partners who are good for us or to attract others who are unsuitable for us—something we would not normally do if our senses were functioning optimally. A common scenario is for women on the pill to find a partner they like and get married. When they decide to get off the pill in order to have kids, they realize that their chemistry is no longer the same, or that they are in the wrong relationship altogether.

Women on the pill also lack the estrous cycle that increases their sexiness at certain times of the month and decreases it during menstruation. The permutations of this effect are striking. For one, women lacking a monthly high are unable to harness their sexual practices. Failing to do this may result in reduced sexual satisfaction, poor bonding with their partners, and, ultimately, relationship frustration.

Figure 8.2. A woman's natural estrous cycle fluctuates in a wave-like way (left), while the the pill has a flat lining effect (right).

Oral contraceptives have a flatlining effect, preventing women from riding the up and down rhythm of nature's monthly cycles. Ultimately, taking the pill to control hormones is like taking antidepressants to control emotions. It may be useful as a short-term therapy, but long-term use (that is, for more than a year) creates a false sense of self built on pharmacology, rather than the natural components of physiology. Consequently, women on oral contraceptives run a risk of biological, emotional, and relationship problems. It is always better to go along with nature, rather than trying to trick or fight nature. In the end, nature always wins.

The pill can also break your heart. The pill is made from the same synthetic hormones as hormone replacement therapy, which are directly linked to increased risk of stroke and heart disease. A university study showed women on contraceptive pills had a 20 to 30 percent increase in plaque in their arteries by the time they reached late middle age.[2]

In her book *Balance Your Hormones, Balance Your Life*, Dr. Claudia Welch quotes numerous studies showing the substantial health risks women face on the pill: "*The Lancet* published the results of a study that showed the use of birth control pills doubled breast cancer risks for women under twenty. In 2005 the World Health Organization classified the pill as carcinogenic to humans."[3]

Thus, the birth control pill is not recommended for long-term use. Women who take it as a hormone regulator, as well as women using it solely to prevent pregnancy, are better served by finding natural ways to accomplish this through herbs, diet, and lifestyle changes and other natural contraceptive methods.

IMPOTENCE

Not too long ago a man who couldn't obtain an erection or perform sex was called impotent, meaning "without power." English vocabulary retains vestiges of the belief that a man's sexual prowess is linked to his vitality. The politically incorrect term *impotence* has now been changed to *erectile dysfunction*, as a way to deflect the stigma of this condition. To go one step further, popular culture and drug commercials have made it even more ambiguous, abbreviating it simply to ED. Thus, "I have ED" sounds as natural as "I drink OJ." But when things seem harmless, that makes it harder to treat the underlying condition. It does, however, promote a drug culture that treats symptoms, not causes, and makes it easier to pop a pill than to make lasting lifestyle changes.

In ayurveda, the underlying causes of impotence are determined and treated, using specific herbs such as ashwagandha (*withania somnifera*), specific exercises like those throughout this book, pranayama, diet and lifestyle prescriptions, yoga asanas, and more. Athletes know that strength is a skill. To gain sexual strength or potency takes a holistic approach that combines mind and body to create wholeness and balance. You can't become a great lover by taking pills any more than you can become a great athlete by consuming sports drinks. The care and help of an ayurvedic coach, trained in *vajikarana* and *rasayana*—two branches of ayurvedic medicine concerned with sexuality and replenishment—are invaluable, as are the daily practices described in part one, because both are designed to restore health to the body and mind.

SEX AND THE DHARMA TYPES

Laborers can have the most sex most routinely. To them, physical appearance is less important than physical comfort, and Laborer types enjoy sex for how it makes them feel, rather than for what it says about them. They can go for long periods without sex as well, but they prefer regular intercourse, which is one reason that the institution of marriage is particularly beneficial for them. With a dedicated spouse, they are able to explore the man/woman mystery, as well as cultivate a large family, more effectively than being alone.

Merchants are next to Laborers in terms of how much sex they can have. The Merchant's art is making sex romantic and enjoyable. They are most likely to "pay" for sex by promoting traditions like giving gifts, buying or making dinners, and otherwise pampering their partners in order to earn their affection. This is the origin of the romantic practices of giving chocolate and flowers, diamonds and lace. Merchants also tend to obsess about appearance; high heels and lipstick are Merchant inventions. Accordingly, they like to have the best-looking partners, regardless of whether these types of people are actually enjoyable to be around.

Warriors treat sex as a competition. They are passionate but, like the flame that flares up and then dies out, they can lose interest quickly. They must be careful not to burn themselves out. Therefore, they are less prone to have sex than Merchant types. They enjoy a partner who's a challenge, and the most challenging is one who stimulates them mentally as well as physically.

Educators have strong passions and desires, but these are mostly in their heads. It is rare for Educators to act out all their fantasies. They prefer to express them through art, music, or their chosen profession. Therefore, in expression Educators are usually the most monastic of the dharma types, restraining themselves sexually due to strong personal or moral beliefs.

Outsiders are not bound by the same moral strictures as the other dharma types. As a result, they freely experiment with alternative modes of sexual pleasure that the other types never sample. Outsiders, or any types in an Outsider life cycle, may oscillate from monasticism to debauchery in their quest to push the limits of discovery. How productive or destructive this behavior proves depends on their personal integration.

In addition, Outsiders may opt for tattoos, piercings, and other identifying marks around the erogenous zones. As social commentators, they may take a role in promoting sexual awareness, traditionally a taboo topic, through television, radio, or print. Or they may enrich the mainstream of sexual knowledge by introducing fresh and new ideas. Madonna is an example of an Outsider who has expressed and profited from her sexual proclivities.

Outsiders tend to have revolutionary attitudes toward sexuality, and often rock the boat with their outspoken opinions. Even lesser-known Outsiders, like author Zora Neale Hurston, who claimed that marriage would only "widen my hips and narrow my options," convey their unorthodox attitudes on sex and marriage and become trendsetters and iconoclasts. But the Outsider's rebellion is not necessarily a loud affair. Independent-mindedness and free thinking are internal qualities, not readily apparent to the naked eye. The Outsider need not make waves to rock the boat; they can steer it with their inner compass and the rudder of their conviction.

9

Nourishing Sex

Optimal Sexual Practices Based on Gender and Dharma Type

In this chapter we will take a look at some traditional sexual values interpreted and adapted for modern times, using tools—not rules—to make sex nourishing to our bodies, minds, and souls. I believe that many of the restrictions or commandments that have come down from ancient traditions are simply tools meant to enhance, not diminish, our sex lives, but we have misinterpreted much of what has been said by hewing to the letter of the law and not its spirit. A literal-minded focus cannot see the forest for the trees. By exploring the forest of wisdom passed down to us, we can find medicine for society.

> **"I am the strength of the strong, beyond passion and desire. I am sex life in accord with natural laws, O Arjuna."**
> **BHAGAVAD GITA (7:11)**

It may be surprising that the land of the Vedas, which gave us the Kama Sutra, also promoted conventional practices like abstinence, monogamy, and sex for procreation. But when we unpack recommendations like these, we find in them an almost subversively humanistic, life-affirming view of sex. It is difficult to know what exactly the ancients intended, particularly when it came to their attitudes toward sex and relationships. Conventions change over time, and we must take what is essential and true from their wisdom while leaving behind the local cultural trappings. We must cull from ancient traditions the pith of what works here and now to make our sexuality, as well as our lives, deeper and more fulfilling.

The laws of nature that govern sex and health haven't changed over the ages, and what was true for Charaka, the author of the seminal ayurvedic text, the Charaka Samhita, remains true today, except for his references to social and literary customs in his time. To understand why tools turn into rules, and sometimes even mysogynistic, repressive dogmas, we must take a step back and look at why traditions become corrupted and how they can be salvaged for modern use.

SEX AND ORAL TRADITION

Religion was the original self-help method and, from psychology to sexuality, the world's religions have addressed humanity's age-old concerns since time immemorial, passing down their teachings through texts and traditions. However, texts can be misunderstood, redacted, damaged, or reinterpreted to suit anyone's agenda. A look around us at the variant views among biblical scholars today on issues as basic as love, sex, and marriage testifies to this.

Understanding these dangers, the sages of ancient India transmitted their most important precepts orally, relying on written devices for more mundane uses, and even then only as crutches. They ensured that their wisdom would endure, not on leaves of parchment but on the tongues of devotees fit to receive and retransmit it. In this way, their knowledge survived as long as its living host remained alive. Consequently, parchment and tablets, and the archaeologist's hunt for buried treasure, become needless: the real treasures of Vedic society are the living bearers of its wisdom. And though human beings, like parchment, will inevitably perish, it is ultimately easier to learn from a living, breathing, spiritual testimony than to decipher the remnants of mute and long-dead ancestors. This, in turn, ensures that we can pass on a living tradition to the next generation.

> **Our ancestors did not all see sex as bad, but wanted to make it good, knowing that deep satisfaction promotes fulfilling relationships and healthy generations to come.**

It has been said that, should all the world's sacred literature vanish, it could be rewritten by a self-realized soul. For people who study ancient traditions today, it is essential to have the guidance of such beacons to shed light on the world's remaining scriptures and to teach us how to read and interpret them for ourselves. In reading with a discerning eye, we may find that many injunctions we hold sacrosanct were intended to enhance, not deny, our enjoyment of sex, and that our ancestors did not all see sex as bad, but wanted to make it good, knowing that deep satisfaction promotes fulfilling relationships and healthy generations to come. Sex, food, and sleep are the three foundations of life, and we must learn to enjoy and regulate them in order to survive.

AYURVEDA AND SEX

To understand how to improve sexuality and well-being, we need to appreciate the rhythms of nature. Ayurveda describes how to align our minds and bodies with nature's cycles. It is the root of what we today call alternative or complementary medicine, and it encompasses various disciplines, from psychology to gynecology, designed to help us get the most out of life. To do this, we want to enhance the pleasurable experiences of our primary human urges for sex, food, and sleep while diminishing their undesirable side effects.

The sages of yesteryear advised regulating these according to our dosha and dharma type, using specific lifestyle and diet, as well as medicine, meditation, exercise, and breathing practices. Much of this was covered in part one. Here we will look at their recommendations for sex, which, like those for sleep and nutrition, are more salutary than sacrosanct. That is, like religious restrictions on eating shellfish, pork, and other "unclean" foods, these injunctions were made to empower us with health, not encumber us with empty superstition. Just as following the daily regimen described in part one can promote health and longevity, following a sexual routine can prolong life, promote vitality, and enhance enjoyment.

In observing nature, the ancients realized that everything happens according to its own season. They understood that when we have sex at the right times with the right people, we are bound to reap more pleasure and vitality than when we go against nature's imperatives. The reproductive cycles of everything from flowers to humans are governed by defined periods of rest and activity. To defy these was considered foolish, because it decreased our enjoyment, and sinful, insofar as *sin* literally means "to miss the mark." There is no supernal penalty or spiritual calamity for one who misuses sexuality, save the very effects thereof. Just as overindulging in pizza and beer the night before can spell indigestion and sluggishness the morning after, the wages of sin are contained within the act itself, and the nature of karma ensures that we suffer its effects sooner or later.

Take sugar, for example. When enjoyed in moderation, at the right time, it's a rewarding treat, but when consumed in excess it can shorten your life and lead to conditions from tooth decay to diabetes. In addition, overindulgence spawns a blasé attitude toward the stuff, so we end up needing more and more to get our fix while respecting it less and less. Overindulging in sex is no different. When the body is dissipated from overuse or misuse of sexual energy, nature robs other systems to maintain reproductive function. From nature's perspective, our most precious possession is the ability to reproduce. That is to say, from an evolutionary standpoint, nature is concerned with propagating the species, investing tremendous energy in maintaining sexual health, even to the detriment of other bodily functions. Therefore, we must learn how to balance sexual enjoyment without depleting ourselves.

SEX FOR PROCREATION: MEN

While most men are capable of ejaculating every day, ayurveda says that this is not advisable, as nature is adept at robbing the body's resources in order to regenerate his reproductive tissue. The effects of this depletion may not be apparent immediately, but will inevitably lead to degeneration of the body and mind if unchecked. Cracking and popping of the joints, arthritis, nervous disorders, compromised immunity and digestion, and mental/emotional issues are all reliable outcomes of chronic misuse of sexual energy. Ayurvedic texts tell us that a man's life juice (shukra)* takes about five weeks to fully regenerate after depletion. What constitutes depletion differs from individual to individual, but the average time for a man to turn raw food into mature, healthy shukra is about thirty-five days.† Therefore, to recover between bouts of sexual intercourse, the sages advised men

---

*In English, "semen" is an incomplete translation of *shukra*, which has a broader definition in ayurveda, including "male reproductive tissue," and "the most refined physical essence of food." In addition, *shukra*, which in Sanskrit means "bright," is also the name for the planet Venus, the second brightest object in the night sky (after the moon). In astrology, Venus also rules male and female reproductive organs, and has the power to bring the dead back to life.
†While sperm count can bounce back within seventy-two hours after ejaculation, healthy, mature sperm and reproductive tissue take longer to develop.

to have sex for procreation. This equates to having intercourse when women are most fertile, which is also roughly once a month. Thus, though women's cycles are more difficult to predict than men's, having sex about once a month aligns the rhythms of both men and women for optimal enjoyment and health.

Number of Days It Takes to Create Healthy Tissues

Rasa (plasma and lymph): 5 days

Rakta (blood/RBC): 10 days

Mamsa (muscle): 15 days

Meda (fat): 20 days

Asthi (bone): 25 days

Majja (nerve/marrow): 30 days

Shukra (reproductive tissue): 35 days

Wait, Only Once a Month?!

There are, of course, corollaries to this principle. Depending on your constitution and your proclivity for sex, that might mean only one session per month, or many sessions over the days before, during, and after ovulation. Why have sex around ovulation? Because studies show that this is when women are usually at their sexual peak and their bodies express desire and readiness for intercourse.* Sex is at its most passionate and satisfying, and partners forge an enduring link, when coupling around this time. Studies demonstrate that a few days before ovulation women become more flirtatious, open, and receptive to sexual advances. Men who pick up on these signals

---

*A couple examples of such studies include Gangestad, S. W., Thornhill, R., and Garver-Apgar, C. E., "Adaptations to Ovulation," *Handbook of Evolutionary Psychology*, edited by D. M. Buss (New York: Wiley), 344–71; Miller, G., Tybur, J. Jordan, B., "Ovulatory Cycle Effects on Tip Earnings by Lap Dancers: Economic Evidence for Human Estrus?" *Evolution and Human Behavior* 28: 375–81.

also become increasingly aroused and resort to displays of quality, like competing for a woman's affection. This behavior in men can take the form of buying gifts, romancing, and even jealously guarding their partner.*

We human beings think that we are above such animal behaviors, but these instincts often operate subconsciously, even convincing our brains they don't really exist. Men and women consider themselves more evolved than that, but behavior tells another story. One of my mentors used to say, "Behavior is everything!" meaning that no matter what people tell themselves or the world, how they act is the final measure of who they are. In the current material age, people's actions ultimately determine their destinies, not their thoughts or even their words.

> Behavior is everything: no matter what people tell themselves or the world, how they act is the final measure of who they are.

In well-documented research, as in long-standing cultural observations, women are known to experience a subtle phase of "heat" midcycle, during which they are more attracted to men and the subject of sex, becoming more receptive to male pheromones,

---

*A few examples of studies examining these topics include Gangestad, S. W., Thornhill, R., and Garver, C. E., "Changes in Women's Sexual Interests and Their Partners' Mate Retention Tactics across the Menstrual Cycle: Evidence for Shifting Conflicts of Interest," *Proceedings of the Royal Society of London Series B* (2002): 269, 975–82; Haselton, M. G., Mortezaie, M., Pillsworth, E. G., Bleske-Rechek, A., and Frederick, D. A., "Ovulatory Shifts in Human Female Ornamentation: Near Ovulation, Women Dress to Impress," *Hormones and Behavior* (2007): 51, 41–45; Haselton, M., and Gangestad, S. W., "Conditional Expression of Women's Desires and Men's Mate Guarding across the Ovulatory Cycle," *Hormones and Behavior* (2006): 49, 509–18; Haselton, M., and Miller, G. F., "Women's Fertility across the Cycle Increases the Short-Term Attractiveness of Creative Intelligence," *Human Nature* (2006): 17, 50–73; Gangestad, S. W., Simpson, J. A., Cousins, A. J., Garver-Apgar, C. E., and Christensen, P. N., "Women's Preferences for Male Behavioral Displays Shift across the Menstrual Cycle," *Psychological Science* (2004): 15, 203–7.

subtle scents that normally repel them during other stages of their cycle.* For their part, men also find the scent of women at this time more pleasant and sexually attractive than in other phases. Women undergo subtle transformations when they're ovulating, including changes to their waist-to-hip ratio, their gait, and even the shape and complexion of their faces! One study illustrates the interesting permutations of these developments. In 2007, the journal *Evolution and Human Behaviour* noted that topless dancers when ovulating made twice as much in tips as when they were menstruating (the opposite end of the reproductive spectrum). Between the peak and valley in their cycle, their earnings fell in the middle of these two extremes. By contrast, participants using contraceptive pills showed no estrous earnings peak.

This is a telling example of the sex for procreation principle at work—when a woman's biological cycles bring out her sexiness, people take notice, as did our ancestors, who advised us to harness the ups and downs of nature's rhythms. This does not mean that a baby has to result from the union. Ayurvedic lore, like other traditions, details methods of birth control for couples not ready to conceive, though none are 100 percent reliable. Neem can be used as a spermicide topically, and, taken orally, will decrease sperm count in men, but it should be used along with other methods of contraception, such as condoms, if conception is not desired. Research suggests that factors besides insemination during ovulation must also be considered for successful pregnancy to occur. According to authors Robin Baker and Mark Bellis, when a woman achieves orgasm well before insemination (forty-five minutes or more) during foreplay, her cer-

*Our word for heat (*estrus*) comes from the Greek word *oistrus*, meaning "gadfly." As gadflies buzzed around cattle they were observed to drive the cattle into a state of frenzy, not unlike the state they entered when they wished to mate—hence *heat*, though a better description would perhaps be "peak sexual interest according to nature's rhythms."

vical filter becomes strengthened, thereby reducing her chances of conception.* However, sex for procreation is not an injunction to only have sex to produce children, but to mate at times that will strengthen a couple's relationship by providing a deeply satisfying mutual experience.

Such a mutually gratifying experience is reinforced by the higher likelihood of female orgasm and bonding hormones, like oxytocin, that peak during this time. When a couple conceives after following the rhythms we shall examine below, they optimally influence the health, nature, and longevity of the children produced from their union.

SEX FOR PROCREATION: WOMEN

Women frequently report being more satisfied with fewer quality sexual encounters than with a greater quantity of subpar experiences. Biologically, women's sexual needs are different from, even opposed to, those of men. A woman's orgasm is difficult to predict, and a partner who can give her one is rewarded with her gratitude for days, weeks, even months at a time. However, when a woman does not get what she wants, she will seek out more and more sexual experiences to scratch the itch left by incomplete lovemaking. Therefore, women end up wanting more and more, while men are able to give less and less.

Because of these differences and in order to satisfy both men and women, ejaculatory sex should be reserved for the height of a woman's sexual cycle, ensuring peak experiences for both parties,

---

*Note that the reverse is also true, according to Robin Baker's controversial book *Sperm Wars* when a woman achieves orgasm during or just after insemination, she may dramatically *increase* the chances of conception. Therefore, men, to avoid pregnancy, make sure your partner has an orgasm well *before* you ejaculate. But to increase chances of pregnancy, have mutual climactic sex.

during which health and vitality, along with love and affection, are amplified rather than depleted. This does not preclude having sex at other times, as we shall see below; it simply means that ejaculatory sex should be reserved for the roughly three to seven days in the middle of the woman's cycle. The most enjoyable time for sex is just before ovulation, though not all women report feeling this way. Improper health and diet, for example, can interfere with this rhythm. Because women's bodies undergo changes during ovulation, such as increased breast and hip size, this transformation may feel uncomfortable, especially if a woman has lymphatic congestion or other health issues. However, nature generally programs women at this time to be receptive to sex, just as nature chemically primes men to respond to them with arousal. By contrast, the worst time to have sex is during menstruation. From a scientific as well as a traditional standpoint, this is when both women and men are more prone to suffer health problems as a result of sex, and are least likely to be fulfilled, especially if the sex for procreation guidelines are already being practiced.

Functionally, a woman's period conflicts with the job of making babies. One is a breaking down of tissues, a "funeral for dead ova," in the words of Dr. Vasant Lad, and the other is a building up; one is downward energy, the other is upward. Biologically, menstruation is a time of cleansing, as the uterine wall sloughs off dead tissue. Therefore, it is best to refrain from any sexual penetration while a woman is menstruating.

Traditionally, women were encouraged to stay home, rest, and contemplate during this time, in deference to nature's low cycle. While menstruating, they may experience emotional fluctuations, physical pain, and other symptoms. This time is ideal for self-reflection and convalescence, and even bathing is frowned upon by ayurvedic tradition while a woman is bleeding. Modern women, on the other hand, are often advised to power through their periods, ignoring nature's imperatives. But it is best to observe menstruation with reverence, and couples should refrain from aggressive activities like sex until this "new moon" phase has passed.

This leaves us with one week during which we can have the most sex (the few days before, during, and after ovulation) and a week to ten days during which we should not have any sex at all (the days before and during menstruation). What, then, do we do with the other (roughly) two weeks of the monthly cycle?

PRACTICE/FOREPLAY

The other half of the month, then, should be dedicated to what for men we will call practice, or cultivation, and for women, foreplay. Let us take the meaning of *foreplay* first. Anticipation of sex can be as arousing and sensual to a woman as the act itself. Such a buildup of positive tension toward a desired outcome constitutes foreplay, and is achieved when a woman has to wait to be satisfied. The sex for procreation principles provide a rich time line patterned after a woman's natural rhythms that shows the most appropriate times for intense activity, rest, and anticipation—the buildup of sexual tension between the weeks of a woman's typically low sexual interest (menstruation) and peak interest (estrus).

This reflects the fasting and feasting cycles present elsewhere in nature. Night is a fast from day, an exhale is a fast from oxygen, and abstaining from ejaculatory sex is a fast from the same old dull routine that will whet your appetite for sex. In sexual terms, fasting stokes the flames of passion, and, as any hungry person knows, after a fast even the stalest of bread tastes like a feast. Abstaining from ejaculatory sex not only builds passion and connection in your relationship, it also improves your health.

TABLE 9.1. SEX FOR PROCREATION
BASED ON A 28-DAY CYCLE

DAYS OF MENSTRUAL CYCLE	RECOMMENDED ACTIVITY
1–6	Rest
7–8	Cultivation
9–15	Sex
16–23	Cultivation
24–28	Rest

Cultivation means sex without ejaculation; *rest* means abstention from sex altogether; *sex* means ejaculatory intercourse is allowed. Daily Devotion may be practiced at any time except during menstruation. Note: Day one is the first day of bleeding.

During this time men and women need to train, not drain, in order to build up their reserves. From Taoist to tantric techniques, there are many exercises to do alone or with your partner to build up your sexual energy. One example is the "microcosmic orbit," a Taoist technique for inner alchemy that circulates sexual energy throughout the body, thereby revitalizing its organs and subtle pathways.* Cultivating with a spouse or partner puts these techniques to work and tests a man's ability to retain self-control during intercourse. For men, solo practice also includes building the size, strength, and endurance of the penis; learning ejaculatory control; and working to boost sexual energy. For women, the key is getting in touch with shakti, the feminine power embodied in all women, but rarely fully expressed.

---

*For more on Taoist sexuality and the microcosmic orbit, refer to Mantak Chia's popular books and programs.

CULTIVATION

Sex for procreation is an effective way to build positive tension in a relationship. During the weeks of cultivation or practice, men can make it a goal to hold on to their life juice and build their energy reserves. It becomes the role of women during their foreplay time—the weeks that men are cultivating—to play and flirt with men and seduce them into giving up that life juice. In this way, the roles are reversed, and men temporarily become the selectors, women the selectees. Such role reversal can be highly arousing for women, who get to enjoy playing the hunter rather than the hunted, enlivening the sensual instincts of both men and women and injecting magnetism into their relationship.

Sex for Procreation Corollaries

+ Depending on individual constitution, age, and other factors, "once a month" could mean one or many sexual encounters during the week or so around a woman's fertile time.
+ Nonejaculatory sex is still practicable during the "off-season," except during menstruation, when no penetration is advised.
+ Outsiders and those in Outsider periods are exempt from some or all of these principles, as are young men in the Spring season of life.

Men and women who want to avoid pregnancy can use a modified version of the sex for procreation method that works outside of a woman's fertile times. For this, using the fertility awareness method, also called natural family planning, a woman determines her fertile window and either abstains from sex or has protected sex to ensure no pregnancy is possible.* This would become her flirtation period,

---

*Excellent books on natural family planning include *Garden of Fertility* and *Honoring Our Cycles* by Katie Singer as well as *Taking Charge of Your Fertility* by Toni Weschler.

and the cultivation period for her partner. Then ejaculatory sex can resume during a six- or seven-day non-fertile window. This practice shifts the timing of sex while keeping the rest and activity periods essentially the same.

Here's what to do during the ten- to fourteen-day period when you are limiting ejaculatory sex:

> **Solo training:** working by yourself to cultivate sexual energy
>
> **Partner training:** having non-ejaculatory sex at least three times for every one session of ejaculatory sex—this model is the optimal way to fulfill the sexual needs of both men and women, and keep them happy over the long term, both inside and outside the bedroom
>
> **Daily devotion:** spending five to ten minutes every day connected to your partner in sexual embrace without thrusting, the practice of Daily Devotion, is a term coined by Diane and Kerry Riley.*

✦ DAILY DEVOTION

To perform Daily Devotion, the woman lies on her back with her knees bent and wide apart.

The man lies between her legs in the missionary position.

The woman wraps her legs around the man's hips and locks her feet together with her arms wrapped around the man's neck. If this is not possible she can bend her knees and wrap her thighs around the outside of the man's thighs and place her lower legs between his legs, or whatever is most comfortable, as long as you are locked together.

The man then puts his lingam (penis) into her yoni (vagina) or she places it in for him.

---

*See also the practice as described in their book *Tantric Secrets for Men.*

Both partners close their eyes and lock together with their mouths, legs, arms, and genitals.

At first there may be just enough movement for the man to maintain an erection, but then be still and enjoy the feeling of joy and gratitude that comes from being in union as one body with your beloved. Drink deeply of this experience, seize the moment, for nothing else matters but this precious time together.

Keep your focus on the parts of your body that are connected and giving you pleasurable sensations. If your mind drifts, gently bring it back to where the genitals are connected and you are sharing each other's nectar. Think of it as mutually beneficial, drinking each other's juices—the woman's yin essence and the man's yang essence.

Maintain this position, with your lips and genitals connected, for five to ten minutes a day to experience a new level of healing in your relationship. Daily Devotion is one of the most secret but powerful tools for improving not just your love life, but saving your relationship as well.

> "Daily Devotion is the opposite of running away from conflict. It involves coming close together, as close as physically possible for two human beings. As a daily ritual it can defuse potential discord before it occurs. It is a far better solution than divorce."
>
> DIANE AND KERRY RILEY,
> *TANTRIC SECRETS FOR MEN*

LIGHTNING AND THUNDER

Just as static accumulates in a cloud, tension builds between lovers who, for reasons of work, health, or simply lack of time, do not have intimate contact with each other. This tension accumulates until, like two electrically charged clouds rubbing together, it is released in a flash of lightning and a burst of thunder. In a relationship, this may take the form of fighting over little things with the slightest provocation. When two people do not have a way of releasing tension daily, or at least regularly, stress builds up. Stress turns into irritation, irritation into anger, anger into resentment, until finally you don't even know why you're mad at your partner.

> **There is a reason why you picked the person you're with: your partner has healing medicine for you, so use it!**

Physical intimacy is important for couples not only if they want to stay together, but also if they want to heal each other and grow as human beings. There is a reason why you've picked the person you're with: your partner has healing medicine for you, so use it! If you're single, there is a reason why you are attracted to the specific partners who come your way: they reflect the type of nurturing you need. Being aware of this can help you nourish yourself when you're with them. Sex is medicine, and like any medication, overdosing can cause more problems than it cures. Practicing the sex for procreation principle, which incorporates periods of rest, activity, and training, is the proper way to use sexual medicine.

Like physical training, sexual training may not always be "fun," but the results it produces go beyond momentary pleasure, extending into every area of life, from career and making money to health and even spirituality. The wise men and women who passed down these techniques knew that successful relationships were built on more than sex, but that sex could be the foundation for other structures in our lives.

In response to a student's complaint that he didn't always feel like doing Daily Devotion, Kerry responds: "Try to understand that Daily Devotion is a means of bonding. Your relationship is more important than how you feel—feelings change. If your relationship is dependent on whether you feel good, you are going to be disappointed a lot of the time."[1]

The dharma of sex is no different than the dharma of caring for your body or your society, it is about long-term fulfillment.

SEXUAL FITNESS

While sex and penetration are still possible during the cultivation phase, ejaculation is not advised. During practice, men need to build energy to perform at their best during the week or so when women are at their peak, so they can climb together to the heights of ecstasy. When a man saves his seed and uses it at the appropriate moment with his lover, he is able to enjoy this ecstasy while maintaining his sexiness. He is never fully depleted, but keeps a bit of his power intact in case he needs it. He remains masculine, strong, and in control of his character.

Have you noticed that men become weak, irritable, and unfocused after too much orgasmic sex? This is because ejaculation exhausts their vitality, and their bodies begin to divert energy from nonessential organs into rebuilding. Men become overly sensitive and susceptible to their environment at this time. But when they avoid depletion they can better face any challenge, be it their relationships, jobs, friends, or even their enemies.

> "No pain, no gain" is obsolete. The new mantra of the savvy modern man is "Work smarter, not harder." That goal is achieved by training, not draining.

Weekend warriors tend to exert themselves to the point of exhaustion in every workout, believing that this is the correct way to exercise. But elite coaches and athletes know that it is imperative to leave some fuel in the tank after every practice, because it is far more difficult to recover from maximal training than from more frequent, submaximal efforts. This is one reason why Eastern European and Soviet athletes dominated sports during the cold war years, because the "Soviet machine" invested millions of dollars in researching the effects of exercise and recovery. The Soviets found that having their athletes fresh and ready for competition produced better results than pushing them to the point of failure in practice. These athletes were required to max out about once a month to test and demonstrate the limits of their endurance. Then they returned to submaximal training to build up to new heights of strength and endurance. The Soviets called this practicing, and we also call it practice, or cultivation.

How fascinating that the secret rules of physical excellence mirror the secret rules for sexual fulfillment. If you're a man, hold your seed and train for a month, then enjoy the full pleasure of maximal performance in your chosen playing field, be it the bedroom or the stadium. In this respect, all of life is exercise, and we can apply these principles to almost any activity. "No pain, no gain" is obsolete. The new mantra of the savvy modern man is "Work smarter, not harder." That goal is achieved by training, not draining. This way, man avoids the weakness, uncertainty, and anxiety that creep in when he loses his power, and, therefore, his masculinity.

> **The very activities that define masculinity also diminish it when misused and overdone.**

Learning how to train and build up his energy is an essential component of a man's maturity. Being able to forego short-term pleasure for a long-term goal, to exercise control in the face of temptation, is a key trait of mature masculinity. By demonstrating self-control, a man creates a "charge" irresistible to the opposite sex. But the more a man indulges in sex, the more his charge is depleted. Ultimately this leads to his effeminization, making him less and less desirable.For this reason, if nothing else, a man must keep his reserves and his masculinity intact. This is done not just by abstinence, but by practicing the three steps of sex for procreation—abstinence, cultivation, and performance.

SOLO CULTIVATION PRACTICES
FOR MEN

Do Kegels. More important than push-ups or squats or any exercise in the gym for your sexual strength are Kegel exercises. They produce intense orgasms and connect you to your primal masculinity. This simple squeeze and release of the perineum is the first step to building legendary stamina and self-control, which lead to confidence inside the bedroom and out.

 ## HOW TO DO KEGELS

Begin by squeezing your PC muscle (that is, the pubocoxxygeal muscle, the one you use to stop urinating midstream) one hundred times in one sitting.

Work up to five hundred Kegels per day over the course of a few days or weeks. You can do them while driving, working, or during practically any other activity.

Try to separate the PC muscle from your anal sphincter; squeezing the latter excessively may block the downward flow of prana and lead to constipation and other problems. It is only the perineum PC muscle you want to activate for this exercise.

After you can do five hundred Kegels without too much work, try the more advanced practice:

Squeeze the PC and count to ten.

Release, relax for twenty seconds, and repeat.

Work up to ten repetitions. Try to visualize your sexual arousal and heat shooting up your spine as you squeeze. This will pull your attention away from ejaculation and train your nervous system to remain in control. It also rejuvenates your body, mind, and spirit.

PENIS BOOT CAMP EXERCISES

Wet towel

To further strengthen and invigorate the penis, try the following routine.

Begin by soaking a small towel in hot water for a few seconds.

Wring it out completely and wrap it around your penis. The towel shouldn't feel very hot, but pleasantly warm.

Hold for five to ten minutes. This vital step opens blood vessels and prepares your tissues for the next exercise. Don't skip it!

Stretching

Hold the head of the penis and gently pull out or up, holding for fifteen to thirty seconds.

Release and repeat up to seven times.

In between stretches, hold the penis by the base and twirl it twenty-seven times in one direction then twenty-seven times the other way. Or, holding at the base, slap the penis twenty-seven times on your left thigh, then twenty-seven times on the right.

Massage

You will need an herbal oil like ashwagandha, bala, or your Vata/Pitta/Kapha abhyanga massage oil. Tahitian monoi oil also works well.

Make an OK sign with your dominant hand, and wrap this around the base of your oiled penis (the same grip you used for twirling and slapping above). Hold firmly, but not so firmly that you can't do the exercise.

Begin to pull down as if milking the soft penis. This is also called jelqing. One stroke should take about one to three seconds.

Repeat with the other hand.

It is important not to become aroused because you can't do this exercise if your penis is hard. If an erection occurs, simply stop and perform Kegels until it returns to normal. A little arousal is okay, as long as it doesn't create hardness, but *do not massage your penis while it's erect*; you can damage blood vessels and hurt yourself, which is counterproductive. Also, try not to turn this into a masturbation session, ending in ejaculation. This is an exercise of willpower meant to build up your reserves, not release them.

Work up to three hundred strokes per session over the course of a few weeks.

Exercise five days with two days off per week to give your tissues time for rest and recovery.

Repeat Warm Towel

Finish with the warm towel for five minutes to allow the membranes to relax and recover.

This step, like the first, should never be skipped; it is vital for recovery.

Between boot camp sessions you can also practice holding *medhra marma* (see the "Oil Is Love—Oil for Sex" box on page 262). You can also practice pranayama, using daily breath extension exercises as described in chapter 4 (beginning on page 106). Not only will these help you gain control of your breath and your mind, but they will also help you rein in your sexual impulses.

Solo practices should be done together with Daily Devotion if you are in a partnership. Daily Devotion is one of the most powerful ways to build energy and stamina, as well as lasting love in your relationship.

SOLO CULTIVATION PRACTICES
FOR WOMEN

Do Kegel exercises (see "How to Do Kegels" on page 257).

It is also important to participate in feminine fitness and other activities that allow women to express their creativity and sensuality. The world abounds in traditions designed to connect women with their sensual feminine nature. Many of these involve circular movements, which emulate the curvilinear shape of nature. Galaxies, seashells, flowers, and DNA are all spirals, and the dance of nature is a vortex. Moving your hips in circular patterns awakens this power within you. Biceps curls at the gym are fine, but women need to cultivate shakti by romancing the spiral. Here are eight examples of solo practices that allow women to connect with their feminine nature:

Hula hoop: Alone or with friends, playing with a hula hoop is both fun and relaxing, while unobtrusively stimulating sexual energy. In addition, it helps you move and tone your hips, arms, and legs in a coordinated, circular way.

Hula: Spirituality and dance combine in Hawaii's traditional art of storytelling through movement. Great for grounding and moving subtle energy in your body, hula incorporates body, mind, and soul into one graceful act of devotion.

Belly dance: The epitome of passion and zest, learning to belly-dance frees your hips and releases the primordial, beautiful goddess in you!

Yoga: This practice is enormously popular among women—women make up more than 70 percent of classes—because yoga provides a safe space for you to sweat, cry, chant, and otherwise express yourself through your body.

Cooking: Learning to cook, if this is not part of your normal routine, is an amazing way to get in touch with your senses. Taking the time to touch, smell, and taste different foods can be a sensual experience that revitalizes your creativity.

World dance: From salsa to kathak to flamenco, learn the steps, get on the floor, and move your hips to get in touch with your passion!

Pole dance: This sexy workout is not just for topless dancers anymore. Soccer moms and executives alike can benefit from this challenging fitness sensation.

A spa day: Treating yourself to a hot stone therapy or lomi lomi Hawaiian massage not only can revitalize your body, but your soul as well. A day at the spa, being pampered and cared for, can automatically make you feel like a new person.

Feminine fitness can be any form of exercise that makes you feel good and free to be a woman. It is not only for the young and fit. New mothers who feel depleted after giving birth can rediscover their shakti and sexiness by practicing forms of feminine fitness, creativity, or restoration. No matter if you are elderly, sick, or depressed, as long as you live in a woman's body, you need to dance. And the best way to move is in a spiral!

> No matter if you are elderly, sick, or depressed, as long as you live in a woman's body, you need to dance. And the best way to move is in a spiral!

Other solo practices for women include pranayama and self-massage. More than for men, exploring your body with daily self-massage is one of the keys to staying young and feeling grounded. Daily breast massage is also essential for staying abreast of any possible changes like fibroids or tumors. Exploring your body doesn't have to be sexual, but it is always sensual.

SELF-MASSAGE FOR WOMEN

Pick a nourishing oil for your mind/body type and take five to fifteen minutes to explore the beautiful and not-so-loved corners of your body.

Pay special attention to your breasts, moving your hands up the sternum and out to the armpits as you massage.

Finish by drawing a hot bath and relaxing for another fifteen minutes, allowing the oil to penetrate into your skin.

This doesn't have to be a lavish affair each time—consistency is more important.

Substituting thirty minutes of TV per night for massage and a bath goes a long way toward creating a stress-free body and mind, which in turn supports healthy weight loss and sensual, loving relationships.

+ + +

For the best spiritual, sexual, and mind/body results from your relationships, follow the rules of sex for procreation: A few days before the onset of menstruation and five to seven days after, abstinence and rest are advised. During the next two or three days, cultivation can begin with nonejaculatory sex. During this time, sexual response will be stimulated and passion heightened, but men should try to save their ejaculatory orgasms for the following phase of sex during ovulation. And then return to the cultivation stage before the next round of abstinence.

Oil Is Love—Oil for Sex

From Medhra Marma to Yoni Pichu

Applying oil to the genitals before sex is a wonderful and stimulating way to lubricate these organs, especially if there is vaginal dryness or other symptoms that make penetration painful. For men, massaging the penis with bala or ashwagandha oil before sexual congress is a great aphrodisiac; you can even make this part of your loveplay together. Men can also use oil on the penis in between sex to combat erectile dysfunction, premature ejaculation, and sexual debility, as described in the "Solo Cultivation Practices" section beginning on page 257. Massaging this oil (almond, sesame, and coconut also work fine) on the penis for fifteen minutes a day, accompanied by stretching and gentle penis exercises, can build up your stamina and make you into a super lover! Simply make sure that you do not ejaculate when performing these stretches, as you will dissipate the built-up energy.

How Does It Work?

Oil has healing properties. Medicated oils like bala or ashwagandha have the added benefit of acting as vehicles for their namesake rejuvenative herbs bala (*sida cordifolia*) and ashwagandha (*withania somnifera*). In this way you get the benefit of the herb and the oil working synergistically.

How Do Men Do It?

Use as described in the cultivation practices above (beginning on page 257). In addition, a special marma (energy or acupressure) point to consider for sexual health, the medhra marma, is located on the dorsal surface of the glands penis. (On women this marma is located on the tip of the clitoris.) Press on the groove about an inch behind the tip of the penis with your index finger (with your thumb on top) and hold for fifteen seconds. Stimulate this marma point while doing your stretching exercises as detailed above. If you have sex an hour after doing your solo practice or stimulating your marma points, you will have better endurance and recovery time.

How Do Women Do It?

A technique called yoni pichu (literally, vagina cotton) consists of dipping a sterilized one-by-three-inch piece of cotton cloth into shatavari ghee, sesame oil, or bala oil and inserting it vaginally overnight or for at least a few hours. Make sure to remove it in the morning. This combats vaginal dryness and can ease painful periods, if done a week before bleeding begins. Don't try this if you are prone to infections or discharge. In such cases, a special yoni pichu oil can be used to fight vaginal infections and restore balance. This oil is available at specialty ayurvedic retailers and usually contains medical-grade alum, which is astringent and antiseptic. An added benefit of this technique is the strengthening of the vaginal muscles, help with prolapsed uterus, improved sex drive, and tightening of the vaginal wall.

For women, shatavari ghee (or Beauty Balm by Banyan Botanicals, which contains shatavari and other nourishing oils) promotes breast health and lactation (for mothers) when massaged on the breasts. You can also take it internally to enhance these effects. Please note that oil should not be used if you have a yeast infection or any irregularity in your vaginal flora. Though regular use of oil will help to build up healthy mucosa in the long term, you should treat any underlying conditions first before using oil intravaginally. And remember the first rule of oil: if you can't eat it, you don't need it.

PART THREE

Love

✦

A Formula for Relationship Longevity

10

The Yoga of Love

Applying Yogic Principles
to Your Dharma Type
and Relationships

In this chapter we will discuss some of the spiritual pillars of daily life and how they relate to the dharma types and your relationships. The first of these is the hierarchy of human needs, as described by the chakra system.

Any relationship has a hierarchy of needs to fulfill in order to make it functional. The chakra system is a body-based, vertical model of human evolution, showing how the building of our life is to be constructed if we are to enjoy a stable, happy, and ultimately enlightening human experience. It works like this:

1. The needs of the previous chakra must be fulfilled before moving on to the next. For example, we need to water the soil of the first chakra before the petals of the second can open to us, which means that we need to have physical security (food, water, shelter) before enjoying sexual satisfaction.

2. The priorities represented by the first three chakras are biological, hardwired drives common to most animals. The next three represent higher human desires, and though not nec-

essary for our survival, they are crucial for our evolution as human beings.

3. The chakra model can be used to represent the needs of a single human being, a relationship between a couple or within a group, or the evolution of an entire country. In this chapter we will use it primarily to show how two people can build a solid, fulfilling life together, but the same rules apply for your own personal evolution.

THE CHAKRAS

First Chakra

The first chakra represents security and survival. It is the instinct for food, air, clothing, and shelter, and, in modern times, the thing that supplies them—money. Money and security are the number one reason couples break up, and the first chakra has primacy because it is the foundation for everything else. Earlier, we saw that female mammals are attracted to males who can provide for them. Even the most romantic relationships break down if the male is essentially helpless to provide for himself or to secure his environment.

This chakra is represented by a square because squares are the most stable shape in nature. Squares also indicate inclusion and exclusion—this is mine and that is yours. When imbalanced this identification leads to jingoism, patriotism, and racism, because these "isms" are all rooted in the same place, the first chakra need for security. The dominant emotion here is fear, especially fear that we won't survive. Statements like "My _____ is better than yours" stem from this kind of fear; a person in a position of strength has no need to make these sorts of statements. Therefore, whether we fill in the blank with *country*, *team*, or *race*, the fundamental impetus behind this sentiment is the same.

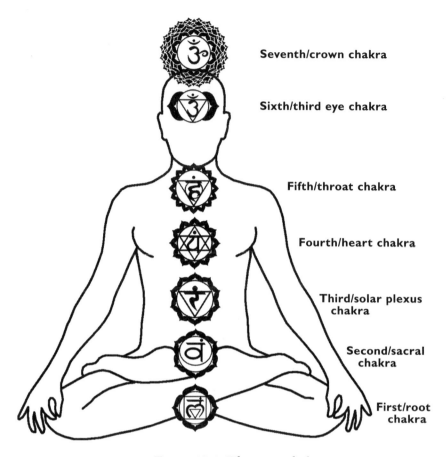

Seventh/crown chakra

Sixth/third eye chakra

Fifth/throat chakra

Fourth/heart chakra

Third/solar plexus chakra

Second/sacral chakra

First/root chakra

Figure 10.1. The seven chakras

That does not mean that we cannot take pride in our ancestors, our land, or our sports teams. However, there is a fine line between pride and obsession. If you are ready to pummel someone because he is wearing the other team's jersey, you've probably gone too far!

First-chakra disorders include lower back pain, constipation, stress (especially over bills and money), joint and foot pain, and fanaticism. If you or your partner suffer from these issues, look at your living situation, using the tools from chapter 5. Begin by eliminating clutter and creating space in the center of your home and every possible room. Unburden the northeast direction and fix leaky faucets. Next, do the same for your body by incorporating the lifestyle suggestions from chapter 4 for at least twenty-one days and see how you feel. It takes twenty-one days to begin changing old thought patterns and another forty-two days for new ones to become embedded in your routine. Finally, while you are doing this, implement the BE FIT system for finding and living your dharma. Follow these recommendations for two months and you will create magic in your life!

Second Chakra

The first chakra relates to the Earth element and fear for survival. Questions of property and ownership are essentially at the root of most wars on this planet. The second-most likely cause of conflict is sex. The second chakra is ruled by Water and this relates to procreation, since all life requires water and at one point originates from water. The symbol here is a crescent moon in the shape of a bowl, filled with creative abundance. If you are experiencing sexual difficulties, hormonal fluctuations, blocked creativity, or reduced pleasure in life, this is the center to address.

To do this, honoring the Water element is important, first, by drinking enough water and doing it at the right times (see chapter 4), and next by allowing it to flow in your life. Water stagnates when it doesn't move; this means sharing your creativity with the world, whether as a hobby or onstage, will improve your hormone balance and sex life. Not the creative type? Allowing water to flow also means sharing your abundance with the world by giving to charity. Living near water also helps.

Second-chakra problems include depression, since our emotions (or lack of them) are largely based on our neurochemistry, and sexual dysfunction. Being by a waterfall or a tropical beach can certainly improve these, at least temporarily, as can following the sex for procreation suggestions in chapter 9.

Third Chakra

This chakra is represented by a downward-pointing triangle, which indicates grace descending to the earth. The desire here is to express your power in the world. It is associated with the Fire element and the outward-moving energy of self-actualization. After basic survival needs are met and our desires for partnership and sex are satisfied by a stable relationship, we naturally turn our minds to self-fulfillment. That is why a good marriage (second chakra) is a stepping-stone for success in the outer world (third chakra). Statistics support this, showing that married couples are self-diagnosed as happier than their nonmarried or divorced counterparts.

The drive to "be somebody" takes precedence here; if it is blocked it can lead to gastric problems like GERD (gastrointestinal reflux disease), Crohn's disease, and sluggish digestion, which itself creates a myriad of health issues, from skin eruptions to compromised immunity. Honor the Fire element and the third chakra by setting good goals and sticking to them. Follow your dharma type, especially its evolution point (see chapter 3), to make the most of yourself in the world. Give yourself time within your relationship to follow your dreams, and talk about this with your partner.

Fourth Chakra

If the third chakra relates to expressing your identity in the world, the fourth is about balancing that expression with acceptance that others have an equal right to express their own identities. This is symbolized by a Star of David—two triangles, one pointing up, one down. This indicates a balance of grace descending down and aspiration rising up. The fourth chakra is not just about *me*, but *us*. Communal and democratic instincts are strong here, as is the desire to preserve life and harmonious relationships. The fourth chakra relates to the Air element, and places that pollute their atmosphere, like large urban centers, also pollute their heart center, typically making them more cynical places to live.

Problems with the fourth chakra include the inability to express vulnerability, which can doom a relationship to mechanistic levels of existence—having dinner together, going to the movies, having sex, and repeating, for years on end. A closed heart leaves a person unable to experience innocence or wonder in life, and can lead to cynicism.

Suggested remedies include traveling and movement to honor the Air element. Travel allows your heart to open up to new cultures, recipes, lifestyles, and vistas, which, in turn, should help you open your heart to your lover. Exposure to Air also means hiking mountains, riding horses, or otherwise exposing yourself to this element. A special, powerful technique is to practice pranayama—yogic breathing. This book has sections that show you how.

The fourth chakra is also about clear communication. The Sanskrit word *anahata* means "unstruck," which relates to a person's ability to hear another's grievances and not take them personally, to not have their egos bruised because they understand the other person's point of view. This ability to empathize makes those who possess it incredible mediators.

Fifth Chakra

The fifth chakra relates to the throat, the Space element, and communication, specifically of higher realities. Space is absolutely pure, a receptacle for whatever it contains. This allows you to be like a mirror and reflect the world around you perfectly. It can also be disorienting, because it loosens the bonds with mundane reality. Disorders of this chakra include speech and hearing loss, as well as loose joints and problems with the spaces of the body, including the synaptic spaces. Dizziness and a lack of groundedness due to an overextended personality are also common—don't lose touch with mundane reality just because you have a connection to other realities. Suggested remedies are similar to those for Outsiders: accept responsibility for everything in life (just as space holds everything), and absolutely refuse to blame others for your problems. Learn to understand the laws of karma and dharma and express your unique gift to the world. You have a body for a reason; use it.

Refuse to put impure thoughts, foods, and words in your body and try to maintain your integrity. If you're a Space element person or suffer from misalignment of this chakra, get your bearings by rooting your life in deep philosophical traditions. Study of the Kabbalah, dharma types, Taoism, or your own religion is indispensible to helping you find your fixed star.

SHARED PURPOSE

Having a shared purpose as a couple can be powerfully binding. When you have compatible ideologies or philosophies, chances are better that you will weather the storms that rock many relationships. That is why sun sign compatibility is so popular in astrology. Comparing sun signs, which is one of many techniques of synastry, or horoscope matching, is a way to gauge a couple's spiritual compatibility. This can mean anything from common political views to a shared religious affiliation. When times get tough, couples who practice a spiritual faith together are more likely to stay married, as opposed to couples who have radically different views or who do not have a shared spiritual community.

Devoting part of your life to a higher purpose is one way to balance body, mind, and soul. This was seen as a normal part of life in ancient traditions.

The pyramid in figure 10.2, which we have seen already, shows three levels of dharma. It also shows a basic breakdown of our daily priorities. Devoting the major part of our day to caring for the body—through eating, sleeping, and other bodily needs—takes up

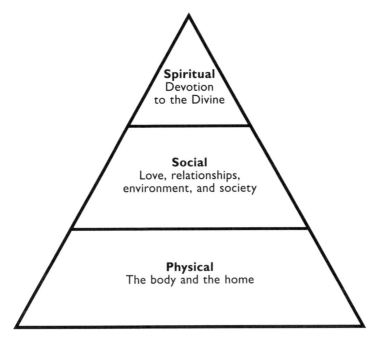

Figure 10.2. Dharma and our daily priorities

most of the twenty-four-hour cycle, which is why the bottom part of the pyramid is the largest.

Social obligations, like work and family (plus our relationship with our spouse), take up the second part of the pyramid. Finally, at the apex we can see that a little time is left for caring for our spiritual self—our relationship with the cosmos. Research shows that developing a relationship with your spiritual roots is just as necessary as brushing your teeth if you want to remain healthy and happy. Let's take a look at the breakdown below.

Self: The Body

8 hours for sleep
3 hours for food gathering/prepping/eating
1 hour for bathing/shaving/applying makeup, etc.
Total: 12 hours

Environment and Society: The Other

8 hours for work

3 hours for leisure, family and spouse, entertainment, sports, community activities

Total: 11 hours

Cosmos: The Divine

1 hour for prayer, meditation, and so forth

These times are estimates and can be adjusted according to individual variables. However we tweak them, it is vital that we incorporate at least some spiritual time in our day to connect to something higher, to anchor ourselves to a greater purpose that puts our daily struggles in perspective. That one or two hours, or even thirty minutes per day, can literally save our lives by giving us hope and insight, and reducing stress and anxiety.

TITHING YOUR TIME

In traditional cultures, tithing was a way to share your bounty, giving 10 percent or more of your income to support the spiritual community. Tithing also works in your daily routine: you can tithe your time. By devoting 10 percent of your day (2.4 hours) to spiritual pursuits, the rest of your life can benefit, just as a society benefits when you tithe your wealth. If 2.4 hours seems like too much, then devote just an hour—less than 5 percent of your day—to connecting with your higher self. Your body, mind, and soul, plus your relationships, will thank you! Suggestions for how to do that are outlined in the Ten Commandments section on page 277.

When a couple shares similar ideas of how to spend this 5 to 10 percent of their day, the rest of their time aligns more easily. When the top of the pyramid is in place, the bottom portions fit better. On the other hand, you may follow the perfect health care regimen, but if you have no friends (social level) or moral backbone (spiritual level), your relationships will never develop beyond that basic physical level.

Having the bottom two levels in place—you take care of yourself; you have a good job and friends, your spouse and family love you—will enrich your life exponentially more than just having the first level in place. But if the top of the pyramid is missing, you are still lacking grace and magic in your life. You are subject to the whims and caprices of natural selection and random pianos falling on your head. Call it luck or divine favor: this level of grace is not earned, but comes about as a side effect of cultivating the top of the pyramid.

A strong relationship to the third level of dharma can minimize suffering at the two lower levels. Have you ever come across people with little food, security, or social mobility who still radiate peace and joy? Have you found those who are content despite having little in the way of physical comforts? And have you witnessed others who, despite enjoying abundance, grow fat and malcontent, sowing distress in themselves and their community? The key is the third level of dharma.

Even if you are not blessed with abundance, we all have equal shares of time, and it is up to us to figure out how best to use that time. We are the generals of this army that consists of *hour* divisions, *minute* brigades, and *second* platoons, and how we command them ultimately reflects on our ability to live in peace with our world, rather than fighting against the crush of time and responsibility.

TABLE 10.1. SPIRITUAL ATTRIBUTES, TENDENCIES, AND BEST PURSUITS BY DHARMA TYPE

DHARMA TYPE	SPIRITUAL PATH	YAMA (RESTRAINT)	NIYAMA (OBSERVANCE)	ELEMENT
Laborer	Devotion, service	Continence	Cleanliness	Earth
Warrior	Karma yoga, austerity	Speaking truth	Austerity	Fire
Merchant	Ritual, charity, karma yoga	Nonstealing	Contentment	Water
Educator	Wisdom, scripture	Nonviolence	Self-study	Air
Outsider	Tantra, mystery	Nongrasping	Divine immersion	Space

TABLE 10.2. SOCIAL ATTRIBUTES, TENDENCIES, AND BEST PURSUITS BY DHARMA TYPE

DHARMA TYPE	PROFESSION	STRENGTH	WEAKNESS
Laborer	Nourish, build community	Solid, dependable	Stubborn, dogmatic
Warrior	Protect, enforce truth, justice	Leader, strong	Cynical, materialistic
Merchant	Happiness brokers, luxury	Fun, motivated	Unreliable, lie
Educator	Wisdom, education	Virtuous	Fickle, weak
Outsider	Innovation, reform	Progressive	Blames others

TABLE 10.3. PHYSICAL ATTRIBUTES, TENDENCIES AND BEST PURSUITS BY DHARMA TYPE

DHARMA TYPE	KOSHA	EXERCISE	FOOD	BRAIN TYPE	EMOTION
Laborer	Flesh	Mechanical	Carb-rich	Cingulate gyrus	Dogmatic
Warrior	Breath	Aerobic	Protein-rich	Frontal lobe	Anger
Merchant	Sensate	Dance	Rich, tasty	Deep limbic	Desire
Educator	Wisdom	Inspirational	Vegetarian, organic	Temporal lobe	Lust
Outsider	Bliss	Exotic	All	Basal ganglia	Anxiety

THE TEN COMMANDMENTS

Many folks don't know that there are ten commandments in yoga, and yoga teachers don't like it when I use that term, preferring the more politically correct *ethical or moral principles*. Whatever you call them, they are great tools for helping you find your spiritual path and focus your 10 percent of spirit time.

The five *yamas* and *niyamas*—the ten commandments of yoga—each relate to a dharma type and give clues to the spiritual discipline most appropriate to each one. They are prerequisites for entering into asana practice. That is, you must have a basic level of cleanliness, honesty, discipline, and strength of character before becoming a yogi: you can't be a lowlife because you will not only disturb other students, but the power of the practice will only make you a worse lowlife. For many sincere students, however, looking at the list of yamas and niyamas can be daunting; even mastering one can be a lifetime challenge. But the dharma type bails us out here again. Here's how it works.

Let's say you're a Warrior. Checking table 10.1 shows that "speaking truth" and "practicing austerity," among the yamas and niyamas, respectively, correlate to your dharma type. Focusing on these will not only give you quick results in your practice, it will also help you master the remaining yamas and niyamas.

Speaking truth means controlling your prana (life energy or breath), since speech is carried on the breath. For Warrior dharma types, this means honoring your prana by using it to speak your truth in ways that promote dharma, and not repressing what you have to say, even if it hurts people's feelings. Speaking truth to those in power is one of the ways Warriors stand up for just causes. It does not mean never telling a lie; where veering from literal truth promotes dharma, that is still truth, as the Mahabharata epic of India famously reminds us.

Austerity, on the other hand, relates to discipline and self-denial for a higher purpose. Having a goal, a mark to strive for, is extremely important for Warrior types, and practicing *tapas*, austerity, helps them get there. Whether it's hitting the next sales target or sitting in lotus position for three hours, Warriors are willing to sacrifice their comfort to achieve their goals.

Spiritual Practices for Warriors

Pranayama in any form

Self-sacrifice and austerity, including asana practice (yoga poses), community work, healing

Fire ceremonies and rituals, including sun worship

For Educators, the primary virtue is nonviolence, which means not causing fear in another creature, including animals and plants. This also means learning to surrender their agenda and open themselves to divine flow. Practicing nonviolence involves respecting your needs and those of your community. This can take the form of using ethically sourced products, eating a vegan or vegetarian diet, or otherwise contributing to peace in your surroundings.

Spiritual Practices for Educators

Self-study—this is another ethical precept for Educators, which means reading, learning, and language are the primary spiritual practices for these types

Mantras, prayers, and scriptural study, including teaching others

Quiet time and meditation

For Merchants the primary precepts are nonstealing and contentment. This means that, even though you can take advantage of others, you shouldn't do it. When nonstealing is understood, contentment comes of its own accord. Because Merchants harbor a yearning inside, they try to fill it with many things. But contentment only comes when they begin to fill others' lives with joy by practicing charity. Tithing is a Merchant invention: do it for yourself and your community.

Spiritual Practices for Merchants

Charity—contributing to the health, wealth, and luxury of others

Good works, compassion in action, and karma yoga

Merchants can also put on lavish rituals and festivals as part of their charitable endeavors, which they appreciate more than most dharma types

For Laborers, continence and cleanliness are the ethical precepts that will bring them enlightenment. This means that practicing the sex for procreation principles in chapter 9 and saving their energy for their primary relationship are vitally important, because these spare them from the drudgery of the mating dance. *Continence* does not mean abstinence; it is a way to focus Laborers on their communal instinct to bring together family and society in harmony.

Cleanliness relates to value. Laborers tend to be more slack with self-care and personal hygiene. For them to optimize their perceived value in society, they have to practice basic cleanliness, and nowhere more so than before the altar. Clean your mouth and body regularly, and make it easier for God and the world to greet you with love.

Spiritual Practices for Laborers

Faith and devotion—chanting, singing, and faith-based prayer

Feeding people, which any dharma type can reap benefits from doing; Laborers, however, have a talent for it and do it better than most

For Outsiders the ethical precepts are nongrasping and divine immersion. This means that, though they spend a good portion of their lives trying new things, grasping at various identities and philosophies, at some point they have to stop and ask themselves who they really are. Because they are able to blend so well into different environments, they can wear many hats, but at some point they need to figure out which hat fits them best. This does not mean giving up their eclectic, experimental nature, only refining it enough to realize that no amount of grasping can give them what they want—their identity. That is a gift they must give themselves.

> **No amount of grasping can give Outsiders what they want—their identity. That is a gift they must give themselves.**

Spiritual Practices for Outsiders

Seeing God everywhere—this is divine immersion

Unconventional spiritual practices, like tantra and aghora

If God is everywhere, then the Divine is in the kitchen and in the toilet as well. For the Outsider, truth is a loose concept, one not grounded in a house of worship. Divine immersion also means God is in you AS YOU; and no matter your predicament, you're only an inch away from grace at any time.

TANTRIC YOGURT

I like to tease my British friends about their accent whenever I can (and they do the same with me). I particularly love to hear them pronounce the word *yoga*, because it comes out like *yogurt*. What follows is a section on delicious tantric yogurt. Try it sometime in the bedroom—you'll love it!

Elemental Love

Making love involves the body on the one hand and the mind, emotions, and spirit on the other. It also involves the five elements. Fire is heat and passion, generated by the friction of two lovers rubbing together. Water is the sweat and taste of your lover. Earth is the scent, the heaviness of your partner; Air is the partner's breath and touch; and Space is the setting, the distance between you, the crucible in which alchemy turns your love into something divine. Tantrics focus their attention on each of the elements to deepen the sexual experience and turn it into spiritual ecstasy.

We can use a two-part process during lovemaking to heighten our awareness. The first is to focus on physical sensations, the aforementioned five elements and their corresponding senses: touch, sight, smell, hearing, and taste.

Sound	Space
Touch	Air
Sight	Fire
Taste	Water
Smell	Earth

FOCUSING ON PHYSICAL SENSES DURING SEX

Isolate each sense and focus solely on it for two to three minutes.

Begin by focusing for a few minutes exclusively on the smell of your lover. The Earth element is related to smell as well as solidity.

As you focus on scent, also let yourself to connect to the solid structures of your lover's body. Feel the gravity of these structures pull you together.

Next, move on to how your lover tastes. This is harder, as you'll have to use your lips to sample different parts of your lover's body.

After a couple of minutes or so, focus on how your lover looks next to you, beneath you, or on top of you. Is your lover sweating? Does his/her skin have goose bumps? Notice your lover's eyes—what color are they? How do they move? Are they looking at you or are they closed? The Fire element relates to the eyes, and they reveal your focus.

Now move on to touch. Feel the weight of your partner's body pressing on you, or your own against your lover's. Even notice the weight of your clothes, or the blankets and sheets on top of you. Then begin to notice the more subtle aspects of touching your partner and how your partner's touch feels on your body. If you're starting to get pretty turned on by now, good. But, men, don't let yourselves go; you have to get through the entire exercise before ejaculating (see tips for avoiding premature ejaculation below).

Then turn your attention to the Space element. Notice the negative space between your bodies and what it would look like on a canvas. What are your surroundings like? What sounds do you hear in the room, and how do they complement your lovemaking? What is your lover saying? How is he or she saying it? What do the sheets sound like as they move underneath you?

Finally, slowly add each sense and element together, stacking them one on top of the next, until you can hold five distinct awarenesses in utter concentration. This is a skill developed with practice.

Avoiding Premature Ejaculation

One way to avoid premature ejaculation is to move with your entire body instead of thrusting only with your hips. Thrusting creates excitement and passion; if this is already at its peak, try resting on your elbows (in the missionary position), and rocking your whole body back and forth. Many women even prefer this to thrusting, as it creates better contact with the clitoris and a wave motion that is highly arousing. Avoiding strenuous positions is another way to prolong sex, because tiring yourself out is a surefire way of losing control. Instead of supporting yourself on your hands, relax on your elbows. Instead of standing, try sitting or lying down. Take your time and do not be afraid to change positions: this is much more preferable than losing control and ending the session by finishing early.

Finally, learn to breathe deep into the lower lobes of the lungs. Shallow breathing creates excitement; deep, yogic breathing brings you back to a relaxed state of self-control. Deep breathing also allows you to stay present without forcing your mind to think of other things, as many men do to avoid ejaculating. It does the same thing for women, though for women slow breathing can help intensify an orgasm, making it deeper and longer. Try playing with the breath the next time you are alone or with a partner and you will see: the faster the breath, the more excited the mind becomes. One secret for prolonging sex is to take two or three deep ujjayi breaths, especially if you feel yourself getting close to orgasm and you want to delay the experience. See page 92 for more on ujjayi breathing.

Drinking Your Lover

After building on the first five senses, we must harness the mind to stay aware and present with our experience. Vedic teachings warn that where your mind goes, your life force (prana) follows. And at the moment of death, where your mind goes, there goes your soul.*

---

*This is why last rites are so important in our spiritual traditions. If the last thing we think of at the moment of death is God, then we reach heaven after death. The Bhagavad Gita discusses this in detail.

If you are fantasizing about another lover at the time of orgasm and conception occurs, the child born from that union will have conflicted consciousness. That child may even have characteristics of the imagined lover, either mentally, physically, or both.

Ayurvedic literature is clear on the influence of our mental projections on the baby before, during, and after conception. There are specific protocols during and after lovemaking that ensure that a healthy, happy child is born from that union. One of these is staying present with your lover during sex.

> "That's why the Christian, at his death,
> Renounces sin with his last breath;
> That's why the Hindu, when he slips,
> Has only 'Rama' on his lips,
> For all religion plainly knows
> That where the mind, the body goes . . ."
>
> FROM THE AUTHOR'S UNPUBLISHED POEM
> "BHAV BALLADS"

 STAYING PRESENT WITH YOUR PARTNER DURING SEX

Try to tap into your partner's energy field and drink it in.

For Men

As you breathe in, imagine molecules of your partner's energy getting sucked into you. Use your third eye as a virtual vacuum to literally aspirate your partner's essence, her pleasure, love, and passion. Don't worry, you cannot suck her dry, as your act of lovemaking creates more of this than you can ingest, unless you're a highly advanced tantric or Taoist practitioner.

Imagine your partner's energy entering through your third eye and streaming down the front of your body until it reaches your sex organs.

Then, squeezing your PC muscle, send it shooting up the back of your spine, up and over your skull, and back down the front of your body. Some of the energy will evaporate out of your head as it does this, which is how you spread your positive vibes through the atmosphere and your environment.

As the energy makes its way back down the front of your body, you draw in fresh new essence from your lover and continue the process.

Another version of this involves pulling your partner's energy up through your penis, but this is usually harder to do for most men.

For Women

As your partner thrusts, imagine his energy not only physically penetrating you, but moving beyond your vaginal canal, filling your belly, your heart, your throat, and your mind's eye with love and passion.

Or, like your man, you can send the energy up your spine and cycle it back down the front of your body, squeezing and shooting it back up again as it reaches your sex center.

> "The mind is its own place, and it can make
> Of Hell a Heaven, and of Heaven, Hell."
> JOHN MILTON, *PARADISE LOST*

If you like, use your own technique for drinking in your lover's energy, one that is specific to you. Don't like the molecule analogy? How about light? Imagine the light of your lover entering and filling your body with different colors, at different centers. Yellow for the root chakra, blue for the sex center, fiery red for the solar plexus, green for the heart, indigo for the throat, and so forth. Make your own game of drinking your partner in so that lovemaking becomes a restorative practice.

Most men experience a sense of depletion after having sex, but if you consistently drink your partner's energy, especially during your orgasm, you can reverse this depletion. After doing the five-element practice and drinking your partner for a while, you should have a good feeling for how it's done. Follow the exercise below to avoid this depletion.

 **DRINKING IN YOUR PARTNER'S ENERGY DURING ORGASM**

Practice the five-element and drinking in your partner exercises for a few sessions without ejaculating. This should build up extra energy in your system.

Then, when you're ready to ejaculate during lovemaking, simply imagine that the energy molecules of the seminal fluid are rising up through your body, just as the fluid is leaving. In that way, what leaves is simply the physical vehicle, while you have ingested its essence.

Like boiling water, imagine the steam of your fluid rising up through you as the fluid leaves. The steam is the essence. The fluid is the dross.

THE PINEAL GLAND

One obstacle to our ability to sense subtle energy is a dormant third eye. Often attributed to the pineal gland, our third eye is the portal to extrasensory perception. Unfortunately, modern diet and lifestyle are not conducive to optimal inner perception; indeed, the Information Age is so outward focused that it is harder than ever to hear the song of our spirit behind the din of daily dialogue assaulting us at all times. Such distraction, coupled with a heavy modern diet, dulls our awareness and drowns out our inner voice.

Physiologically, the pineal gland is part of the endocrine system and is thought to be, along with the pituitary, the master gland associated with orchestrating hormone/neurotransmitter release in the body. Little is known about this seemingly innocuous gland, aside from the fact that diets high in soft drinks (colas especially) and fluoride products accelerate its calcification. For most adults, the pineal gland is effectively shut down; they are unable to perceive anything besides the blatant material world. Calcification of the pineal gland is thought to be normal, in that no discernible deleterious side effects have been observed from this condition.

In India, *kumkum*, or red sandalwood paste, is placed on the forehead to symbolize opening the third eye. Done daily, it brings awareness of the unseen into our mundane reality. Otherwise, life becomes mechanistic and dull; we are imprisoned by the tyranny of the five senses. Worse, being enslaved to our physical senses, we don't even realize that we're in prison; we don't know what we're missing.

When couples marry in Vedic ceremonies, they put this red dot on each other's third eye to symbolize seeing each other as more than flesh and bones and attitude. We are more than the sum of our physical parts and, to recognize that, we need to begin waking up the third eye. No more colas, fluoride, or artificial sweeteners. Exercise and meditate, and the best meditation for couples is seeing your lover fresh and new every day.

Flesh gets used to flesh and habits become stale when you live with someone. When you can't see beyond the five physical senses it is easy to take your partner for granted, which can create problems that lead to breakups and divorce. Taking your lover for granted is spiritual laziness and relationship suicide. The more you work on opening your third eye, the more you will fall in love with your partner every day, over and again.

Flesh and Bones and Attitude

So, how do we decalcify our pineal gland and open our third eye? One of the best ways is to practice regular pranayama, breathing exercises. Alternate-nostril breathing, Phantom Breath, or the following technique, which I call Shiny, Happy Breath, all work to scrape the mud off the mirror of the inner eye and help reveal the divinity reflected within.

Skull shining, or *kapalabhati*, is useful for kindling agni, balancing hormones, and revitalizing the brain. It consists of active, rhythmic exhalation, using the abdomen and passive inhalation. The reputed benefits of this pranayama are staggering. Oxygenation of the brain is one, and it is thought to counter cognitive decline, brain fog, and even Alzheimer's disease. Because of its mood-enhancing effects, it is also a practice for people with mild to moderate depression, though those with serious psychological problems should consult their doctor first.

Ayurvedic physicians sometimes prescribe this pranayama for elevated cholesterol levels and high lipid profiles, as well as for patients suffering from obesity and anorexia. Finally, advanced practitioners report that joint pain and inflammation disappear with high-level practice, on the order of a thousand or more kapalabhati per day. Pain is a symptom of blocked or misaligned prana. By doing regular breathing practice, you not only keep stagnant life force moving, you can remove discomfort from the body as well.

However, beginners should start with only fifty to a hundred repetitions, and work their way up. Because of its intensity, this pranayama is not recommended for anyone with elevated blood pressure, glaucoma, a detached retina, a recent heart attack or other heart problems, nosebleeds, a hernia, ulcers, recent surgery, pregnancy, or menses. If you experience light-headedness or vertigo, stop and lie down, and reduce the number of repetitions the next time.

SHINY, HAPPY BREATH, OR KAPALABHATI

The key to this exercise is to keep your face and body relaxed: if it feels like you're straining, you're doing it wrong. Remember why you're doing yogic breathing in the first place—to relax and strengthen your body, not to stress yourself out.

Start by forcefully exhaling through the nose, using your belly button to drive the air out.

Allow the inhale to come in naturally through the nose, keeping the focus on the forced exhale.

It helps to look at yourself in a mirror when you do this, to see your facial expressions. Try a light, easy smile when performing this exercise.

You can lift your hands above your head for a more intense practice, in the style of kundalini yoga. Keep them there for fifty to a hundred breaths.

With your hands lifted, you can also twist to each side for fifteen to thirty breaths, bringing prana into your liver, spleen, and kidneys on each side.

Oil Is Love—For Super Immunity and Stress-Free Travel

Karna purana is the practice of filling the ears with five to ten drops of warm sesame oil or garlic-infused sesame oil. It has been used for centuries to boost resistance to colds and flu, calm the nervous system, and encourage smooth, stress-free travel. It is part of a daily practice that will keep you strong and calm in the face of stress.

How Does It Work?

In ayurveda the ears are gateways to the inner nervous system and must be protected to avoid shock and irritation that can lead to stress, fatigue, and compromised immunity. Ardent surfers and swimmers know that if they protect their ears they can swim in colder water much longer than if their ears are not protected. Karna purana, or lubricating the ears with oil, is your under armor for the ears. It is also used to ease ringing in the ears and TMJ.

How Do I Do It?

You will need two cotton balls, an eye-dropper, and warm sesame oil. Use regular (nontoasted) sesame oil, or make your own garlic-infused sesame oil. (Do not buy the darker, toasted sesame oil from your grocery store or Asian market—that is used for cooking certain Asian dishes, but is not for external use.) To make your own garlic oil, add one clove of garlic per ounce of sesame oil in a saucepan and heat slowly over medium heat until the oil is hot.

Remove from heat and let it cool. Pour this oil into a glass bottle and label it for karna purana. This bottle should last you for some time. You can also use a bit of this oil to cook with, but be careful if you are a Pitta type; it will heat you up quickly!

Warm a small glass bottle of this garlic oil by putting it in hot water. Never, ever microwave this! Do not use plastic bottles, as they will leach chemicals into the oil. You can buy inexpensive empty eye-dropper bottles online or at your local pharmacy. In five minutes the oil should be a nice lukewarm temperature (not hot) and ready to put in your ears. Always test the oil first. Dip your pinky finger in the oil to make sure it is the right temperature, lie on your side, and put a dropper-full of this oil into the ear that is facing up. You will feel a sensation of being underwater as your ear fills up and sound becomes dulled. That's okay. Maintain this position for five to twenty minutes. It is best if you're lying down; this can be profoundly relaxing and you want to take advantage of the oil's soporific properties. Many people go to sleep like this.

When you're ready, put a cotton ball into that ear and turn over. The oil will be absorbed by the cotton and not spill out. If you find it spilling, just make the cotton ball bigger. Now repeat for the other ear. When you're done, you should feel relaxed and shielded from the outside world. You can leave the cotton balls in your ears as long as you like. It is best to do this at night and leave the oil and cotton balls in as you sleep. You will wake up refreshed and ready for your day.

Try this practice once a week and see how you feel. In the winter months and during the cold and flu season, you can do this up to three times a week or as needed, as it helps prevent colds and flu. Also, whether you're traveling by car, bus, or plane, this is a great way to ensure that your body stays healthy and balanced during long trips by reducing vata aggravation—the effects of noise, movement, and stress. Before you leave for a trip, do karna purana and you will get to your destination more relaxed than ever.

The Quickie

Alternatively, if you don't have time to do the full version of karna purana, you can simply put some oil on your pinky finger and use it to lubricate each ear canal. This can be done daily as part of your morning routine. It will ensure enhanced immunity against the onslaught of noise and stress in your day.

Or, if you're a Q-tip user, dip your Q-tip in (preferably warm) garlic-infused sesame oil and swab as you would normally. Be very careful not to go too deep into your ear canal as you may cause painful and even permanent damage. You will see how much better the oil helps to clean out and moisturize the ear canal.

11

Love in the Stars

Astrology for Timing Sex, Marriage, and Other Aspects of Life

Timing is everything. From drinking water to having sex, the *when* is at least as important as the *how* and *how much*. We have seen in chapters 4 and 6 that timing your food and water intake is crucial to clearing ama, kindling agni, and getting the body you want. We discovered in part two that sex for procreation times sex according to nature's rhythms to give you the best experience possible. We also saw that, over the course of a lifetime, initiation into sexual activity should happen according to different schedules for young men and women.

In this chapter we will look at your body's diurnal rhythm—the twenty-four hours between sunrise and sunrise—and how to align each part of your day for success. The Vedic art and science of jyoti-sha provides elegant metaphors for linking the cycles of the heavens with our diurnal rhythms, just as ayurveda gave us the template to study the dharma of our bodies in parts one and two.

The sages of ancient India did not create jyotisha to make nature fit its concepts. Instead, they observed and created a system of symbols to fit nature, and in so doing help us understand and predict nature's cycles. It is not because Taurus looks like a bull that the constellation was invented, but because they observed that when planets cross that part of the sky, agriculture is affected. This is a simple explanation of a complex science that perhaps is better served by seeing it in action: you don't have to believe in astrology to benefit from its wisdom. Take the daily rhythm for a spin in your life and observe its usefulness for yourself.

THE DAILY RHYTHM: AS ABOVE, SO BELOW

Our bodies have diurnal cycles that relate to the apparent movement of the sun in the sky, and our ancient ancestors learned how to harness these biorhythms for optimal success. Did you know that there are moments in the day when it is better to ask for a raise than others? Did you know that sex and romance are juicier during certain hours, and that there is an optimal time to eat your biggest meal? Let's take a look at how these work.

In striving to understand the movement of the heavens, the sages of antiquity noticed correlations between the macrocosm up there and the microcosm in our bodies. For example, when the sun is at its zenith, they found that hunger and digestive juices were also at their peak. They correlated the inner agni (digestive fire) with outer agni (the sun) and postulated that midday was the best time to have your biggest meal, since the fires outside and within our bodies were at their peak. They also noticed that when the sun is at the opposite point in the sky, exactly below the earth, there is a second kindling of digestive fire—something known to us in the West as the midnight snack phenomenon. This is the time for agni to do its inner cleaning, and they advised against eating then so as not to overburden our liver and metabolism. Instead, going to bed before agni's second wind is preferable, optimally before 10 p.m.

These sages also pictured the movement of the sun through

different parts of the sky they termed "houses." The ancients then assigned meanings to each house based on their observations of reality (see figure 11.1). At first these meanings might not make sense. But a closer inspection reveals how they mirror both our internal and external realities.

The First House (5–7 a.m.)

What is the first thing you notice when you wake up? It is probably your body and its location in time and space. Just before you may have been sailing the high seas or soaring through the heavens as a bird in the world of dreams, but as soon as you wake up you become aware of your mundane reality and the body that anchors you to it. Accordingly, the first house is the time to attend to the body's needs by doing things like brushing your teeth, getting dressed, eating, exercising, and excreting. It is also the best time to study. Getting to bed early and studying in the sattvic morning hours is the optimal way to train the brain to hold and retain information. Sattva begets knowledge and wisdom, and is present in the early morning and early evening hours. (See pages 226–27 for more on the sattvic, rajasic, and tamasic portions of the day.) Cramming late at night may help you pass a test, but that does not promote long-term wisdom.

The first house also relates to sunrise, the "birth" of the sun over the horizon and the transition from night to day. The dawn heralds the beginning of your day and beginnings are important in any tradition. How you start a relationship, a business, or even a lifetime has great bearing on how those work out. That is why the way in which you spend the morning is vital to the success of the rest of your day. In part one we discussed daily self-care, most of it focusing on the first hour or two of the day. We also related the early morning hours to the early years of life, as posited by Dr. Claudia Welch, and suggested that healing practices like pranayama and meditation

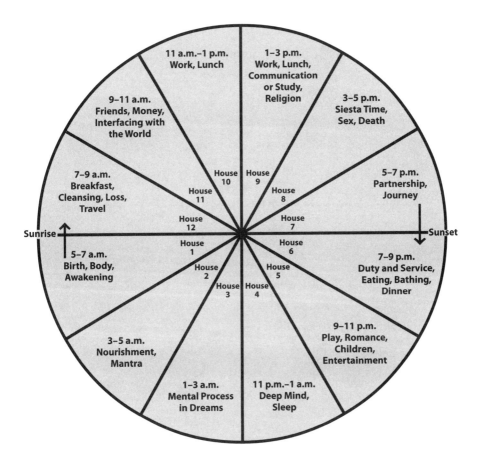

*Figure 11.1. The twelve houses and
their times of day and optimal activities*

done in the morning can help to heal traumas from those years (see page 71). This concept has even permeated the English language. Consider the word *orientation*. *Orient* means "east," and to orient oneself is to literally face east, where the sun rises.

It is not surprising, then, that so many cultures historically worshipped the morning sun, and that millions of people today greet the sunrise in temples and in homes with prayer and devotion. A good practice first thing in the morning after your bathroom duties is to face the sun—to *orient* yourself correctly for the day. Saying a few words of appreciation and intent, making an offering or otherwise acknowledging your personal connection to nature helps to ground you to your inner and outer realities. The Sun Salutation is a yoga practice done for just this purpose—to connect your body (first-house microcosm) with the rising sun (first-house macrocosm). Sacred movements like yoga, t'ai chi, and qigong, which combine physical exercise, mental focus, and energy alignment, yield good results when done in the morning.

When Is It?

Different systems allocate different times to the beginning, duration, and end of each house. This is further complicated by the fact that days are longer or shorter, depending on the season and your latitude north or south of the equator. Nonetheless, here's an easy practical reference: the first house begins with the first appearance of light in the sky. Note that this happens during the early twilight hours, well before sunrise. It ends after the sun has fully risen above the horizon and begun to make its way upward, usually thirty to sixty minutes after official "sunrise." Another rough way to measure the duration of the first house is to count an hour before and after sunrise. Ultimately it is best to feel the changing of the houses in your body and mind; with a little practice, this will become second nature.

The Twelfth House (7–9 a.m.)

The first house ends about thirty to sixty minutes after the sun has completely crossed the eastern horizon. The best way to know this is to feel what is happening in your body. Do you feel a bit of a slump, a slight tiredness come over you, or an urge to get away from your house? If you're still in bed it will be hard to get up, since the twelfth house represents bed pleasures, something experienced by those who luxuriate in sleep past the sunrise hours. Sleep is sweetest during this time, as anyone who has hit the snooze button in the morning can attest. However, the twelfth house also represents loss and dissipation, and one who lingers in bed loses out on precious daylight to make productive use of the day. Dissipation also relates to the use of sexual energies, and though sex is allowed during the sun's tenure in the twelfth house, it may sap the vitality we need to fire us through the day. This is why ayurveda typically frowns on daytime sex.

The twelfth is also a house of extended foreign contacts and travel. If you think about your morning commute, this makes perfect sense. From ancient times, when people left the home to go to the market or pursue their trade, to the modern-day commute, the twelfth house hours represent the time when most of us get in our cars and leave for work. This is both travel and extended foreign contact, since we typically don't return home until after an eight-hour workday, which takes up most of our diurnal routine. How the ancients devised this remains a mystery. Why it is still applicable today, thousands of years after it was observed and systemized is not—human beings are the same now as they were then, and are subject to the same forces and drives as our prehistoric ancestors.

The Eleventh House (9–11 a.m.)

During the next portion of the day a typical person moves into his work routine, visiting with friends, catching up, or having meetings. The eleventh house rules all these things, and is the time to socialize and enjoy the company of one's peers. Chatting up coworkers at the water cooler and engaging in social and professional liaisons and other group interactions work well here. This is the best time to ask for a raise, as the eleventh and ninth houses are considered "lucky" and good for wish fulfillment. Waiting to ask that special guy or gal on a date? Wondering what is the best time to call the debt collector? Do it now, when spirits are at their highest. Text or call and that special someone should respond well to you; even if she lets you down, she will let you down easy! Hold your meetings, pep rallies, and strategy sessions during the eleventh house if you want to succeed. Absolutely avoid the eighth house for these things.

The Tenth House (11 a.m.–1 p.m.)

After the meetings are done, it is time to put your nose to the grindstone: the tenth house is the time to get to work. It represents the sun's peak in the sky, when the fire principle is most promi-nent. Fire in the body means enzymatic activity, which makes us hungry. Throw anything at the sun, from comets to planets, and what happens? They're gobbled up. In the same way, anything you put in your mouth is more likely to be digested at this time. Fire in the mind also means more mental acuity and ambition, driving us to work hard and leave our mark in the world. The tenth house is the time to fully showcase our personalities through our profes-sions. If there are executive decisions to be made, make them now. No matter what your position, you delegate with more authority at this time.

Even if you are unemployed or work from home, this is the time to finish chores: vacuuming the house, paying bills, shopping, and attending to all the duties that await you. The tenth house is an active time and you should not be idle while the sun is here. However, be careful with exercise. Because it is an inherently hot time of day, whether you're indoors or out, overheating and over-training are more likely. Therefore, reserve your workouts for later, during the sixth- or fifth-house hours, when the sun is below the horizon. In ayurveda this is considered Pitta time, when the fire principle is most active in the body. Regardless of the external tem-perature, if you do train during this time, pay special attention to keeping cool.

The Ninth House (1–3 p.m.)

An extension of the optimal lunch period, the ninth is also a house of education, travel, and communication. If there is research to be done, phone calls to make, or emails to send, the ninth house is a good time to take care of those chores. The ninth is another favorable period to hold meetings and communicate strategy. Its energy is also optimal for learning and high-minded ideas. The mood turns philosophical, and this is one of the best times to plan your future, motivate yourself, and communicate your intentions. During this time, lunch is being digested and there is a feeling of relaxation and satisfaction. The effects of too much food or bad food combinations do not become apparent until the next house, when indigestion and sluggishness may overtake the body.

If you don't leave your home by the time the ninth house rolls around, you may find yourself feeling a bit stir-crazy, imprisoned by the four walls of your abode. That is because houses twelve to nine are optimal for dealing with things outside your skin, your home, and your immediate environment. These resplendent daylight hours encourage outdoor activity, which is why nine to five is a common work schedule all over the world. Even if you just go out to get the mail, go shopping, or go for a walk, make it a point to get outside while the sun is transiting these houses.

The Eighth House (3–5 p.m.)

The eighth is perhaps the most important house of the horoscope because it is also the most pernicious. It represents the infamous afternoon blahs—the slump everyone feels whether they live in New Zealand or Nova Scotia.

The eighth house rules endings and death because it is here that the sun begins its steady slide down to the horizon. It is a "dead time" during which the human biorhythm is at its lowest point and tamas pervades the atmosphere. You don't have to be a yogi to feel the eighth-house slump. It happens every day to everyone, and it is a great way to tune in to the inner and outer rhythms of nature.

During the eighth house, people are more likely to be irritable and negative, so this is not the time to ask for a raise, hold meetings or rallies, or call your special someone. It is the time to retreat within yourself by putting on your headphones and immersing yourself in work, cultivating silence, or, best of all, taking a nap. Some cultures wisely dub this "siesta time," when merchants close their shops and go home to rest and refresh themselves. Sleep harnesses the heaviness of tamas and allows you to recharge. It also prevents accidents, which the eighth house also rules, as home in bed is one of the safest places you can be. During this period the body is using its resources to digest food, and your mind can become sluggish and inattentive. Avoid operating heavy machinery, exercising, or undertaking dangerous work when the sun is in the eighth house; this is the house of death and trauma for a reason.

Exercise at this time runs the risk of pushing the body too hard and pulling muscles or causing injury. The body is tighter and less responsive, and nurses report more severe injuries in the ER during this period. However, one exception to the no-exercise rule is sex. The eighth house is a place of lust and carnal pleasure. Sex has a more intense, physical, even vulgar quality here. If you have pent-up tension or trouble generating passion in your relationship, consider eighth-house sex an option, though the best time to engender love and romance is during the fifth house.

The Seventh House (5–7 p.m.)

The seventh house is a place of transitions and journeys. For working folks, it represents the end of the workday, the drive home, and the shift to one's home environment. Sunset is the end of the day and the beginning of night. It signals a change in priorities, during which we go from outwardly expressing ourselves to inner reflection. For the average person, this may simply mean going home, kicking up your feet, and watching TV. For others, sunset is a time for meditation or prayer, or a moment to share with your beloved. The seventh house is the place of the other, particularly the significant other. It is when we rejoin our beloveds after a day spent away from them. Sex is possible during this time, though the half hour or so before and after sunset should be actively avoided.

Ancient traditions speak a similar language. Vedic astrology agrees with ayurveda and yoga that one should not have sex at sunrise or sunset because these mark the birth and death of the sun. It is not customary to observe birth and death with sex, but with contemplation. This is also a time of sattva, and should not be disturbed by rajasic activities like vigorous exercise, intense work, or sex. Instead, use the togetherness energy of this house to take a walk with your partner or take in the sunset; it will help you work up an appetite for the period to come.

The Sixth House (7–9 p.m.)

The sixth is a house of duty, work, and diet. This is not the work of the outside world, however, for the sun has ceased to shine on external activity. During the sixth house it is time to finish household tasks, rest from a hard day's work, bathe, and eat dinner. Obligations to your body and family take precedence. Cooking and cleaning, for example, are types of family duty, while working out, getting a massage, or going to the chiropractor are examples of treating your body. Ancient cultures, especially those in the tropics, observed at least twice-daily bathing rituals—in the morning to wash off sleep, and in the evening to rid themselves of the burdens of the day. This corresponds nicely to the first and sixth houses in astrology.

If you work a nine-to-five schedule, the sixth house may be the only time you have to make a home-cooked meal. Make the most of it; we already discussed the benefits of cooking at home, like improved sensual awareness, family cohesiveness, and even weight management. Use this time to sow the seeds of health and romance that will sprout in the following house.

Because it is a place of duty, and the least romantic house in astrology, sex is not advised during this time; wait an hour or two until the fifth house. It will feel less perfunctory and more satisfying then. It makes sense to eat dinner and relax first before rushing into sex. Take your time and enjoy the transition. But be careful: if you don't get to the dishes before the end of the sixth house, you may lose any inclination to do them at all.

The Fifth House (9–11 p.m.)

A house of play, leisure, creativity, sport, and lovemaking, the fifth house represents recreation in all its aspects, including making babies. This is the best time to have sex, especially if a healthy, happy child is desired. But even if children are not the aim, the fifth house is a good time for creative loveplay and sport.

It is no wonder that major sporting events are also held during these hours. Russian coaches during the cold war reported better performance from their athletes, who broke more records when meets were scheduled between 7 and 10 p.m. than during the day.* Famous musicians have also commented that their playing improves at night, as the musical muse favors the fifth house, allowing a smoother flow of their creative juices. This is true for nonartistic types as well. People who work during the day enjoy entertainment at night, whether by creating it in the form of parties or get-togethers or simply observing it by watching movies and television.

---

*Note that, depending on the season, the fifth house may occur as early as 6 p.m. The best way to know is to feel yourself transition from the sense of duty in the sixth house (cooking, eating, washing dishes) to relaxation (entertainment, play, a night on the town).

Sex is best during the relaxed evening hours when the body and mind have settled in. This is when it becomes all right to let our guard down and relax into a creative expression of our physical and spiritual natures particularly in the NNW part of your house—the lover's nook (see page 119). The natural segue into sleep allows our bodies to recover from sexual play and feel rejuvenated the next morning.

The Fourth House (11 p.m.–1 a.m.)

The fourth house represents the unconscious/subconscious mind. It is the deep delta wave of sleep and rest, and you should be in bed before 11 p.m. to harness the energy of this period. Transitions are vitally important in sacred societies, and they are observed in everything from exercise to meditation to sex. The transition from the fifth house of sex and enjoyment into deep, pleasurable sleep is a natural one. Going to bed with a smile on your face, the result of a day spent in harmony with the rhythms of nature, is the ideal way to enter the netherworld of sleep. Recall from part one the importance of eating a relaxed, deeply satisfying lunch in order to optimize hormone levels, rejuvenate your body, and release stress. The same is true of the midnight period, the counterpoint in the sky to lunchtime. Here again we should feel ourselves relaxing into the arms of sleep so we can come out of it fully recharged the next morning.

Every house constitutes a transition from one state to another, an organic sequence that follows the macrocosm of the sun's course through the heavens. In yoga asanas, transitions are called *vinyasa*, and they are crucial for taking the body from a state of inactivity to intense movement and back again to alert relaxation. The transition to and from sleep is just as important, as it determines whether we will benefit from our sleeping hours or wake up dull and tired.

This is also the time of the midnight snack. Note that during the fourth house the sun is directly underneath us, which makes it lunchtime for someone on the other side of the globe. Let them have their lunch; you should allow your body to run its internal cleansing cycle without burdening it with food. If you must eat, consider a light protein drink, a glass of milk, or some juice. But no steak dinners at midnight!

The Third House (1–3 a.m.)

If the fourth house is the deep unconscious, the third rules the active mind and REM (rapid-eye movement) sleep, during which your brain discharges accumulated tensions from the day. It is marked by dreams and mental activity, though not on the conscious level. Interestingly, it is a house of learning; while sleeping, the skills practiced during the day become hardwired into our body and mind. How the ancient sky watchers figured this out is unclear, but their correlations suggest that if you want to get good at a skill (third house), REM sleep should not be interrupted. Here, the mind is busy sorting the experiences of the day into well-organized information for future use. When sleep is disturbed during these hours, learning and judgment may be impaired.

The Second House (3–5 a.m.)

The second house rules nourishment. This is when the fully digested food from dinner (the sixth house) begins to build our tissues and create an anabolic environment in the body. This is when we experience a testosterone spike. Body builders often train in the early predawn hours to take advantage of their anabolic properties. But you don't have to be an athlete to notice the effects of extra testosterone: men across the planet are very familiar with the intense erections that occur during this time. This is also because the second house reflects the lusty sex energy of the eighth and sex is allowed during this time for householders.

The second house is used by spiritual practitioners for meditation and prayer. Four to five in the morning is the *brahma muhurta*, the most sacred hour in the day, according to Vedic tradition. Think of the brahma muhurta as a spiritual mist that hangs low during the early morning hours and vaporizes with the first hint of day. It is the best time to come into contact with your deep, silent self, and God is more likely to take your call then, as the line is not too busy.

However, this is not a time for pleasant or casual meditations, for spiritual practices performed here take a toll on the body, depriving it of sleep and succor. Since these hours are dedicated to nourishment, we are, in effect, trading physical nutrition for spiritual sustenance, and these hours are therefore reserved for the serious practitioner. But for those hardy enough to practice during brahma muhurta, spiritual attainment comes rapidly indeed.

The second house rules all forms of nutrition and, just as babies cry for milk at this hour, if you're up you can have a light, nutritious snack as well. Any nutrients you take in at this time are metabolized more easily by the body. That is why having a nutritious, protein-rich drink is desirable, since protein is necessary for building muscle and taking advantage of the anabolic properties of this house. During extended fasts like Ramadan, people often eat in the predawn to nourish the body while fasting during daylight hours, thereby ensuring that they have made the most of the nutrients they've eaten.

The second house also rules wealth, which nourishes us as adults. This means that if you want to be rich, you must rise during the predawn hours to outdo the competition. It is a simple fact, corroborated by millionaires and billionaires, that early to rise makes one wealthy and wise. Take a poll among your richest friends and the wealthiest people in the world, and you will find that rising early is a common trait among them.

✦✦✦

The twelfth, eighth, seventh, fifth, and second houses and their times are noted for sexual activity, with the fifth being optimal.

Since nature wants us to reproduce, you can have sex at practically any hour. But to create fulfillment, build intimacy, and reap magnified enjoyment, be aware of the energies that surround your lovemaking and use them to shape your relationships.

The first, eleventh, sixth, fifth, and second houses accommodate sports and physical activity, with the first being optimal for personal training and the fifth for team sports and activities.

The eleventh, ninth, and fifth houses are considered lucky, with the eleventh being the most opportune time to ask for favors, hold meetings, or organize activities.

Finally, the eighth house is to be actively avoided for any auspicious undertaking except sex. It is a time for death, introspection, and altered states of consciousness, not necessarily fun and games. Use it wisely.

THE LOVER AND THE SPOUSE

In astrology, there are two fundamental houses for relationships: the fifth and the seventh. The fifth house represents the lover or courtesan, the seventh the spouse. The fifth is also a house of fun and entertainment, wrestling, play, and sport. The seventh, on the other hand, also represents war, conflict, and one-on-one confrontation. Our ancestors understood the disparate roles of lover and spouse and apportioned them accordingly in the horoscope.

Interestingly, however, these houses are in a positive sextile, or secret friends, relationship. This means that, though the spouse may be jealous of the intensity of attention given to the lover, and the lover may resent the time and devotion accorded the spouse, functionally the two roles support each other. The spouse offers stability and deep love, and the lover provides a temporary outlet, a relief from the day-to-day routine of married life. In this way, spouses who take a lover may return to their marriage refreshed and able to shower their long-term partners with more love and devotion. Lovers, in turn, may find a semblance of relationship and support without a long-term commitment. Today this is highly controversial, and goes against the message of this book, which is that, for lasting physical, psychological, and spiritual fulfillment, a life partner is highly desirable for most people (Outsiders and those in Outsider periods excepted). However, our ancient ancestors felt it important enough to recognize these institutions not only in astrology, but in society as well.

Having a paramour as a teacher may strengthen the bonds of long-term relationships by helping couples discover and develop their sexuality. In societies where this institution was encouraged, the paramours were the teachers of men, women, and couples, helping them have better sex, romance, and intimacy. They were the Dr. Ruth or Dan Savage of ancient societies, but with a kick: a combination of porn star and marriage counselor rolled into one. And they were not exclusively for men or women, but for both.

In some cultures it was normative for women to take a younger lover at a certain age. Not only did this take some of the pressure off the husband, but it released tension from the wife and eased the marital relationship. And this approach is in lockstep with the sex and training rule described in this book, wherein younger men need older women to guide them in the first steps of love so they can become better partners to their eventual spouses. Here again the favorable relationship between the two astrological houses is illustrated: the lover (the older woman) helps the young man's future spouse by teaching him how to talk to, touch, and treat a woman—things he can't learn nearly as well by watching television or reading books.

Thus, the paramour relationship need not be inimical but may actually support long-term relationships. Of course, it is not for everyone, just as the sex and training principles are not for every young man. But the choice to engage in these relationships should be discussed openly within society, and by couples with each other.

A Lesson in Astrology

Astro-logos means making sense of the sky, aligning the macrocosm with the microcosm. The diurnal wheel modeled after astrology's twelve houses is a metaphor that allows us to align the internal rhythms of our body/mind with the natural rhythms of the day, particularly the sun.

Our bodies are inextricably tied to the rising, setting, culminating, and anticulminating of the sun, represented by the east, south, west, and north directions in the Northern Hemisphere. Everything from work schedules to clocks and calendars is based on the sun's movement.

Every day the sun courses through discrete portions of the sky called the twelve houses, six above the horizon (day) and six below (night). Beginning with the first house, where it crosses the horizon at dawn, the sun moves clockwise, finally setting in the seventh house. It then continues its course back again into the first house in a twenty-four-hour period. The sun spends roughly two hours in each house, though this varies depending on your locality and the season. An easy way to establish more or less how long the sun will sojourn in each house is to determine the duration of the daylight hours and divide them by six. This is done by looking up the sunrise and sunset times for your city and the date. Multiply the number of daylight hours by 10: this will give you the average minutes the sun will remain in each house that day. Then multiply the number of daylight minutes, if any, also by 10. This will give you the average seconds. Add these two together to get the total average time the sun will spend in each house.

For example, let's say sunrise is 7:00 a.m., and sunset 6:30 p.m. This gives us 11 hours and 30 minutes of daylight. Multiplying 11 by 10 results in 110 minutes. Next, multiplying 30 minutes by 10 gives us 300 seconds. Converting 110 minutes to hours gives us

1 hour, 50 minutes. Adding 300 seconds (five minutes), results in an average time of 1 hour, 55 minutes that the sun spends in each house. While this is not a major change from two hours, this technique makes more sense when applied to very short or very long days and nights.

Calculation methods are useful for the technical minded or those who wish to pursue astrology further, but it is also important for us to develop the ability to observe these transitions naturally, both in the environment and within our bodies. Haven't you noticed that a stillness overtakes the land before sunset and sunrise? Animals are keenly attuned to the sattvic quality in the environment at these times. We human animals also have this unconscious capacity, though it is sometimes trampled over by the waking conscious mind. Likewise, there is a noticeable, though perhaps more subtle, juncture between each of the houses, as the sun travels each day to visit the mansions of the sky estate.

In this explanation day and night are assumed to last twelve hours each, something that technically occurs only on the spring and autumn equinox. But once you understand the principle, we can apply it to more extreme periods when day and night are of unequal length, as in midsummer and midwinter.

FATE OR FREE WILL?

"Do you really think the stars predict our fate?" asks Jane as I look at her Vedic life map. It is a question astrologers get often, and skirt with stock responses, like "The planets indicate potentials only to be realized when you apply your free will: they impel, but don't compel" or "The chart is the map, and your life the territory." But the progenitors of Vedic astrology (jyotisha) were pretty clear that the planets were not only indicators of our karma, but compellers as well—deities to be respected as well as appeased. In a typically

Eastern way, they put the power in our hands to work with them through rituals, mantra, and other remedial measures called upayas.*

However, despite our best efforts, some karma cannot be changed. This is because there are three levels of karma: fixed, mixed, and nonfixed. Where nonfixed karma prevails, we certainly have a choice in our lives. But where fixed karma is at work, very little we do can change its momentum. Consider your gender, eye color, or height—these are pretty fixed karmas. No matter how hard we work, the best we can do to change these is to provide a crutch, like a colored contact lens or a taller shoe, or hormone replacement. To alter your fixed karma is not easy, and your chart can help you see in which areas you have fixed, mixed, or nonfixed karma. For example, if your seventh house of relationships shows positive fixed karma, you are likely to easily find love and stability in your partnerships. No matter how much you act like a jerk, people still love you. If it shows undesirable mixed karma there, you are likely to experience poor effects at first, but with assiduous self-improvement and work, you can turn that around into positive outcomes. By working on your communication skills, performing rituals, and otherwise inviting love into your life, you can have lasting harmony in your relationships. Reading this book is an upaya, a tool for self-improvement that can help you conquer negative nonfixed, mixed, and ultimately even fixed karma.

> Reading this book is an upaya, a tool for self-improvement that can help you conquer negative mixed, nonfixed, and ultimately even fixed karma.

The karma (free will) you exert today produces a result that you experience as karma (fate-effect) somewhere down the line.

Upaya means using skillful means to attain a goal. Any self-directed measure taken to alleviate a particular defect is an upaya.

Ultimately, there is no free will, since we are all living the conse-quences of our past actions.

This is not something we like to think about, expecially in the West, where we believe we have a choice in every area of our lives. However, if that were so, tools like the dharma type, your ayurvedic constitution, and any other typing system simply wouldn't work. Do men behave like men, women like women? Sure they do. Because they are influenced, or impelled, by the dictates of their gender to behave in ways that typify their sex. The words *man* and *woman* would have no meaning if men and women randomly acted like each other. Likewise, if you are a Pitta constitution, you are likely to behave in predictable patterns, encouraged by the hot, light, and subtle elements prevailing in your body and mind.

Other astrologers and I use the life map as a counseling tool to help clients understand their dharma type, their personality traits, and their behavior patterns. You can use the date, time, and place of your birth to reveal if you're scientifically minded or artistic, mar-riage material or a loner, or even if you like cats or dogs. For a layper-son, that can be a revelation. But that is only scratching the surface.

> **"Millionaires don't use astrologers; billionaires do."**
> **ATTRIBUTED TO J. P. MORGAN**

I look up from my study of Jane's life map. "You know, a long time ago astrology wasn't for common folks like you and me, because what we did really didn't matter to the kingdom. Astrology was reserved for people whose decisions affected the fates and fortunes of thousands of people. And these folks weren't interested in their sun sign or whether they were nice or spiritual. They were more intent on expanding their coffers and their kingdoms—their power and wealth.

"Thus, astrologers were queried about important state matters, like royal marriage and war, to find times that favored the best outcomes.

And back then, if your predictions weren't up to snuff—" I pause, drawing a finger across my throat—"you were done for. Period."

Astrology wouldn't have lasted five thousand years if it didn't have a successful track record, a long line of accurate predictions. And that's why, at the highest levels today, bankers, brokers, and investment and insurance companies continue to use astrology to help predict trends in the financial markets. Much to the chagrin of fundamentalist scientists, astrology continues to enthrall the hearts and minds of people around the world, because it is at once magical and mundane, science and art rolled into one.

Jane is quiet for a moment, then asks, "So what do you think of all those horoscopes in the newspaper?"

"Well, they're misdefined. A horoscope is the chart for a specific event, literally the vision of a moment. It is erected for the specific minute, hour, and day of an event. (The Sanskrit word *hora* is a cognate with the English *hour*.) Your newspaper sun sign guide, on the other hand, types you based on twelve signs where everyone born within a one-month period is classed into one sign. This really should be called a *masa* scope—a glance at the month, not the moment!

"Even so, this can still shed light on the workings of your psyche, and some astrologers have suggested (rightly) that these can even be used for market profiling to increase sales and a company's bottom line."

"I didn't realize you could use astrology to make money—no offense!" says Jane, a little embarrassed.

You can, but you have to be very careful where that money goes. If you use jyotisha to glorify your ego, making yourself fat and rich using what is essentially a spiritual science, the attendant negative karmas are unpleasant.

"I'll tell you a story. This summer while watching a particularly eventful World Cup game, a thought came to me: jyotisha should show who will win! And as I whipped out my laptop to pull the chart for each game, I discovered the predictive power of this ancient tradition. Over a short period I began to predict winners, and even put my money where my mouth was!"

"So what happened?"

"Well, I forged on, betting on underdogs and favorites until that first tiny investment turned into a pile of money."

"What? You got rich gambling with astrology?"

"You know, Robert Svoboda's mentor Vimalananda said something like this: 'It's not gambling if you know who's going to win.' But the truth is that it's jyotisha that won. No, I didn't get rich, though we did win a lot of money. The truth is, you can't keep that kind of money around if you want grace to continue to follow you. It has to be shared or given to charity."

"So can you do this all the time? Why don't you make a computer program or teach seminars on this stuff?"

At this point, some of my folly comes back to bite me. I tell her emphatically that jyotisha, though a royal science, still remains a mystical, spiritual art.

"It would be like squaring a circle or making jyotisha a prostitute at the beck and call of every sleazy gambler, if we forced ourselves upon it for our own selfish pleasure—the ego-drive of money and desire. Besides, jyotisha does not operate independent of grace—those are the two wings of this airliner—and to ignore or eliminate one is to fall from the lofty heights and perish on the hard ground of your karma. I learned that the hard way when I thought my system didn't need grace to make it work, and I lost a big chunk of change as a result.

"Jyotisha is a living, breathing spirit that lingers with you, if you're lucky, but can leave you just as quickly. So to answer your question: no, you can't turn it into a computer program open for everyone to use. If I had to make the same bets from this summer using only tricks and techniques I would probably lose my shirt! You can't calculate a concerto, square a sonata, or imprison jyotisha with the chains of reason. Reason and logic are one wing, grace and inspiration the other. Use them both to soar. Neglect one at your peril!"

THE ASTROLOGY OF RELATIONSHIPS

Synastry is the art of matching horoscopes for compatibility. Because family was so important to social cohesiveness, our ancient ancestors used many tools for assessing a couple's compatibility, including synastry, socioeconomic factors, spiritual direction, physical appearance, and psychological suitability. Looking at a couple's potential from these points of view allowed both the families involved, as well as the couple themselves, to feel certain in their choice of partner. In the Vedic tradition, some techniques remain that give insight into just how detailed the matchmaking process can be.

In traditional societies, marriage was less about infatuation than integration, knitting the dharma of your family, society, and spiritual traditions together over time. How your relationship affected society was just as important as how a couple felt about each other. And, as Elizabeth Gilbert says in *Committed*, her follow-up to *Eat, Pray, Love*, "The emotional place where a marriage begins is not nearly as important as the emotional place where a marriage finds itself toward the end, after many years of partnership."[1]

Infatuation and lust are typically not sound foundations for a strong relationships, because they are not sustainable states. The brains of infatuated people show patterns of dopamine release much like those of drug addicts. And, like addicts, these brains require more and more of their drug to feel high. Thinking about and being with the partner becomes a fixation, and, like most addictions, things usually end badly. Such states cannot be sustained over the long term because they are not built on a solid foundation. Typically, an infatuated brain only sees projections of who the partner is, but over time reality has a way of intruding into these fantasies and bursting our bubble. Our grandparents and ancestors knew this, and sought to keep us from the perils of addicted love—at least as precursors for serious life relationships. Everybody is free to indulge as they wish, as long as they know that, as sweet as it may seem in the short term, every drug is likely to become bitter in the end.

Lasting fulfillment is built on understanding the reality of your partner. How you two fit together sexually, spiritually, philosophically, and psychologically, and the effect your relationship has on the world around you, have a lot to say about your relationship's success. Let's begin with the good stuff—how two people match when it comes to sex.

THE SIZE THAT COUNTS?

In the Vedic system there are several ways to match couples in terms of sexual compatibility. One is physical, based on the size of their sex organs. Another measures the potential for emotional and psychological fulfillment from lovemaking. In the first method, the size of a man and a woman's genitalia is categorized into three groups (see table 11.1).*

TABLE 11.1. COMPATIBILITY BASED ON SIZE OF SEXUAL ORGANS

SIZE	WOMAN	MAN
Large	Elephant	Horse
Medium	Mare	Bull
Small	Deer	Rabbit

---

*The relative size measurements attributed to the yoni and lingam types are five, seven, and nine inches for small, medium, and large, respectively. However, size measurements differ according to culture and race. Even within these sizes, there is room for interpretation: use these as a guide, not as a literal classification.

Basically, like a good pair of shoes, you want your partner to fit you just right—not too loose, not too snug. Large fits best with large, medium with medium, and small with small. Medium can do relatively well with the other two sizes, but pairing couples with large and small genitalia may feel, at least metaphorically, like an elephant having sex with a rabbit.

Note that this is purely on the physical level: a couple may have good compatibility in other areas, but if they are mismatched by size, they may have trouble being physically fulfilled by sex. A case study illustrates this.

Judy and Carl were deeply in love. They had courted for many months, and their love gradually blossomed as they dated and and eventually moved in together. Curiously, six months into their relationship, they still had not had sex. Carl was reticent, and she didn't push. Perhaps something cautioned them to wait until their love and comfort with each other grew into deep intimacy. On the night they finally consummated their union, Judy found that Carl was unusually large— a horse in the Vedic scheme—while she was more like a deer (small). This caused a problem, at least initially, as the each of them tried to reconcile their anatomy with the other's. Finally, because they had overall good compatibility and because their yoni matching was excellent (see below), they managed to fulfill each other sexually, despite their anatomical differences. With oral sex, manual stimulation, and gentle intercourse, they found ways to please each other and remain together. Today, Judy and Carl are happily married with two children.

It is important to note that with extended foreplay and careful use of sexual positions, almost any size difference can be accommodated. Such positions are not detailed here, but can be found in good books on the topic.*

---

*See Nik Douglas and Penny Slinger's *Sexual Secrets, The Alchemy of Ecstacy*, which summarizes the sexual teachings of several Eastern traditions, including the Kama Sutra and Ananga Ranga.

BIRTH ASTERISMS: YOU SEXY BEAST

Using the relative position of the moon in each partner's horoscope, the yoni, or the psychological and emotional fulfillment a couple derives from sex, can be determined. This requires knowing which nakshatra, or birth asterism, each partner's moon occupied at the time of birth.* There are twenty-seven such asterisms. Each asterism contains four parts for a total of 108 sounds (27 × 4 = 108). This number is sacred across cultures, and specifically to Vedic traditions.

TABLE 11.2. NAKSHATRAS CHARACTERISTICS

NAKSHATRA	PART 1	PART 2	PART 3	PART 4	ANIMAL	GENDER	INCOMPATIBLE ANIMAL
Aśvinī	Cu	Ce	Co	La	Horse	Male	Buffalo
Bharaṇī	Li	Lu	Le	Lo	Elephant	Male	Lion
Krittikā	A	I	U	E	Sheep	Female	Monkey
Rohiṇī	O	Va	Vi	Vu	Serpent	Male	Mongoose
Mṛgaśīrṣā	Ve	Vo	Ka	Ki	Serpent	Female	Tiger, Dog
Ārdrā	Ku	Gha	Ṅga/pha	Ccha	Dog	Male	Rat, Dog
Punarvasu	Ke	Ko	Ha	Hi	Cat	Female	Monkey
Puṣyā	Hu	He	Ho	Ḍa	Goat	Male	Dog, Rat
Āśleṣā	Ḍi	Ḍu	Ḍe	Ḍo	Cat	Male	Dog, Rat
Maghā	Ma	Mi	Mu	Me	Rat	Male	Cat

Note that these vowel sounds are pronounced as they are in Japanese or Spanish: E is pronounced "eh," not "ee," and I is pronounced "ee." Other sounds that are unfamiliar to English speakers can be approximated, but it is best to consult a Sanskrit speaker for clarification.

---

*For more information on birth asterisms refer to *Light on Relationships* by Hart de Fouw and Robert Svoboda.

TABLE 11.2. NAKSHATRAS CHARACTERISTICS (con't.)

NAKSHATRA	PART I	PART 2	PART 3	PART 4	ANIMAL	GENDER	INCOMPATIBLE ANIMAL
Pūrva Phalgunī	Mo	Ṭa	Ṭi	Ṭu	Rat	Female	Cat
Uttara Phalgunī	Ṭe	Ṭo	Pa	Pi	Bull (cow)	Male	Tiger
Hastā	Pu	Ṣa	Ṇa	Ṭha	Buffalo	Female	Horse
Chitrā	Pe	Po	Ra	Ri	Tiger	Male	Cow
Svātī	Ru	Re	Ro	Ta	Buffalo	Male	Horse
Viśākhā	Ti	Tu	Te	To	Tiger	Female	Cow
Anurādhā	Na	Ni	Nu	Ne	Deer	Female	Tiger, Dog
Jyeṣṭhā	No	Ya	Yi	Yu	Deer	Male	Tiger, Dog
Mūlā	Ye	Yo	Ba	Bi	Dog	Female	Tiger, Deer
Pūrva Āṣāḍhā	Bu	Dha	Bha	Ḍha	Monkey	Male	Dog, Goat
Uttara Āṣāḍhā	Be	Bo	Ja/śa	Ji/śi	Mongoose	Female	Serpent
Śravaṇā	Ju/śu	Je/śe	Jo/śo	Jha	Monkey	Female	Dog, Goat
Dhaniṣṭhā	Ga	Gi	Gu	Ge	Lion	Female	Elephant
Śatabhiṣā	Go	Sa	Si	Su	Horse	Female	Buffalo
Pūrva Bhādrapadā	Se	So	Da	Di	Lion	Male	Elephant
Uttara Bhādrapadā	Du	Kha	Ña/ jña	Tha	Cow	Female	Tiger
Revatī	De	Do	Ca	Ci	Elephant	Female	Lion

Note that these vowel sounds are pronounced as they are in Japanese or Spanish: E is pronounced "eh," not "ee," and I is pronounced "ee." Other sounds that are unfamiliar to English speakers can be approximated, but it is best to consult a Sanskrit speaker for clarification.

Knowing one's birth nakshatra was vital in Vedic societies, and is equally important today in India, as it plays an enormous role in personal, social, and spiritual rituals. For example, to this day, babies born in a particular nakshatra are often named for that nakshatra's sound. Because your name is the word most associated with you during life, it is vital that it reflect your personality, your dharma, and who you are on a deep, primordial level. People with misaligned names are thought to have a harder time making their way in the world and expressing their talents. (See "Naming Ceremony," pages 160–61.)

Since the moon remains in one asterism for a little over twenty-four hours, a person's brith nakshatra is relatively easy to calculate using a *panchanga* (a Vedic almanac). A precise birth time is not necessary. This makes it handy for even rural folk in India to know their nakshatra and thereby gain valuable information about themselves, including the type of profession, partner, and spiritual practice appropriate for them.

YONI CHART

Rules for Interpretation*

+ When a man's moon is in a male nakshatra and a woman's moon is in a female nakshatra, and their nakshatra animals are not inimical, there is excellent compatibility.

+ When both moons fall in either both female or both male nakshatras, and their nakshatra animals are not inimical, there is good compatibility.

+ When a man's nakshatra is female and a woman's nakshatra is male, there is average compatibility, provided their nakshatra animals are not inimical.

---

*For more on this see *Light on Relationships* by Hart de Fouw and Robert Svoboda.

✦ When a couple's nakshatra animals are inimical, as in Horse and Buffalo, there is no compatibility.

Note that there are not many inimical placements. Perhaps this is because nature essentially wants us to procreate, and the psychological and emotional bond forged by sexual satisfaction is important for the creation and rearing of children. Table 11.3 indicates the relative compatibility of each nakshatra animal.

This yoni compatibility is just one of ten vital combinations, called *poruthams* or *kutas*. Poruthams are a complex set of tools used in Vedic societies to match couples in relationship and must be used together for optimal results. Because the rules of matchmaking can be harrowing, they are sometimes considered archaic. But when they work they can provide fascinating insights, predicting a couple's financial success, social recognition, and even their health and longevity together.

Sometimes couples pair up wonderfully for sexual fulfillment, but have poor prospects for longevity or prosperity. Tom and Jackie were a good example of this.

Tom was a graphic designer who worked for high-end clients. One day, Jackie, a new customer, walked into his office and it was infatuation at first sight. The palpable energy between them soon erupted into a dizzying affair. In the bedroom they were a formidable match, but they could not agree on career, money, and even food choices. Soon, despite his objections, she took a job promotion in another town, and he was too sick to protest, having come down with a tough cold that wouldn't go away for weeks.

Yoni compatibility and other combinations in their horoscopes (like a tight Venus to Venus opposition) showed powerful sexual chemistry. However, other factors like their mutual health, finances, and overall life direction didn't jibe. Vedic analysis of a couple's compatibility includes these as well as other considerations, all of

TABLE 11.3. COMPATABILITY OF NAKSHATRA ANIMAL ON A SCALE OF 1 TO 4

	HORSE	ELEPHANT	SHEEP	SERPENT	DOG	CAT	RAT	COW	BUFFALO	TIGER	HARE	MONKEY	MONGOOSE	LION
Horse	4													
Elephant	2	4												
Sheep	2	3	4											
Serpent	3	3	2	4										
Dog	2	2	1	2	4									
Cat	2	2	2	1	2	4								
Rat	2	2	1	1	1	0	4							
Cow	1	2	3	1	2	2	2	4						
Buffalo	0	3	3	1	2	2	2	3	4					
Tiger	1	1	1	2	1	1	2	0	1	4				
Hare	1	2	2	2	2	3	2	3	2	1	4			
Monkey	3	3	0	2	2	3	2	2	2	1	2	4		
Mongoose	2	2	3	0	1	2	1	2	2	2	2	3	4	
Lion	1	0	1	2	1	1	2	1	2	1	1	2	2	4

which have to be assessed before compatibility can be pronounced. Here are some of the areas in which compatibility is traditionally analyzed:

Sexual alignment: both physical and emotional, as explained above

Love, respect, and devotion: one-sided or mutual?

Happiness through children: the happiness that children bring to the couple, their ease of child rearing, and the children's own health and satisfaction

The social standing of the couple: do they become a synergistic unit that soars together, or do they bring each other down in the eyes of their families and the world?

Temperament and personality: can they live together or will their moods and conflicts tear them apart?

Health and longevity: will their habits create health and long life or shorten their years together?

Prosperity: will one or both partners enhance the other's prosperity, or will they sink their marriage in debt?

Obstacles: how will they face life's challenges together?

For millennia, these and other criteria have formed a comprehensive approach to relationship stability that has helped India's couples stay together. But the rapid modernization of traditional cultures has led to increasing divorce rates, in part because the advancement of women's rights and the democratization of society allow couples more freedom to do as they wish. This is a great step forward: Western influence has brought progress by replacing outdated practices, but we shouldn't throw out the baby with the bathwater by abandoning all ancient practices, especially those that nurture our dharma as couples and individuals. Abandonment of these ancient compatibility techniques, at least in part, has increased the chances of mismatched relationships and, ultimately, divorce.

Synergy

The categories above indicate just how important synergy becomes to a relationship. One plus one does not always equal two. Sometimes two average people come together and achieve extraordinary results—a case of 1 + 1 = 3. On the other hand, consider the famed star-crossed lovers Romeo and Juliet, who perhaps enjoyed compatibility on a physical and emotional level but lacked dreadfully in the "social standing" and "health and longevity" categories. Their negative synergy was so overwhelming that it led to premature death, scandal, and the destruction of their families—a case of 1 + 1 = 0.

In much the same way, children can also bring blessings and prosperity to a couple, or so burden an otherwise functional relationship that it ends in divorce. This synergistic effect must be judged by looking at the charts of the people involved to gauge how well they match, and how having children will affect their relationship.

EXALTED OR DEBILITATED SIGNS

In astrology, there are terms for planets when they're in their own signs, in their exalted sign, or in their sign of debilitation. A planet in its own sign is comfortable and happy. This is like Bill Gates at home, relaxing in his underwear watching TV. An exalted planet, on the other hand, is powerful and influential (for good or ill). This is Bill Gates on the job, where he is practically a god. Exaltation is where we are at our best and people look up to us. Finally, a debilitated planet is at its point of weakness, like Bill Gates in the middle of the jungle, with only bugs and snakes around and no technology or use for his formidable wealth, power, and intellect. Debilitated, we feel useless, our efforts are futile, and our worst qualities tend to come to the fore.

In relationships, it's important to see our partners exalted, doing what they love, for at least a little while, so we can better appreciate them. When we first fall in love, this is how we usually see our significant others—as amazing, admirable people with whom we want to spend our lives. But too often we lose this respect, especially when we move in and reach a level of comfort together, like planets in their own houses. We become content to see each other in pajamas, without makeup, not doing anything in particular to exalt our talents. Too much of this leads to "getting used to" and "taking for granted" behavior. Stop it. Make plans to exalt each other. Get out of your comfort zone and explore exaltation and debilitation, because nothing stimulates romance in a comfortable relationship like novelty.

Bill Gates at home is Bill Gates—a husband, dad, all-around average guy. Bill Gates working on his business or his charitable endeavors is a superhero—a man adulated (and perhaps hated) for his iconic status in the business and tech worlds. It is good for spouses and partners to see each other in their respective exalted space, to marvel at each other's genius, to appreciate each other's talent.

It is also important to see how our partners function under "debilitated" conditions sometimes. Your transmission breaks down in the middle of the desert? How do you handle that? You get fired from your job and can't take care of the bills—that's a definite challenge. All too often our Merchant culture throws us financial threats that keep us on the edge of anxiety and in fear for our futures. We don't need this kind of debilitation. However, deliberate debilitation, like fitness adventures, horror movies, and other temporary uncomfortable situations can be fun ways to see your partner under adverse conditions. When done right, temporary shared deprivation can be a nice way to bring two people together. Can you think of three deliberate debilitations you can do with your partner this month? How about these:

Dancing lessons (if you're not already dancers)
Horseback riding (if you don't ride) or any kind of activity that
    you have no experience in
Fitness boot camps
Relationship classes

Don't have an exaltation? Well, let's find one. Every planet has an exaltation point, but it has to walk through eleven other signs before it reaches that. Take a walk through your life and see where your skill set is particularly appreciated.

 FINDING YOUR EXALTATION

Get five friends to write your top ten worst qualities and your top ten best qualities. (If you don't have five friends, ask whoever knows you best—your mom, your dad, the kid down the block, etc.)

Now write your own list.

Compare the results. Which ones match? Which ones are new to you?

Focus on the best three qualities. What do you see there that you can build on?

Compare these to your dharma type. How can you use your dharma type to spotlight and express these three items? What about the negatives—how do they express the low side of your dharma type, and what can you do about them? If you're stuck, go back through the exercises in the BE FIT chapter 3 to recapture your essence and find your exaltation.

For example, Joe is really good with kids, but he doesn't have any of his own. Joe is a retired musician, and when he's around kids he's the rock star—cool and funny but also caring and firm. Joe could take a date along to see him around kids. A nice way to get an immediate boost in personal morale is to play to your strengths. It is one thing to know you're good at something; it is something else altogether when someone you like admires your talents. As a bonus, this is also an instant cure for mild depression. Doing your dharma is not always thrilling, but it can earn you the respect and admiration of the people you love, and that is a high that remains with you.

MARRIAGE TIMING

In traditional communities, no major event is planned without consulting the skies. An auspicious undertaking like marriage or opening a business should harmonize with the environment in which it takes place. You wouldn't consider throwing a baby shower at midnight, disco dancing in a morgue, or selling cupcakes in a rainstorm. There is a time, place, and season for everything under heaven, and knowing the best (or at least the better times) to do anything will give your relationship or business a leg up.

Consider Facebook's initial public offering on May 18, 2013. High hopes were shattered as it quickly became what the *Wall Street Journal* dubbed a "fiasco" and "a big bomb." Had Mark Zuckerberg waited a few days after the major solar eclipse of May 20, he might have experienced vastly different results, according to astrology's rules of timing. Considering the billions of dollars at stake, waiting a few days might have been an acceptable hedge for this business and its stockholders. Of course, at the time of this writing, the stock has picked up again and is trading well above its initial offering price, proving that a fundamentally strong business or marriage can ultimately overcome environmental factors pitted against it. But for months it faced enormous challenges and devaluations, and who knows where it would be now, had its inception not been so disastrous? Why not avoid such challenges if we can?

Here are five rules for planning a good marriage.

1. Hold the ceremony when the moon is bright, six or more days before or after a new moon. The moon is water, juice, and emotion. Emotions are made up of the chemicals and hormones in our bodies. We have to surf our inner neurochemistry to experience life's emotional richness. When the moon is dark, depression and lack of juice are more likely. Darker emotions come to the fore. Avoid this by marrying when the moon is still large and juicy, and preferably waxing. This applies to any endeavor in which we want success, prosperity, and enjoyment. (Some auspicious things to do on a dark or new moon include spiritual practices, preparation of certain medicines, and ancestor worship.)

2. Wed on a benefic day. The benefic days of the week are Thursday, Friday, Monday, and Wednesday, with the first two being best. Actively avoid the malefic days—Saturday, Tuesday, and Sunday (in that order). Just like Facebook's IPO, wedding on a Saturday does not immediately spell doom for a long-term commitment, but it does make it so more challenges have to be met. Why not just do it on a Friday instead? Friday belongs to Freya, the Norse goddess equivalent to Venus in Roman mythology. In the Latin languages, *vendredi* (French), *venerdi* (Italian), and *viernes* (Spanish) all correlate this day with the goddess Venus—the goddess of love and romance.

Thursday is associated with Thor and, in Roman mythology, Jove. Jovian sentiments include generosity, agreeableness, and prosperity. Getting married on a Thursday encourages mutual respect, loyalty, and wisdom in couples.

3. Do it at the right time of day. Do not marry at night, or within four hours of sunset. Avoid the junctures of the day—sunrise and sunset—as well as the eighth house. As we saw earlier in this chapter, the eighth house encompasses the afternoon blahs, when children get fractious and parents irritable. Best to avoid it, and wed during the eleventh house.

4. Avoid the ancestral fortnight. Halloween is the sanitized holy day of the dead so popular in American culture. The unsanitized version, and still widely practiced fortnight* of the dead, occurs every year and ranges from September through mid-October. Checking when this is going on can help you avoid getting married at a time when much of the world's population is focused on grieving and honoring its dead. You wouldn't get married during a funeral, would you? It's best to avoid the ancestral fortnight for anything requiring an auspicious beginning, including starting a business, buying a house, or the like. Do use this time to honor your departed relatives, however.

5. Match it to your chart. For best results, matching your own horoscope to the timing of your special event is the best way to minimize negative expectations and optimize the positive. This can be done by a trained professional astrologer.

---

*Astronomically, a fortnight is fifteen days—the time it takes the moon to go from new to full, or full to new. Though *fortnight* in English is literally fourteen nights, perhaps it meant fourteen nights and most of the day. That would make it technically accurate; the mean average between a full and new moon is 14.77 days.

12

Love and Dharma

How Knowing Your Dharma
Can Strengthen Your Relationship

Today there are countless methods for matching people in love. Popular websites such as Match.com, E-Harmony, and ChristianMingle bank on pairing couples based on personality questionnaires as well as shared racial, religious, and sexual values to help them find love. But before we talk about love, it is best to define it.

WHAT IS LOVE? DON'T HURT ME

Love as I define it is not an emotion, or a biological imperative, like lust, attraction, or infatuation. Love is not a transient chemical response to the world that is dependent on hormones, mood, or the fluctuating states of the body. The body engineers situations optimal to its survival by producing appropriate physical reactions to different people and phenomena. Studies show that even the microbes in our guts exert a huge influence on how we feel, what we like and don't like, and the foods we eat.* To certain degrees, we are all subject to

---

*"Microbes have the capacity to manipulate behavior and mood through altering the neural signals in the vagus nerve changing taste receptors, producing toxins to make us feel bad, and releasing chemical rewards to make us feel good," says Dr. Athena Aktipis, director of human and social evolution at the University of California–San Francisco.

our biological needs; it is the aim of spirituality to raise us above this base animal nature to an experience of being truly human. Love is this quintessential spiritual experience, precisely because it is independent of the animal instinct. So what is love? As cheesy as it might seem, it is useful to revisit Paul's famous missive from the Christian Scriptures:

> Love is patient, is kind. It does not envy others or brag of itself. It is not swollen with self. It is not wayward or grasping. It does not flare with anger, nor harbor a grudge. It takes no joy in evil, but delights in truth. It keeps all confidences, all trust, all hope, all endurance. Love will never go out of existence. Prophecy will fail in time, languages too, and knowledge as well. For we know things only partially, or prophesy partially, and when the totality is known, the parts will vanish. It is like what I spoke as a child, knew as a child, thought as a child, argued as a child—which, now I am grown up, I put aside. In the same way we see things in a murky reflection now, but shall see them full face when what I have known in part I shall know fully, just as I am known. For the present, then, three things matter—believing, hoping, and loving. But supreme is loving. (1 Corinthians 13:1–13)

What we commonly call love is often simply chemical intoxication, whose symptoms are desire, obsession, and infatuation. Love is not possessive—it is not afraid that something will leave it, because fear lives in the impermanent world of time, whereas love abides in a timeless state beyond mine and yours. The late B.K.S. Iyengar gave a good definition of this in his book *Light on Life:* "What we call love is . . . one impermanent entity seeking an enduring link with another impermanent entity."[1]

This scenario is bound to fail, since what is impermanent cannot take the place of what is real, permanent, and beyond time. Love is beyond time; desire is rooted in objects. Love is timeless, obsession temporary—a conflation of the egoic self with the object of its attachment, to continue with Iyengar's definition. In short, the ego cannot love; only the spirit can. What we think of ourselves, our identity, is the ego. But the ego cannot know love, only attachment, for it is rooted in the material mechanics of natural selection, personal individuation, and survival of the fittest. In a sense, this is the devil the Bible warns us about, the worldly self that tempts us to indulge in selfish, impermanent pleasures, such as those that tempted Jesus in the desert. *You can have all this, if you will only serve me!* Such is the siren song of the egoic self, the temptations of the flesh. It will always seek to come first, before another, but love gives itself up for the sake of another.

It feels good to be around the object of our infatuation, but love is not always about good feelings. Love is not easy. How can we have love for our own offspring, yet kill another's? Animals love their own brood, but a male lion will kill his rival's cubs to gain a chance to mate. This is biological competition, not love. The love of a mother for her children is genuine, but it is mixed with biological attachment to such a degree that it becomes difficult to separate the two. If it were only spiritual love, she would see all children as her own. A man would love all women as sisters, mothers, and children. A child would respect all elders as mother and father. True love is everywhere. It begins in our biology, by giving us a taste of its potential; it is up to us to take it from the material level to its highest expression, as exemplified in the Corinthians passage above.

When Jesus said to his disciples, "He who does not leave his father and mother for my sake does not deserve me!" (Matthew 10:37), he challenged just this sort of biological love, of parent for child, or child for parent. He fought to spiritualize and purify his disciples' attachments to worldly imperatives. If it was so hard for those few who had personal contact with him, how hard must it be for the rest of us, who do not have such an immanent example to guide us? How do we navigate through our daily relationships? How do we distinguish between what is pure, spiritual love and what is selfish desire? The dharma types offer guidance here, and can teach us how to love, each in our own unique way.

Educators love and nourish with wisdom. Wisdom teaches them to control their senses and become exemplars of temperance and virtue. Warriors give love by protecting and generously offering their energy, prana, to those who need it. In its highest expression, Warriors give their lives to protect others. Merchants cater to our emotional and sensual needs, making life fruitful and joyous, while Laborers feed our bodies, minds, and souls with affection, nourishment, and touch—all natural expressions of their love.

Everyone expresses love differently: what works for me may not be appropriate for you; and what comes naturally to you may seem artificial or contrived to me. We must each find our own best expression by following the guidelines of our dharma type and making it our own.

RELATIONSHIPS
AND THE DHARMA TYPES

Our ancestors understood that most humans are incomplete without an intimate partner, a soul mate to share life's journey. So they developed a system of analyzing relationships to allow people from a young age to find a suitable a life mate. By comparing maps of the heavens at the time of birth, two astrological charts were analyzed to gauge a prospective couple's levels of physical, emotional, and spiritual compatibility. This deeply detailed analysis encouraged joyous relationships by fostering healthy sexual, social, and professional integration. Among the secret techniques employed were methods for discovering the sexual compatibility of a couple, their potential for financial success together, and more, as discussed in chapter 11.

Imagine being paired with someone with whom you have phenomenal chemistry, someone who shares your life goals and supports you in pursuing them. Imagine someone who is your best friend and greatest ally in achieving your dreams. Imagine finding true love early in life, escaping the trial-and-error desperation of the mating game. So much of an adult's time and energy is tied up in searching for companionship, sex, and love that we spend the better part of our lives concerned with how we look, act, and whether or not we will be accepted by the opposite sex. Only a few are spared the trials and tribulations of this lifelong chase. Recognizing this deep need for bonding, our ancestors encouraged marriage for all but the most dedicated of spiritual practitioners, for whom celibacy and worship of God substituted for the marriage vow. In this way, they all but eliminated pornography, rape, and crime by filling the void in humankind with wholeness and satisfaction.

> Imagine being paired with someone with whom you have phenomenal chemistry, someone who shares your life goals and supports you in pursuing them. Imagine someone who is your best friend and greatest ally in achieving your dreams. Imagine finding true love early in life, escaping the trial-and-error desperation of the mating game.

The rishis relied on their ability to attune to nature and interpret nature's symbols for the benefit of the community: to know what plant cured which disease and what star related to which earthly phenomenon. These insights evolved into the complex sciences of ayurveda and jyotisha that continue to be used to this day and have survived, from guru to disciple, even over the expanse of continents and generations.

And just as we can compare two charts for harmony, we can use dharma type compatibility to match people in relationships, be they personal or professional. The dharma types align to create harmony or disharmony just as signs and planets do, but give us quicker and simpler insights into which relationships work and which ones need work. In addition, when we compare life cycles we can see why people who start off well can sometimes drift apart as a result of a change in life direction. Using the skills inherent in each type, we can also make suggestions about how to improve our relationships for our personal, financial, and spiritual benefit. Let's take a look at the major relating patterns of the types, at how they match up in compatibility, while also analyzing the pitfalls that lie in wait for the unwary.

COMPATIBILITY

Vedic astrology is used traditionally in India to assess the compatibility of prospective mates. However, it requires the exact birth details of both partners and a well-trained astrologer to sift through the complex system of Vedic matchmaking. Lacking competent astrologers or accurate birth times, we can still use dharma type compatibility to render a quick general assessment of relationship dynamics. If birth data is available, one can go further and gauge the life cycles to come up with an even more insightful look at one's relationships.

Dharma types match up best with people from their point of evolution. That is, Educators with Warriors and Laborers with Merchants. Each type is attracted to qualities present at its integration point. Merchants are attracted to the substance and sensuality of the Laborer while Laborers appreciate the charm, wit, and variety of the Merchant type, though this is only when the types are relatively healthy.

Just as a hale body will crave food that is good for it, while a toxic body craves sweets and other foods that feed its toxicity, so it is with dharma types. Dysfunctional Educators may not like hanging around Warriors because they challenge these Educators to be their best. Devolved Merchants won't want to hear what Laborers think of them, even though it is for their higher good. Therefore compatibility between these types may not always be easy, though it is usually evolutionary for both parties.

Dharma Type Compatibility in Relationships

Excellent compatibility: Educator–Warrior, Merchant–Laborer

Good compatibility: Educator–Educator, Merchant–Merchant, Laborer–Laborer, Warrior–Warrior, Outsider–Outsider

Average compatibility: Educator–Merchant, Laborer–Warrior

Poor compatibility: Laborer–Educator, Merchant–Warrior

Warriors are drawn to the Educator's culture and wisdom, while Educators are pulled to the Warrior's strength and leadership ability. Of course, every type appreciates its own qualities as well, and this makes for good compatibility for same-type pairings, while average compatibility is present for those who are neutral to each other, namely Warriors with Laborers and Educators with Merchants. Finally, people whose partners represent their point of devolution may find themselves repulsed by surface qualities in their partner, though they may love them for their inner character. Poor compatibility is not a death sentence to a relationship, but partners must work harder to accommodate each other than in good-compatibility relationships.

Outsiders have the freedom to merge with any type and are not bound, as you may guess, by ordinary rules of compatibility. There are three main points to observe for Outsiders:

1. They are best understood by their own kind, and often find other Outsiders good company, both in marriage and in other relationships.

2. Outsiders take on qualities of the other types. Therefore, they will share the compatibility preferences of the type they most emulate. An Outsider playing a Merchant should have the best compatibility with Laborers; he will have good compatibility with other Outsiders and Merchants, average compatibility with Educators, and poor compatibility with Warriors. Also, an Outsider playing a Merchant will get along better with another Outsider playing a Merchant than with an Outsider playing a Warrior. In the latter case he will have poor compatibility, though not as poor as a regular Warrior/ Merchant combination, for the Outsiders' affinity toward each other tends to soften the effect.

3. Along with others of their kind, Outsiders also share a special affinity with Laborers. One reason for this may be their long-standing position on the bottom rung of the social ladder. Outsider and Laborer types have suffered at the hands of the so-called higher castes, due to the perversion of wisdom and lack of understanding present in the Dark Age of the last five thousand years. They also both value community, and where others may exploit, reject, or otherwise mistreat them, Outsiders and Laborers are accepted by and share a fundamental bond within their own groups that does not exist in the same way for other types. Warriors may see other Warriors as competition, and the same goes for Merchants. Educators may be jealous of other Educators—but Outsiders and Laborers generally tend to be more accepting of their own types, especially within a group or community.

As we turn toward a new Golden Age, we can reestablish the original spirit of the dharma types and invoke the undeniable equality and right of every type to life and liberty, and, more than the pursuit of—the map and directions to—happiness and fulfillment. We can take the original directives of the rishis and revise them in a fresh and new spirit for the benefit of everyone.

How It Works

Compatibility implies more than attraction, which can exist between any of the types. Compatibility is the ability to generate and sustain mutual attraction in a healthy, long-term relationship. It is a spiritual connection between two people that enhances the good qualities in each. Lust can exist between all the personalities and sexual relationships can be enjoyed by everyone, regardless of compatibility. The freedom to engage in a sexual relationship with anyone we choose is the basis of modern Western social attitudes toward sex and relationships. It does not, however, guarantee satisfaction. If anything, too much freedom creates a void that leaves us always wanting more, while retarding the development of relationship skills and further feeding the cycle of emptiness and desire.

Understanding simple interactions between the dharma types can help us develop the skills we need to properly contextualize and navigate our day-to-day relationships. These skills, in turn, translate into a more fulfilling experience of human dynamics while retaining the freedom, so cherished in the West, to be who we are. Being with the right person can bring out your natural self more exquisitely than anything else—just as being with the wrong person can as quickly suppress it!

With respect to relationships, the attitude of the ancients was simple: enjoy yourself with whomever you please—but if you want lasting happiness, pay some attention to the laws of nature, starting with your dharma type. This was their attitude toward human behavior in general: honor the natural laws that made you, and enjoy the divine favor of the universe; disregard them, and sweat out existence on your own. This is the true meaning of "By the sweat of your brow shall you earn your bread" (Genesis 3:19). Instead of being a blessing, this is a sentence for those who choose to turn away from dharma, and, like Sisyphus, fight an uphill battle that they must eventually lose.

Relief comes when we drop the stone and ask for help, and the rishis are revered in Vedic society for establishing the systems whereby freedom and happiness may be enjoyed by everyone who embraces them. Far from being an isolated or strictly religious doctrine, dharma is universal and encompasses everyone, from the Outsider to the Educator, uniting them into a society that recognizes their equality and celebrates their distinctiveness.

Our points of evolution challenge us to become our highest selves. Positive compatibility between the types, however, should not conjure up a happily ever after–like fantasy. Instead, types with good and excellent compatibility challenge each other to evolve and grow, invoking the best qualities in the other person and making each of them even better. Incompatible types, by contrast, bring out the worst qualities in each other and challenge growth in different ways. These relationships act like harsh purgatives, cleansing and purifying a couple of their worst traits and destroying the personality structures that constrain them, whereas compatible couples build on the positive structures and make these grow.

But relationships between compatible types can also be difficult, especially when we are reluctant to step into a full expression of our essence. For example, Educators learn that they cannot threaten, bully, or intimidate Warriors; therefore, their only recourse is the humility, mildness, uprightness, and integrity that are their virtues. In return, Warriors learn that their anger, force, power, and intimidation are useless where the innocent are concerned, and can only harm others when misplaced. They learn discrimination and self-control.

Merchants learn the value of their word, to be accountable for their actions, and to appreciate human effort. In return they gain sustaining nurturing from the Laborer type. The Laborer, on the other hand, is challenged to learn how to prosper himself and become savvy in the world. He is brought out of his shell by the Merchant and stimulated to constantly see the world fresh and new.

Types with excellent compatibility feel their strengths highlighted and their weaknesses minimized when they're around each other. Each type feels they can be at their best. This is like actors on a stage or star athletes on the field: the venue of excellent compatibility allows them to showcase their talents. On the other hand, types with good compatibility feel at home with each other. They are understood by their partner. This is like actors or athletes after their performance or their game, cozying up in their favorite chair and sipping hot chocolate. Good compatibility is based on same-same pairings, and it is easier to be yourself and relate to someone who is fundamentally like you than it is to relate to someone basically opposed to you in nature.

The point of evolution is a case of "opposites attract," where opposite qualities nurture positive change in a partner. On the other hand, devolution points invoke an "opposites repel" vibe, in which different qualities chafe and irritate, rather than complement each other. You have a sense of discomfort, of feeling misunderstood, when you're dealing with an incompatible type.

Relating to types where compatibility is neutral, on the other hand, is like being in a stranger's house for whom you have neither enmity nor love. There is neither tension nor excitement, but a neutral ground of civility and social respect. Like standing with someone you don't know in an elevator, the conversation between neutral types can build into something interesting, or it can dissipate into uncomfortable or frivolous chatter. Let's take a deeper look now at the neutral and incompatible dynamics, as they often offer the greatest opportunities for growth through self-examination and purification.

Neutral Dynamics
Warrior–Laborer

Warriors enjoy the company of Laborers because they have much in common: they both appreciate hard work, are both plain speaking and concerned with truth, and they both like the challenges of the natural world. However, they are also opposed in many ways: Laborers love to build, but Warriors often have to destroy. Laborers are passionate about community and maintaining the status quo, but Warriors are leaders and tend to be solitary. Laborers live by concrete principles, while Warriors live by austere philosophies. Despite their many differences, Warriors and Laborers nonetheless respect each other. There is a link between them that is even more primal than their dharma type. During stress and hardship, these two are the likeliest to survive. They are the strongest dharma types, and that is why they represent the male/female archetypes, as noted earlier.

And like man and woman, they are fundamentally different but conspicuously attuned to each other, so much so that society cannot survive without them. In the most basic survival mode, a Warrior hunts while the Laborer gathers; the Warrior keeps enemies away by force, while the Laborer reinforces their shelter and feeds the community.

But this book is about more than fulfilling our basic biological imperatives. In such a world, Warriors and Laborers are basically compatible. But in a world where each type has time for introspection and the ability to strive for something more than survival, the Warrior and Laborer types move in different directions to gain fulfillment.

Warriors need to be constantly tested, to achieve one goal and move on to the next one. They are sprinters rather than marathoners. Laborers, on the other hand, don't mind sticking with the same job or living situation for years and even decades; they are in it for the long haul. In the end this can be tiring for Warrior types, whose problem-solving minds need challenge and improvement. Like the Fire element that corresponds to this type, Warriors need something to consume, lest they consume themselves. As an example, consider two different pastimes, baseball and football.*

Baseball is a Laborer sport, a sweet, slow, family-oriented game. The season is long, sometimes with two games played by the same teams in one day. Their season begins in the spring (a Laborer time), and baseball players tend to have greater longevity, sometimes playing into their forties. Football players, on the other hand, have limited longevity. They are specimens of strength and power, but, due to the intensity of the game, they tend to burn out sooner. Their season begins during late summer and fall, the Warrior time of year. But perhaps most telling is the fact that baseball has no time limit; it can go on indefinitely, like the sturdy, long-enduring Laborer type.

Applying themselves to Laborer-style activities can be a great source of relief to Warriors when there is nothing else to quench their fire. Warriors love to learn new skills and to adapt themselves to new situations. Learning a trade—be it painting, cabinetmaking, or tilling fields—can be a useful antidote to the Warrior's impatient spirit. However, the danger is that he will get bored and abandon these activities when his lust for challenge can no longer be satisfied. This is where the Laborer's mistrust of the Warrior type arises. Sensing that he may be overtaken at any moment by a desire to leave and seek something else, the stable Laborer type cannot fully trust the Warrior. Conversely, the Warrior may feel trapped and stifled in

---

*Comedian George Carlin's famous riff on the differences between these two sports is a classic.

the Laborer ranks, and find it hard to trust those who cannot trust him. He may also miss the Educator's sage advice when surrounded by the quieter logic of the Laborer mind.

Educator–Merchant

The mutual uneasiness felt between these two types arises out of their sense of inadequacy around each other. Merchants may feel "uneducated" (or undereducated) and prosaic next to the Educator's perceived worldliness and savoir faire. Conversely, the Educator feels impractical and useless around the Merchant, whom he perceives as clever and streetwise—qualities the Educator painfully lacks. These views are both a matter of perception, and can be resolved when mutual respect is extended and judgment held in check. Give credit where credit is due, and allow each other's strengths to shine. If the Educator is clumsy in Merchant affairs, why not enlist the Merchant's help? If the Merchant finds herself in a sticky moral or intellectual situation, why not consult the Educator for advice? This is a way to foster mutual respect.

When the Educator needs someone to help her negotiate a deal, such as in buying a car, she can call on the Merchant type for help. When the Merchant needs help on a question that requires diplomatic sensitivity, such as confronting her boss about a troublesome coworker, she can turn to the Educator for advice. This is the basis of the barter system, which draws out people's best talents and makes them work together rather than estranging them from each other, as the financial markets do. This is also the basis for sharing between two neutral types, who have neither animosity nor great natural love for each other.

Incompatible Types

Incompatible relationships between dharma types are a misnomer because they can often turn into the most fulfilling relationship dynamics. But the couple has to want to work at their relationship. Long-term personal relationships that involve incompatible personalities (Laborer–Educator, Warrior–Merchant) result from strong karma between two individuals. Because it takes a lot of work to keep incompatible types together, their mutual karma must be as strong or stronger than the natural forces working to pull them apart. The word *karma* in this sense carries the common Western definition, meaning an undesirable, often unavoidable situation that one just has to go through.* This karma may come in the form of economic or social restrictions that force people together, family duties, or fiduciary obligations. Whatever the cause, differences between incompatible types can be minimized by understanding and appreciating the other in a spirit of compromise.

Relationships between incompatible types can be dramatically improved when each party understands the motivations of the other and make concessions. Sometimes the deepest spiritual bonds are formed between people who have worked the hardest to sustain their relationship. Ultimately, awareness and compromise are the best tools for overcoming inconsistencies and incompatibilities in any relationship, and cultivating that kind of awareness and compromise is the purpose of this book.

For incompatible types to forge a relationship, they must engage in spiritual work. Those who want smooth, harmonious relationships should stick with their compatible types. However, sometimes it is impossible to avoid working with incompatible types in love, family, or work environments. Yet keep in mind that these situations offer the greatest opportunity for spiritual growth, and are often fated areas of our personal development. A person may have harmonious work relations and good friendships but suffer in love,

---

*Technically, this refers to undesirable fixed karma. The three levels of karma are discussed in chapter 11.

or she may be lucky in love but have challenging family dynamics. In whatever area of life you encounter incompatible types, you must apply the following rules, not only to minimize the pain they can bring, but to optimize your own learning and growth. Once you have learned to relate to incompatible types and witness the personal growth and character you cultivate as a result of these interactions, you may wish to continue challenging yourself with incompatible type relationships for a lifetime. They are the bitter green vegetables that are both purging and nourishing, and though sometimes difficult to swallow, are ultimately good for the body and spirit.

> **Dharma types expressing their highest qualities get along with everyone.**

Please note also that dharma types expressing their highest qualities, who are integrated and following their dharma, get along with everyone. This is the most important point to take away from this chapter. It is the secret of compatibility and the beauty of self-actualization. If a Laborer is evolved, expressing love, devotion, and service, she can get along just as well with Merchants as with Educators. An Outsider who is honest with himself and shares his gifts with society derives insight and understanding from everyone, and is admired by the world. When a person takes refuge in her dharma, dharma makes her self-sufficient. Then she does not need anything from the outside, nor is she reactive to other types when things go awry.

In chapter 7 we explored the mechanics of attraction. There is nothing more attractive than men or women at one with their life purpose. These kinds of people are a blessing to the world and attract others with their light. Even setbacks, pain, and suffering are borne by them with dignity befitting their type. Where there is trauma, conflict, and friction, it is only to burn away the dross of our egoic attachments. Incompatible types challenge us to become one with our dharmas, and that is the most valuable lesson we can learn.

When incompatible types meet, they admire the qualities in the other that they feel insecure about in themselves. The Educator sees the Laborer type's practicality and wishes she had it. The Laborer sees the Educator's intellect and wishes he had it. The Warrior sees the Merchant's people skills and wishes he had them; the Merchant sees the Warrior's authenticity and discipline and wishes she had them. What these types see in each other is the projection of their hopes and insecurities. This is wanting your neighbor's lawn, without fully appreciating your own.

> There is nothing more attractive than men or women at one with their life purpose. These kinds of people are a blessing to the world and attract others with their light.

If the Warrior had the Merchant's people skills, he could not be a Warrior. If the Educator had the Laborer's practicality, she could not fully operate as an Educator. Different fuel runs different engines. Diesel works well in diesel engines, just as regular gas does in automobiles. When you put one type of fuel into another's engine, disaster results.

In dynamics between incompatible types, people must take care not to covet the qualities of the other. To want these is to go against the nature of your type. This is the lesson of the evolution/devolution points: it is desirable to want the qualities of your integration type; it is undesirable to want the qualities of your disintegration type. Thus, it is good for Merchants to want to be like Laborers; it is good for Warriors to mold themselves after Educators. But when Merchants struggle to become Warriors, or Warriors Merchants, a breakdown of purpose ensues that eats up a person's integrity and results in their destruction.

Here are some guidelines for improving your ability to relate with these types as well as becoming embodiments of the virtues of your own.

Educator–Laborer

If they are to get along, Educators and Laborers must avoid imposing their belief systems on each another. Educators are sure they know what is necessary for a Laborer type. And Laborers are certain that what works for them will work for the Educator. They are both wrong, because imposing one law for both the lion and the ox amounts to oppression.

That is not to say that these types cannot benefit from learning from each other. It's just that the lessons need to be absorbed, not pounded into, the other person. Laborers must be allowed to learn at their own pace, and Educators to assimilate Laborer wisdom on their own terms. The best way to do this is to model behavior—to be the best self you can be—and let others profit from your example. When Educators step up as examples of temperance, compassion, and wisdom, people can't help but love them and follow their counsel. When Laborers stand strong as pillars of good faith, love, and service, they win the blessings and admiration of the whole community, if not the world. This live and let live attitude is crucial for any incompatible types to get along.

Educators can become exasperated with a Laborer's lack of subtlety, inability to recognize nuance, and reluctance to embrace refinement. For their part, Laborer types get fed up with the Educator's laws and regulations, their judgments and impracticality, and their inability to keep their word and walk the walk.

Educators and Laborers are ruled by the Air and Earth elements, respectively. Too much air erodes the earth with its harsh gusts of criticism and judgment; too much earth encloses air and makes it stale, unable to move and rise to the heavens. If this sounds like your relationship, please take time to understand the effect your element has on others. Let your partner fly if she's an Educator, and allow your lover to be her solid, earthy self if she's a Laborer, for both types wither when abused, and cannot offer their unique gifts to the world.

Laborers admire the Educator's worldliness and wisdom when they first meet. They are enamored of his intelligence and high-mindedness. But as they get to know the Educator, they become disappointed by his inability to stand up for what he believes, his feckless, wishy-washy nature. They become repulsed by his lack of motivation, particularly in matters of mundane practicality. They are let down by the Educator's weaknesses, and his inability to live up to the philosophies he espouses. And they become fed up by the Educator's needs for solitude, diet, introspection, and other special considerations. Eventually, they move on to someone not as high-minded, not as intellectual, but more real to them than the ephemeral Educator, who is too much in the air to be caught and tethered to the earth.

For their part, Educators initially appreciate the Laborer's direct, plain-speaking attitude. They like the Laborer's earthy sensuality, and may fall in love with his loyalty and devotion. Laborers have a way of making you feel at home and cutting through the uneasiness of social situations, which Educators appreciate. Laborers are real, a welcome contrast to Educators, who work in the realm of ideas and theories. Laborers are all heart, and their affection can nurture anybody back to health, including an ailing Educator. The problem is, you cannot go home with your nurse. The practicalities of daily living with a Laborer type become unsettling for the subtle Educator. Physical gruffness, insensitivity, and materialism turn off the Educator to a Laborer partner. Ultimately, while Laborers and Educators admire each other, they do not understand each other. When a person wants to be understood by her mate, she will find that pairing with his devolution point will make it harder to convey her real identity, to become fully known to her spouse.

If they are to get along as friends, lovers, or spouses, the Laborer needs to give her Educator partner room to fly. This often means plenty of solitude or time alone, during which the Educator can develop those qualities that do not get full expression around her Laborer counterpart. Educators feel stifled because they cannot express all aspects of their complex personality around Laborer types, and need other outlets to articulate their various talents. This could mean other friends, hobbies, or pursuits. The Laborer partner should not begrudge the Educator these pastimes, because they are crucial to improving their relationship.

On the other hand, Educators need to demonstrate patience and forbearance toward Laborer types. They need to learn to "speak their language" and be more direct and down-to-earth, present in their bodies and minds, not flying off thinking about the math problem at work while they are in bed with their partner.

Every type has specific intelligence, as described in *The Five Dharma Types*. Being Renaissance types and the quickest learners, Educators need to apply their skills to understanding the needs of their Laborer partners. They need to be present at every moment to discern exactly what is being said and understood. This is good practice for both types, as releasing Educators to fly teaches Laborer types to drop their attachments—and forbearance teaches Educators to forestall the judgments that result from a lack of mental presence. These are the toughest lessons each type has to master, and Educator/Laborer pairs are very good at teaching them to each other. They must master them if they are to get along.

For instance, natural urges of the body, such as sneezing, coughing, scratching, and snoring, are expressed with great relish by Laborers. To more sensitive Educators, this may seem barbaric. Nonetheless, it is the first point of respect and compromise between these two: understanding the physical habits of the other and learning to adapt your own. Relaxing artificial constructs and accepting the reality of the body's everyday needs is part of the Educator's struggle to understand her Laborer type partner. Conversely, education and culture can hew and polish the rough edges off the Laborer's sometimes gruff external persona, and benefit him immensely in turn.

Warrior–Merchant

Much of what was said above regarding Educator/Laborer compatibility, and the tools necessary to make incompatible types succeed in relationships, applies here. Please take a moment to read it again, substituting the Warrior/Merchant dynamic for Educator/Laborer. For Warriors not to betray themselves, and for Merchants to enjoy themselves, they have to allow each other to be who they are.

Warriors must respect the Merchant's right to make money, with the understanding that this money is used for their enjoyment and to respond to the needs of others who can benefit from the Merchant's prosperity. Merchants need to allow Warriors the opportunity to challenge themselves and not grow stale. What makes Merchants happy may not provide lasting enjoyment for the Warrior type. Parties and entertainment can only go so far in fulfilling a Warrior, who may need to go hunting, hiking, biking, or otherwise express his Warrior energy. When the Warrior and Merchant types create adequate space for each other to do the things they need to do to fulfill their dharmas, mutual understanding and happiness is the result. The way to do this is to learn as much as possible about the other type, her integration and disintegration, her duties and priorities, and to encourage, or at least not stand in the way of, her fulfilling these. Refer to the chapter 10 of *The Five Dharma Types* ("Element, Season, and Taste") for more details on the Fire/Water, Warrior/Merchant relationship.

Warriors are often too serious for Merchant types, like a chaperone on a date. When one prevails the other can't have any fun; when the Merchant wins, the Warrior's honor is compromised. Either way, whoever comes out on top, the other suffers. For them to get along, the Warrior needs to lighten up, while the Merchant needs to understand the consequences of her actions.

Warriors must learn when it is okay to have fun and when it is not appropriate. This requires the judgment to discern when fun is just fun and when it can generate negative fallout. *Viveka* (discrimination) is the Warrior's sword, and Merchants help her keep it sharp against the whetstone of their constant testing. Warriors must also learn that, against the Water element of the Merchant type, her fire is basically useless. Her fire is not meant to destroy water but to turn it to creative uses, like cooking, cleaning, and otherwise driving the pistons of society.

SOUL MATES

The idea of two incomplete souls coming together as one stems from Plato's philosophy and has been popularized in the New Age movement. It is romantic to believe that there is one soul in the world for whom you have been destined. It also makes the search for that one soul very difficult. The Vedic model, if there is one, is a bit more complex. The self is complete in itself; it needs nothing to complete it. However, as limited identities driven by karma, past tendencies, and associations, we are propelled toward certain people and situations that allow for the resolution and discharge of that karma. Let's take a look at the Vedic model of karma and how it is understood to play out in our lives. There are four levels:

> **Total karma:** This is the sum total of karma of the individuated identity that is beyond our ability to assess and fathom.

It spans multiple, countless lifetimes, and is stored for us to experience. It is impossible to know what portion, when, and how this karma will become activated at any given time.

Lifetime karma: This is the sum total of karma we are set to experience in the present lifetime. This level is knowable by looking at our horoscopes. Lacking an astrology chart, we have only to look at our lives to see where destiny, our lifetime karma, has put us. It has three levels—fixed, mixed, and nonfixed. (For more on this see "Fate or Free Will?" beginning on page 309.)

Present karma: This is the karma that you are experiencing now. If lifetime karma is destiny, present karma is free will. Remember, karma is both fate and free will, separated by time.

Future/potential karma: Potential karma is simply action that has not yet been performed. It is that portion of the lifetime karma that has not been experienced, and that portion of our free will that we have yet to exercise. Just as sex is stored in the genes of a prepubescent youth, to be enjoyed at an appropriate time in her evolution, so future karma stays locked inside as potentiality, until its time comes. The life cycles work with this type of karma, and help us to prepare for it in advance.

It is not absolutely necessary to understand these four levels to appreciate that karma in the Vedic sense is more complex than we conceive of it in the West.

In addition, anybody we relate to has karmic ties to us, some strong and some only fleeting. Therefore, in a sense, everyone with whom we have karma is a soul mate; everyone with whom we have unresolved conflicts is a soul mate. Jesus taught that, even as we sit to pray, if there be even one who may harbor something against us, we should get up and make amends first. And if someone has wronged us, we should forgive him before petitioning the Lord and pretending to the spiritual life. How pertinent is this to the universal description of the soul mate for the spiritual practitioner, and how much more far-reaching than the basic Platonic view! For the spiritual man and woman, everyone with whom we interact is a soul mate, capable of galvanizing us to growth, evolution, and even salvation.

And yet, are there some with whom we are meant to have more meaningful exchanges in this lifetime? Is there one with whom we are bound from life to life, a constant companion on the cosmic journey? The Vedic answer is an emphatic yes. And, more intriguing than the New Age concept of twin souls, the answer is both intricate and simple.

The limitless self is perfect and needs nothing to complete it. But in the relative world, where very few experience this reality, there is nothing as stabilizing, nurturing, and conducive to success in the journey of life as a partner; a friend and ally, a lover—a lifetime companion in the human search for wholeness. So much suffering, loneliness, and hardship are avoided when there are two together on the road to salvation. The spirit is eternal, but the body's needs in the temporal world are both immediate and constant. The needs for sex, food, and sleep are best addressed in a personal union that is recognized by society. That way a couple becomes a fortified pillar, uniting to bolster the greater edifice of the community, and supported by it in turn.

But is the soul mate just one person? When our karmas with one person expire, what then? And if we are destined for just one soul mate, how are those who are widowed, or have lost a mate, to find true love again with another? These questions hearken back to karma and its various levels.

When a couple is ideally matched they can stay together indefinitely, as long as they work to evolve and become ever more perfect expressions of themselves. However, when one or both members give up, or indeed have not been matched perfectly, the soul mate effect sometimes expires. Two people who thought themselves destined for each other find that, after some time, the flame of love and friendship has gone out, and their karmas begin to pull them apart. Their mutual support wanes into indifference, or worse, enmity.

Practically, this can be gauged by consulting the Vedic horoscopes of each partner. Is there a lifetime worth of karma shown in these horoscopes, or just a fleeting moment? This practice is done before marriage to ensure lasting compatibility. Personality, psychology, and spirituality, as well as the life cycles, as we'll see below, all affect how we relate to others. Finding someone with whom we are well suited is a task that transcends momentary passion and infatuation; it takes looking beyond the immediate physical phenomena that captivate two souls to see if there is anything else to keep them together after the flames of lust and romance have died down.

Sometimes we have to come across many soul mates before finding the one for this lifetime. These are purification and preparation experiences that prepare us to love. Without learning to love, even soul mates grow apart and relationships die. But how can this be avoided? How do those who stay together happily for decades manage the ebbs and lulls of the karmic tide? In a moment we shall see how the life cycles steer us this way and that. Ultimately, it is up to us to navigate the high seas of our romance, to build a mast that's keen and strong and a rudder that's true, so we may sail on toward our destiny and destination and weather the gusts and storms of fierce misfortune.

In a Golden Age, when truth and understanding prevail, when the seas are tame and the winds benefic, it is easy to maintain love's true course. But in the current age of dark storms and wretched seas, when the ocean convulses with sickness, we must be heroes to traverse the choppy waves where so many fall and drown, or are shipwrecked, stranded and alone. It takes great skill to court disaster and resist the sirens of temptation, while remaining true to course.

Find Your Soul Mate

So, just where do you find a soul mate? Your soul mate is where your dharma is. The best place to meet a potential mate is where you feel most comfortable, confident, and at home (aside from your home!). The place that affords the best expression of your dharma is the place to meet those with similar tastes. You do not have to go out looking for God and love; they are on your path—find that, and you find them both. And if they are not in your life, take a look at yourself. Are you where you want to be? Examine your personal, work, and domestic situations and ask yourself: Is this where I want to be? Does this truly express who I am?

In working your profession, not your job, you attract the highest good. By going in the direction of your point of evolution, you attract a life partner at your level. When you disintegrate and move away from your dharma, you also find people to complement that state, but these bring you down instead of raising you up. In a practical sense, these also become soul mates because they make you see the contrast between where you are and where you want to be. These difficult or karmic relationships force you to turn your life around and find the path of your highest self. However, because these kinds of relationships can be a slow and painful way to learn about self-actualization, it is better to find someone who positively supports your goals and needs instead.

If you want to date movie stars, it makes sense to move to Hollywood. In addition, you might want to get involved in moviemaking yourself. Become part of the action that you seek, and it will become part of you. You do not have to pack everything in the station wagon and head for the hills, but plan and start slowly on the path you feel is yours. Does your local community college offer acting or production classes? Begin with small steps first, and the journey will take you to your goal.

Another way to meet people is to frequent places favored by the types you are trying to attract. Merchants like nightclubs, but an Educator may prefer spending time at a bookstore. To meet like-minded people you have to go where they gather. It might be a cooking class, for a Laborer type, or tennis camp for the Warrior. Outsiders may find their one true love at the tattoo convention or the New Age gift shop. Think like the type you are trying to attract, and go there. Better yet, think like your own type; demonstrate excellence in the things you naturally do, and this will attract others to you. Being good at something is one of the most powerful ways to bring positive attention to yourself, for that is the major force of attraction.

Dissatisfaction and depression motivate us and help us kick ourselves into gear. The role of depression in spirituality is pivotal. The Bhagavad Gita begins with Arjuna's dejection. His redoubtable teacher guides him to turn this dejection into a new awareness. Dissatisfaction and dejection can be powerful tools to dredge out what is useless in our lives and kick-start us to pursue something new, but help is usually necessary to accomplish this. A teacher, catalyst, or coach—sometimes even an article or a book—can give us the guidance necessary to proceed.

It may take a while, for example, if your body is not in the shape you want it to be. You may have to join a gym or take a dance class. But each step along the way presents you with people who are on your own path, who can help catapult you to new levels of achievement. Eventually, the guiding light of your dharma will cross the ray of that one person who matches your own, and these two will form a new radiance, brighter than the sum of its parts, that becomes a beacon and a blessing to others.

LIFE CYCLES AND COMPATIBILITY

The idea that compatibility is influenced by the flow of life should come as no surprise, since we can see this throughout nature. A river that begins strong may split into tiny streams or change its course so that it never reaches the ocean. It may court the snaking valley depths, or find its way altered by geology and time or dammed by human efforts. Or it may rush headlong and meld into the arms of its ocean lover.

Everyone in your life right now is your soul mate, because they are agents of your karma at the moment. One way to judge the ever-changing course of compatibility is to analyze the life cycle you are in.* People in compatible life cycles are likely to experience greater affinity than people in incompatible ones. This is irrespective of their basic dharma type. Let's take a look at an example.

Robert is a Merchant type. He normally gets along well with Laborers and other Merchants. But Robert just entered a Warrior life cycle. As a result, he finds himself doing things he never thought he'd do (like taking boxing classes) and going to places he would not normally have thought to go. One day while hiking, he meets Samantha, another Warrior who happens to be in a Warrior cycle herself. By virtue of association and their shared experiences, they grow close and begin to date, eventually moving in together. The relationship progresses until, four years later, they begin to consider marriage.

But just at that time, Robert's Warrior cycle starts to wane, and an Outsider period takes over. Now, even though Outsiders and Warriors are not inimical to each other, Robert begins to lose the sense of closeness and camaraderie he enjoyed with Samantha and a

---

*When taking the dharma test at the beginning of this book, two types typically stand out—one is your dharma type, the second is the life cycle. For a complete look at life cycles, refer to *The Five Dharma Types*.

wanderlust begins to consume his soul. Abruptly one day, he decides that it's time to leave and calls off the engagement, leaving Samantha wondering what happened.

Robert began to grow close to Samantha when he entered his Warrior cycle. This is because she was also a Warrior, but the attraction was especially strong because she was in a Warrior period. The attraction would have been just as potent if she were in an Educator period, as Warriors and Educators share good compatibility. Like two people who find themselves together on a plane, a type of friendship or camaraderie emerges because of the environment you share. You can't help but exchange phone numbers or recipes with someone who sits next to you for twelve hours. In a sense, you can reinvent yourself and be someone else in a new place and in new company. You can experience this on the job or, in some more extreme examples, when confronted by war, disaster, or other calamities. People grow close when they share powerful experiences—positive or negative. Thus, soldiers in war or strangers at a rock concert will share a bond as long as the experience lasts, and sometimes far longer.

Let's take a look at another example.

Mary, an Educator, is a pre-med student. During her junior year she seizes an opportunity to study in Africa for a year, gripped as she is by an Outsider life cycle. During her trip she falls in love with the customs, environment, and people of the region. She develops a special fondness for one of her interpreters, Henry, with whom she eventually falls in love. For ten months they live and work together, while her stay in Africa proves an enormous success.

At the end of her tenure, she is heartbroken and loath to leave. Nonetheless, having no alternative, she returns home to her eager and solicitous parents. For a long time she remains in contact with Henry, talking on the phone and writing letters. Finally, after four years, three more trips abroad, including one to Africa, and a medical degree, she and Henry eventually lose contact and the letters stop. She meets and eventually marries a man from her hometown, and begins her life as a doctor.

In this scenario, Mary entered an Outsider period during which she journeyed far away from her routine environment to learn about a radically different culture. She may have also picked up new languages, fashion styles, and other idiosyncrasies that distinguish the Outsider from everyone else. She also fell in love with a local man, Henry, with whom she had a protracted, long-distance romance. It is important to note that, as long as her Outsider period lasted, she kept in touch with the man and the mystery that was her African connection. But as her Outsider life cycle ended, so did her relationship with Henry, as she moved into a new phase of life.

That is not to say that just because you change life cycles your relationships have to end. The world would be full of divorces if that were the case. The love and affection we build during our close times is the glue that keeps us together during difficult times or times of separation. Traditional societies know this well and prepare couples for the inevitable rough spots.

BREAKING UP

Doctors and chemists tell us that the strongest drugs known to humankind are produced in the body itself. Perhaps the most powerful catalyst in this chemical laboratory is love. The neurochemistry associated with being in love is addictive. There is no greater high than the rush of true love and no greater low than the heartbreak of splitting up. When our limbic system bonds with another person, we depend on him for the continued creation of the emotion cocktail our brains churn out. When this link is severed, we may suffer heartbreaking withdrawal that is both physical and emotional, devastating us psychologically as well as spiritually. Splitting up can create physical heartbreak, and we have the science to prove this. Better to stick together and understand the different life cycles that we as couples move through, and allow each other the freedom to experience them.

That is why it is vital to have a life partner with whom to ferry across this dangerous and lonely world on the way to the far shore of self-fulfillment, a soul mate to help us pull the oars and share the journey with us. In sacred societies, at the end of life's Spring season and after young men and women have enjoyed the tutelage and experimentation of youth, they are wed for life to ensure their continued happiness. The blessings they receive from this union are manifold: their wedding present to themselves is improved physical health and immunity, longer life expectancy, greater financial reward, and improved social integration. Successful marriage has always been the foundation of personal happiness as well as social cohesiveness, and the proper way to ensure it is to match couples based on deep levels of compatibility.

The life cycles are like the storms and weather on a long journey. The dharma types are the vessel and its crew. When the storms prevail we are set awash and left helpless, waiting for a change in tide to bring us safely to shore. When our dharma type is dominant, there is no sea and no storm that we cannot conquer, held firm and fixed by the bonds of dharma and steered by the rudder and sail of wisdom and experience. In the end, our essential character, and the degree to which it has been actualized, determines our ability to sustain loving relationships.

Life Is in Your Hands

At the beginning of this book I told you that life is full of roles—boyfriend, girlfriend, parent, lover, sibling, friend—and that each has a dharma, a duty, associated with it. I also noted that how we execute that duty is up to us. I've tried to show you how to fulfill the dharma of the body through self-care and an optimal daily routine, the dharma of your environment and living space, as well as the dharma of compatibility and relationships.

Shakespeare said, "All the world's a stage, and all the men and women merely players." How right he was. The key to being a successful actor is to know your part and not expect it to be anything else. Understand the strengths and weaknesses of your dharma type, the needs of your body, and the function of your various social roles. Play your part to the fullest, so that when the play is over and the curtain falls you have poured your heart, sweat, and soul onto the stage. There is nothing left to give, nothing left to say. That is the mark of a life well lived and of a beautiful production, one that people stand up to cheer, one that invites a glorious encore.

May your life be such a blockbuster that it leaves your audience speechless with joy and you fulfilled and proud, like the radiant and successful author-actor that you are! Thank you for joining me on this journey, and remember: live with purpose!

Notes

INTRODUCTION.
DISCOVERING YOUR DHARMA

1. Robert Svoboda, *Aghora: At the Left Hand of God* (Albuquerque: Rupa Publications, Brotherhood of Life, Inc., 1993).

3. BE FIT

1. Sivaya Subramuniya Swami, *How to Become a Hindu: A Guide for Seekers and Born Hindus* (Kapaa, Hi.: Himalayan Academy, 2000), 287.
2. Dawn Baumann Brunke, *Animal Voices, Animal Guides: Discover Your Deeper Self through Communication with Animals* (Rochester, Vt.: Bear & Co., 2004), 84.
3. Ibid.
4. Pandit Rajmani Tigunait, Ph.D., *Seven Systems of Indian Philosophy* (Honesdale, Pa.: Himalayan Institute Press, 1983), 7.

4. FROM AMA TO AGNI

1. *JAMA International* (February 2014); doi:10.1001/jamainternmed .2013.13563.
2. "An Early Bedtime May Improve Your Heart Health," http://

sleepeducation.blogspot.com/2009/05/early-bedtime-may-improve-your-heart.html; and Christopher Ryan King, et. al., "Short Sleep Duration and Incident Coronary Artery Calcification," *The Journal of the American Medical Association* December 24, 2008: http://jama.jamanetwork.com/article.aspx?articleid=183124.

3. Dr. D. Y. Patil, "Effect of Water Induced Thermogenesis on Body Weight, Body Mass Index, and Body Composition of Overweight Subjects," *Journal of Clinical and Diagnostic Research* 7, no. 9 (September 2013): 1894–96; doi: 10.7860/JCDR/2013/5862.3344; Epub September 10, 2013.

4. Candace Pert, Ph.D., *Molecules of Emotion: The Science behind Mind-Body Medicine* (New York: Simon & Schuster, 1999).

6. PHYSICAL DHARMA AND THE DOSHAS

1. Adam Hadhazy, "Think Twice: How the Gut's 'Second Brain' Influences Mood and Well-Being," *Scientific American* February 12, 2010: http://www.scientificamerican.com/article/gut-second-brain/. See also Michael Gershon, *The Second Brain* (New York: HarperCollins, 1998).

2. Timothy Ferriss, *The 4-Hour Body* (New York: Crown Archetype, 2010).

7. THE LAWS OF ATTRACTION

1. David DeAngelo, *Attraction Isn't a Choice* (2007), http://doubleyour-dating.com/catalog-attractionbook/.

8. SEX IN A SACRED SOCIETY

1. Jonathan Margolis, *O: The Intimate History of the Orgasm* (London, Random House, 2004), 134.

2. Ernst Rietzschel and Jennifer Mieres,"Oral Contraceptive Use: More Carotid and Femoral Atheroschlerosis Later in Life," *New England Journal of Medicine* (2007): 357.

3. Jane Bennett and Alexandra Pope, *The Pill: Are You Sure It's for You?* (Crows Nest, New South Wales: Allen and Unwin, 2008); *The Lancet* (June 1996): 347.

9. NOURISHING SEX

1. Kerry Riley and Diane Riley, *Tantric Secrets for Men* (Rochester, Vt.: Destiny Books, 2002), 91.

11. LOVE IN THE STARS

1. Elizabeth Gilbert, *Committed: A Love Story* (New York: Penguin Books Ltd., 2010), 41.

12. LOVE AND DHARMA

1. B.K.S. Iyengar, *Light on Life* (Emmaus Pa.: Rodale, 2005), 195.

Suggested Resources
on East/West Wisdom

Dr. Vasant Lad

www.ayurveda.com

Dr. Lad is perhaps single-handedly responsible for training more Westerners in authentic ayurveda than any other teacher. His institute is a haven for all who thirst for Vedic wisdom, and a port to higher knowledge. He teaches with compassion and an uncanny understanding of a student's needs.

Robert Svoboda

www.drsvoboda.com

The original Ayurvedic Westerner, Svoboda holds the distinction of truly honoring India's spiritual traditions in his books as well as in his life. A must read for those wanting to explore ayurvedic alchemy and the mysteries of sacred India.

Hart deFouw

www.vedicvidyainstitute.com

What Dr. Vasant Lad is to ayurveda, deFouw is to jyotisha—a living, breathing embodiment of the art and science of Vedic astrology. The first Westerner to authentically imbibe and carry on a Vedic tradition normally inaccessible to Western students, his books and classes on jyotisha make for tough reading but set the standard in authentic instruction.

Robin Gile
www.robingilepalmistry.com
Author of *The Idiot's Guide to Palmistry,* Robin is a practicing palmist and archetypal symbolist in the Albuquerque, New Mexico, area. Few can match his talent and uncanny insight born of forty years' experience.

Graham Hancock
www.grahamhancock.com
This far-out journalist cum spiritual seeker has trekked the globe looking to uncover man's ancient civilizations and their connections to the modern world. Voracious in his thirst for knowledge and truth, here is an Outsider-Educator combination that makes us stand up and take notice. Even if you don't agree with his conclusions, his body of work cannot be ignored.

Pavel Tsatsouline
www.dragondoor.com
Pavel is a Master of Sports, the title of highest achievement accorded in the old Soviet system—akin to a Ph.D in both athletic understanding *and* practice. Revolutionary in his approach, he transformed the Western fitness scene by introducing the kettlebell and other little known training secrets to America. He makes difficult concepts simple to digest and is as compassionate in his delivery as he is brutal in his excoriation of what doesn't work. A true Warrior-Educator evolution. Check him out!

John Douillard
www.lifespa.com
John Douillard is a true admixture of East and West. A triathlete turned doctor turned Ayurvedic physician, his insights on modern Western integration of Ayurvedic principles, especially in athletics, are unique and enlightening. Buy his books.

B. K. S. Iyengar
www.bksiyengar.com
Well known to the West, Iyengar was largely responsible for making yoga safe and understandable to the Western practitioner—all without diluting the essence of his tradition. Iyengar was one of few among the yoga multitude who kept his sincerity, integrity, and tradition intact over the years. For that, he remains a jewel to yoga culture.

Krishna Das
www.krishnadas.com
Not an author but a musician, Krishna Das is the East-West link to devotional Indian music and chanting. By the grace of his guru, he carries the spark of an ancient tradition in a modern Western voice that's guaranteed to make you sing along (just don't send him your speeding tickets).

For more information, or to find a dharma ttype practitioner near you, visit
www.spirittype.com or write **siddhadeva@yahoo.com**.

Index

Numbers in *italics* indicate illustrations

BOOKS OF RELATED INTEREST

The Five Dharma Types
Vedic Wisdom for Discovering Your Purpose and Destiny
by Simon Chokoisky

The Complete Illustrated Kama Sutra
Edited by Lance Dane

The Heart of Yoga
Developing a Personal Practice
by T. K. V. Desikachar

Sacred Sexual Union
The Alchemy of Love, Power, and Wisdom
by Anaiya Sophia

Advanced Spiritual Intimacy
The Yoga of Deep Tantric Sensuality
by Stuart Sovatsky, Ph.D.

Desire
The Tantric Path to Awakening
by Daniel Odier

Slow Sex
The Path to Fulfilling and Sustainable Sexuality
by Diana Richardson

Tantric Sex for Men
Making Love a Meditation
by Diana Richardson and Michael Richardson

INNER TRADITIONS • BEAR & COMPANY
P.O. Box 388
Rochester, VT 05767
1-800-246-8648
www.InnerTraditions.com

Or contact your local bookseller